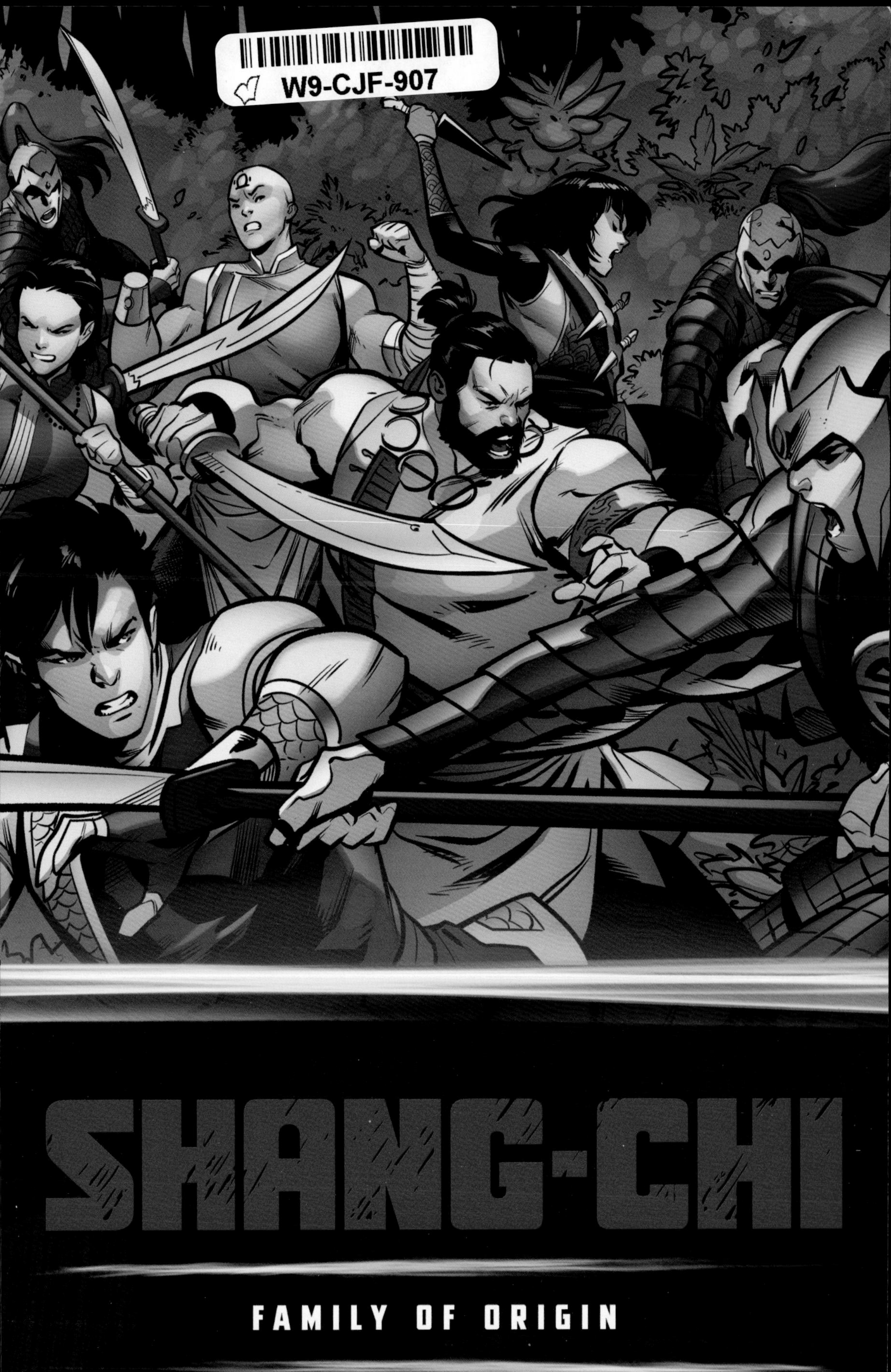

SHANG-CHI

FAMILY OF ORIGIN

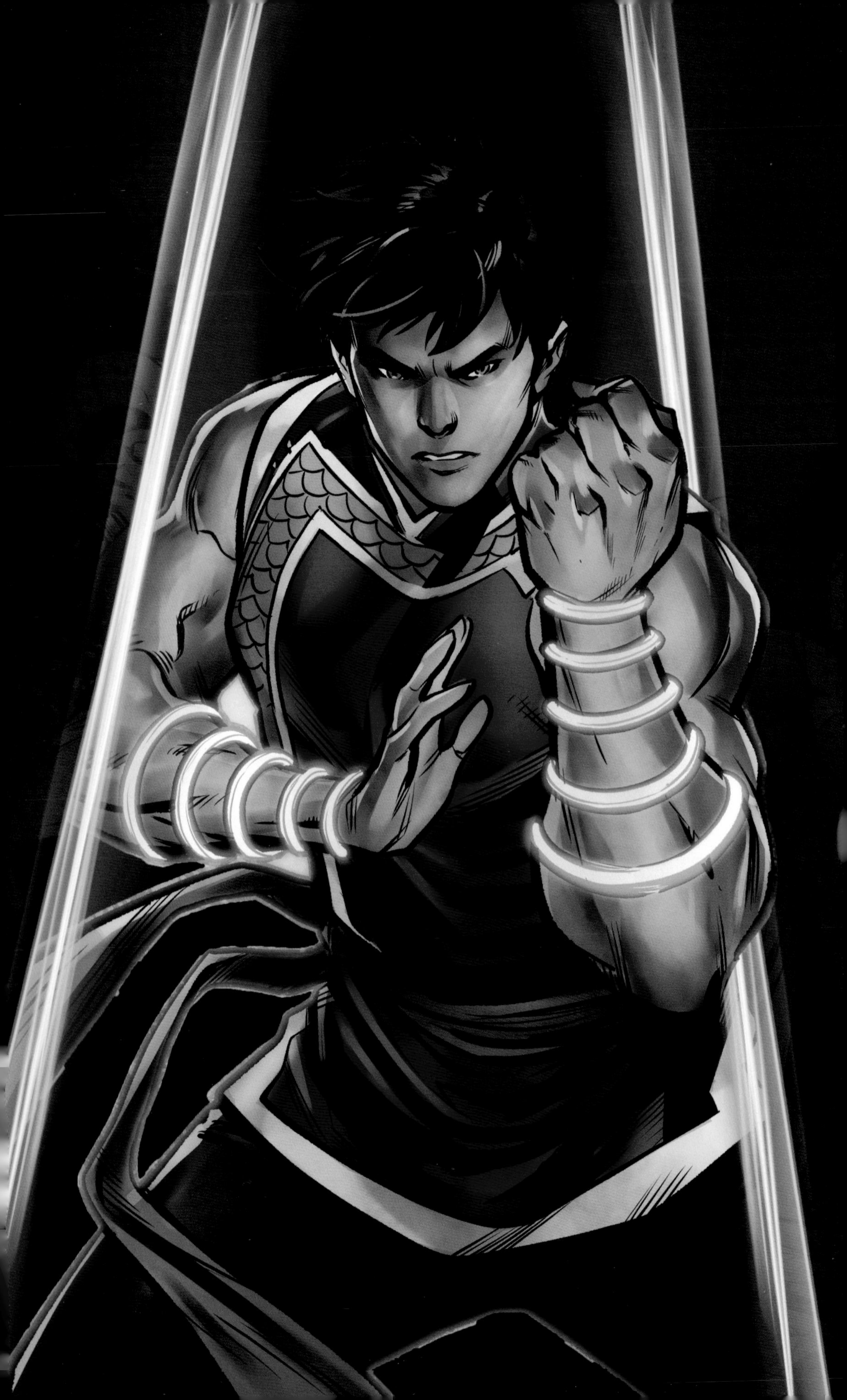

FROM THE DAY HE WAS BORN, HIS EVIL FATHER TRAINED HIM TO BE A LIVING WEAPON. HIS MIND, BODY AND SPIRIT HONED TO A RAZOR'S EDGE, HE NOW USES HIS ABILITIES TO STRIKE DOWN INJUSTICE AND ATONE FOR HIS FAMILY'S MISDEEDS. HE IS...

SHANG-CHI

FAMILY OF ORIGIN

FOR HUNDREDS OF YEARS, THE FIVE WEAPONS SOCIETY HAS OPERATED IN THE SHADOWS, WORKING TOWARD WORLD DOMINATION. THEY HAVE INTIMIDATED, STOLEN AND KILLED IN ORDER TO ACHIEVE THEIR GOALS.

NOW SHANG-CHI HAS TAKEN CONTROL OF HIS FATHER'S CULTLIKE ORGANIZATION. BUT CHANGING THE SOCIETY AND HIS FAMILY'S EVIL WAYS HASN'T BEEN EASY.

SHANG-CHI APPREHENDED BROTHER SABRE AND HANDED HIM TO THE AVENGERS. HIS OTHER SIBLINGS NOW DON'T KNOW WHERE SHANG-CHI'S LOYALTY LIES. BUT SHANG-CHI'S PROBLEMS ARE NOT JUST FAMILIAL AS HIS PAST ENEMIES ARE NOW CONSPIRING AGAINST HIM, WITH THE HELP OF AN INSIDE SOURCE.

BUT HIS MOTHER HAS SECRETS TOO, AND SHE'S FINALLY READY TO TELL SHANG-CHI THE TRUTH ABOUT HER DISAPPEARANCE.

WRITER **GENE LUEN YANG**

ARTISTS **DIKE RUAN** [#7-8] & **MARCUS TO** [#9-12]

COLOR ARTISTS **TRÍONA FARRELL** [#7-8], **SUNNY GHO** [#9] & **ERICK ARCINIEGA** [#10-12]

LETTERER **VC's TRAVIS LANHAM**

COVER ART **LEINIL FRANCIS YU** WITH **SUNNY GHO** [#7-11] & **ROMULO FAJARDO JR.** [#12]

MARVEL VOICES: IDENTITY
"WHAT IS VS. WHAT IF"

WRITER **GENE LUEN YANG** ARTIST **MARCUS TO** COLOR ARTIST **SUNNY GHO**

LETTERER **VC's JOE SABINO** COVER ART **JIM CHEUNG & ROMULO FAJARDO JR.**

ASSISTANT EDITOR: **KAT GREGOROWICZ** EDITOR: **DARREN SHAN** SPECIAL THANKS TO **TOM BREVOORT**

COLLECTION EDITOR DANIEL KIRCHHOFFER
ASSISTANT MANAGING EDITOR MAIA LOY
ASSOCIATE MANAGER, TALENT RELATIONS LISA MONTALBANO
DIRECTOR, PRODUCTION & SPECIAL PROJECTS JENNIFER GRÜNWALD
JEFF YOUNGQUIST VP PRODUCTION & SPECIAL PROJECTS
STACIE ZUCKER WITH SALENA MAHINA BOOK DESIGNERS
ADAM DEL RE SENIOR DESIGNER
DAVID GABRIEL SVP PRINT, SALES & MARKETING
C.B. CEBULSKI EDITOR IN CHIEF

SHANG-CHI BY GENE LUEN YANG VOL. 3: FAMILY OF ORIGIN. Contains material originally published in magazine form as SHANG-CHI (2021) #7-12 and MARVEL'S VOICES: IDENTITY (2021) #1. First printing 2022. ISBN 978-1-302-9302 Published by MARVEL WORLDWIDE, INC., a subsidiary of MARVEL ENTERTAINMENT, LLC. OFFICE OF PUBLICATION: 1290 Avenue of the Americas, New York, NY 10104. Printed in the U.S.A. KEVIN FEIGE, Chief Creative Officer; DAN BUCKL President, Marvel Entertainment; JOE QUESADA, EVP & Creative Director; DAVID BOGART, Associate Publisher & SVP of Talent Affairs; TOM BREVOORT, VP, Executive Editor; NICK LOWE, Executive Editor, VP of Content, Digital Publishi DAVID GABRIEL, VP of Print & Digital Publishing; SVEN LARSEN, VP of Licensed Publishing; MARK ANNUNZIATO, VP of Planning & Forecasting; JEFF YOUNGQUIST, VP of Production & Special Projects; ALEX MORALES, Director of Publish Operations; DAN EDINGTON, Director of Editorial Operations; RICKEY PURDIN, Director of Talent Relations; JENNIFER GRÜNWALD, Director of Production & Special Projects; SUSAN CRESPI, Production Manager; STAN LEE, Chairman Emeri For information regarding advertising in Marvel Comics or on Marvel.com, please contact Vit DeBellis, Custom Solutions & Integrated Advertising Manager, at vdebellis@marvel.com. For Marvel subscription inquiries, please call 888-511-54 Manufactured between 5/27/2022 and 6/28/2022 by SEAWAY PRINTING, GREEN BAY, WI, USA.

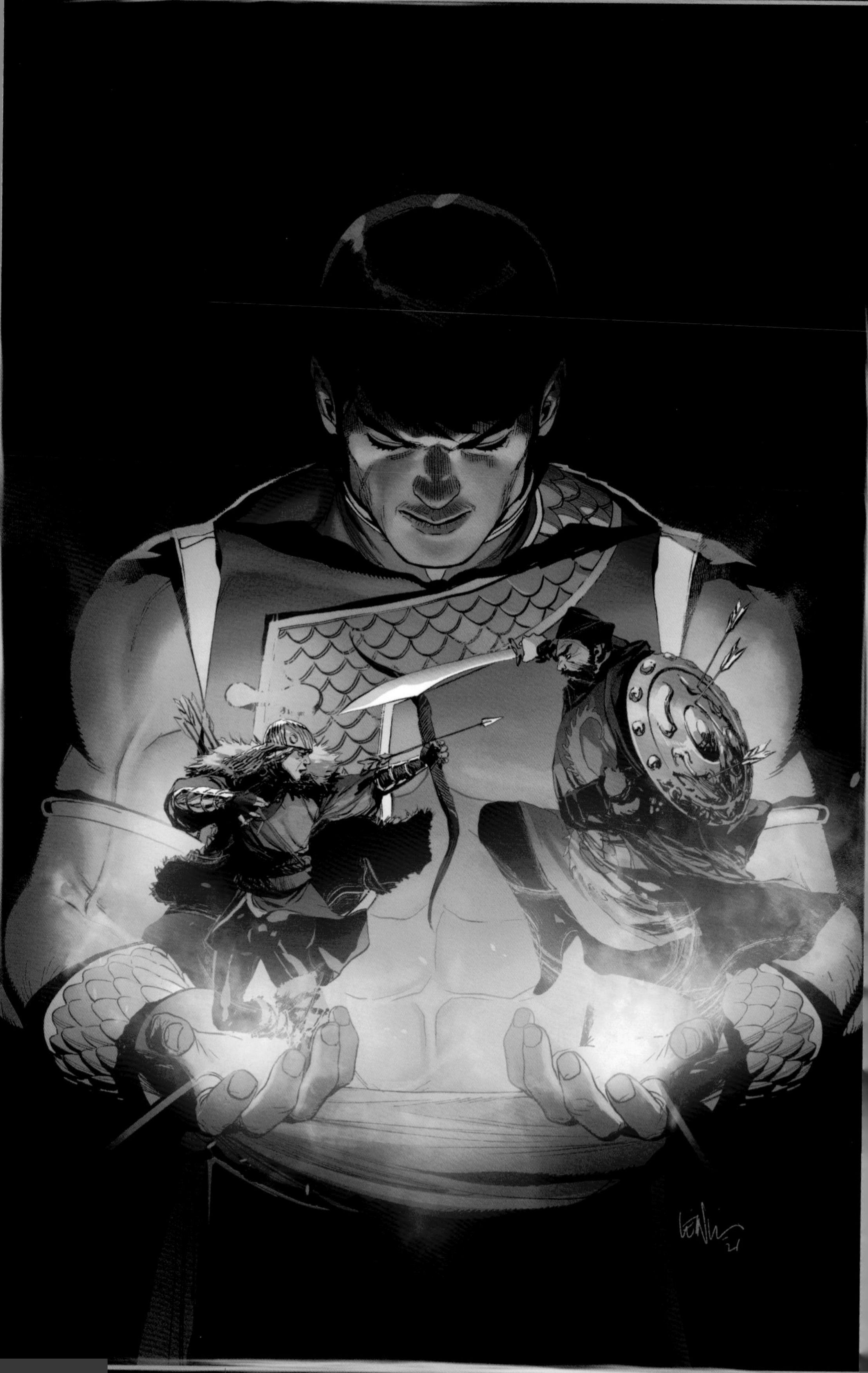

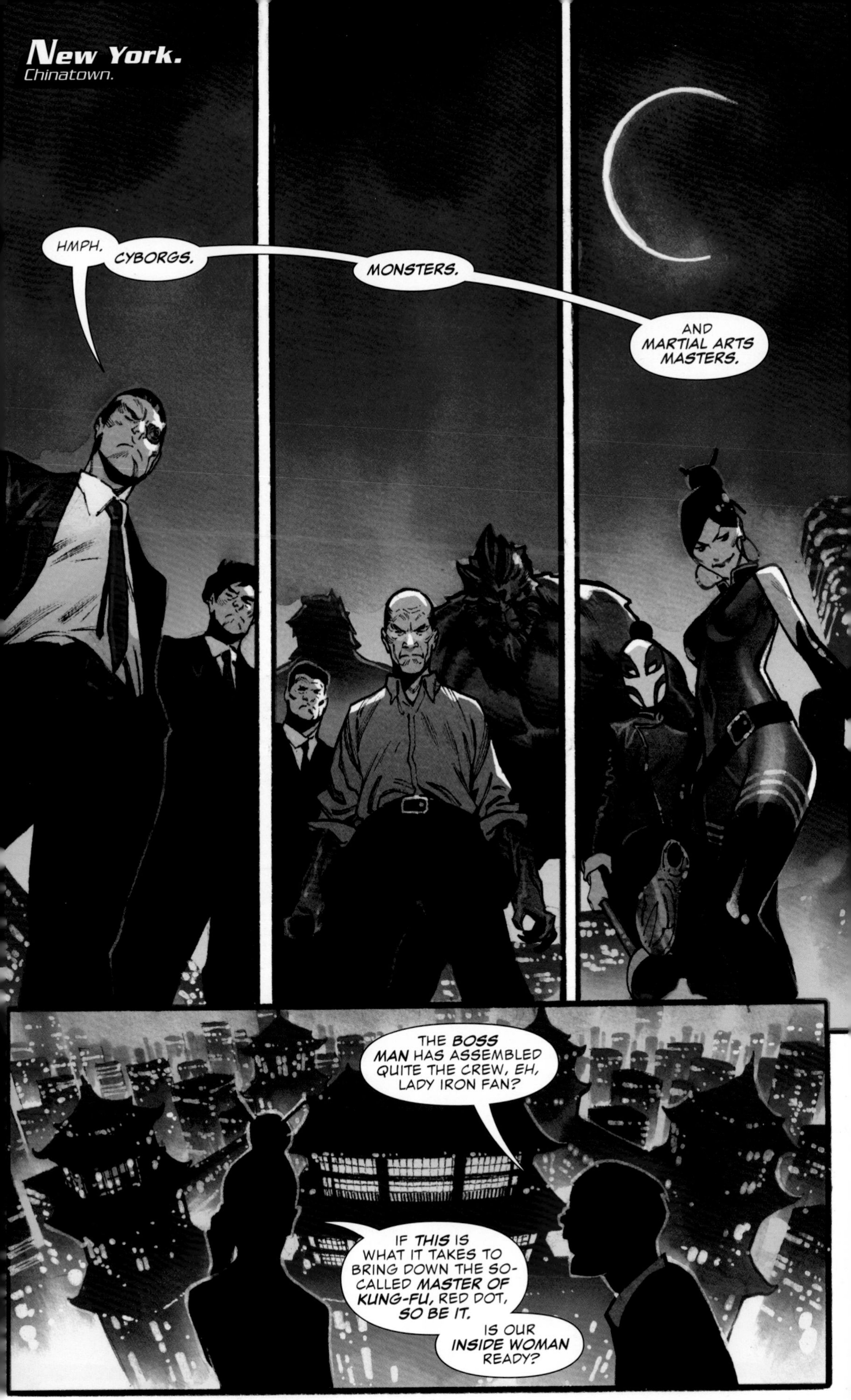
New York.
Chinatown.
HMPH.
CYBORGS.
MONSTERS.
AND MARTIAL ARTS MASTERS.
THE BOSS MAN HAS ASSEMBLED QUITE THE CREW, EH, LADY IRON FAN?
IF THIS IS WHAT IT TAKES TO BRING DOWN THE SO-CALLED MASTER OF KUNG-FU, RED DOT, SO BE IT.
IS OUR INSIDE WOMAN READY?

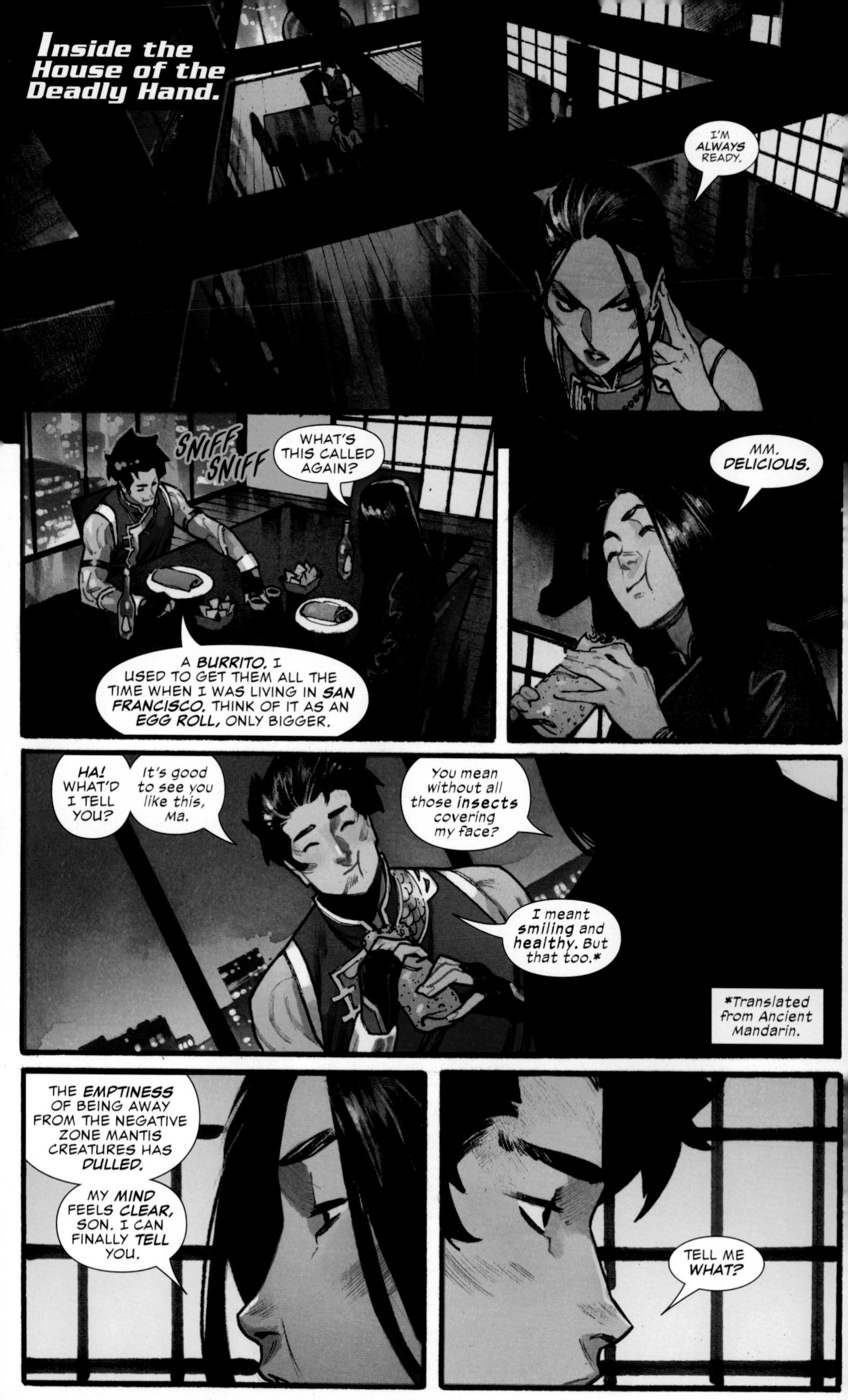
Inside the House of the Deadly Hand.
I'M ALWAYS READY.
SNIFF SNIFF
WHAT'S THIS CALLED AGAIN?
A BURRITO. I USED TO GET THEM ALL THE TIME WHEN I WAS LIVING IN SAN FRANCISCO. THINK OF IT AS AN EGG ROLL, ONLY BIGGER.
MM. DELICIOUS.
HA! WHAT'D I TELL YOU?
It's good to see you like this, Ma.
You mean without all those insects covering my face?
I meant smiling and healthy. But that too.*
*Translated from Ancient Mandarin.
THE EMPTINESS OF BEING AWAY FROM THE NEGATIVE ZONE MANTIS CREATURES HAS DULLED.
MY MIND FEELS CLEAR, SON. I CAN FINALLY TELL YOU.
TELL ME WHAT?

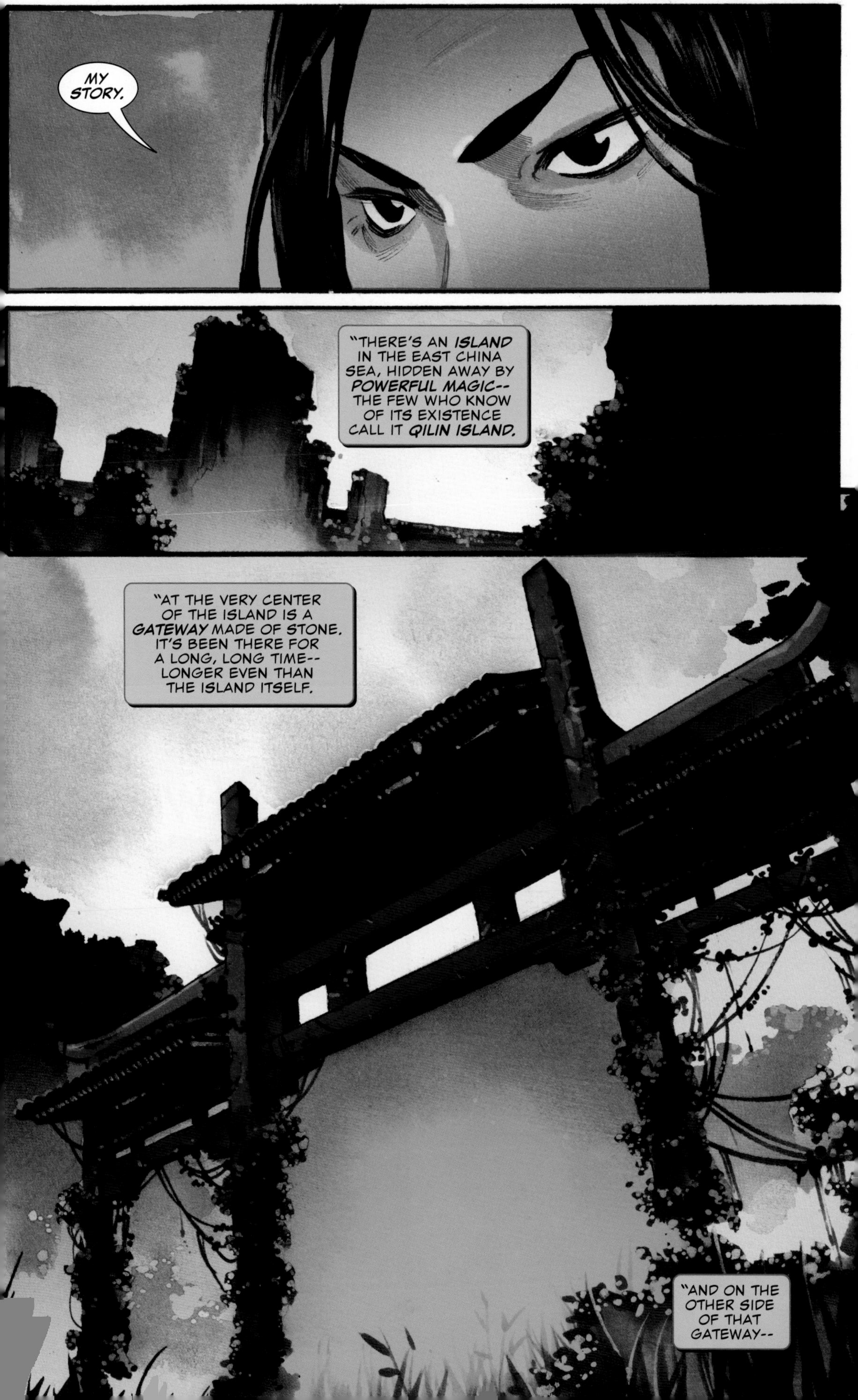
MY STORY.
"THERE'S AN ISLAND IN THE EAST CHINA SEA, HIDDEN AWAY BY POWERFUL MAGIC-- THE FEW WHO KNOW OF ITS EXISTENCE CALL IT QILIN ISLAND.
"AT THE VERY CENTER OF THE ISLAND IS A GATEWAY MADE OF STONE. IT'S BEEN THERE FOR A LONG, LONG TIME-- LONGER EVEN THAN THE ISLAND ITSELF.
"AND ON THE OTHER SIDE OF THAT GATEWAY--

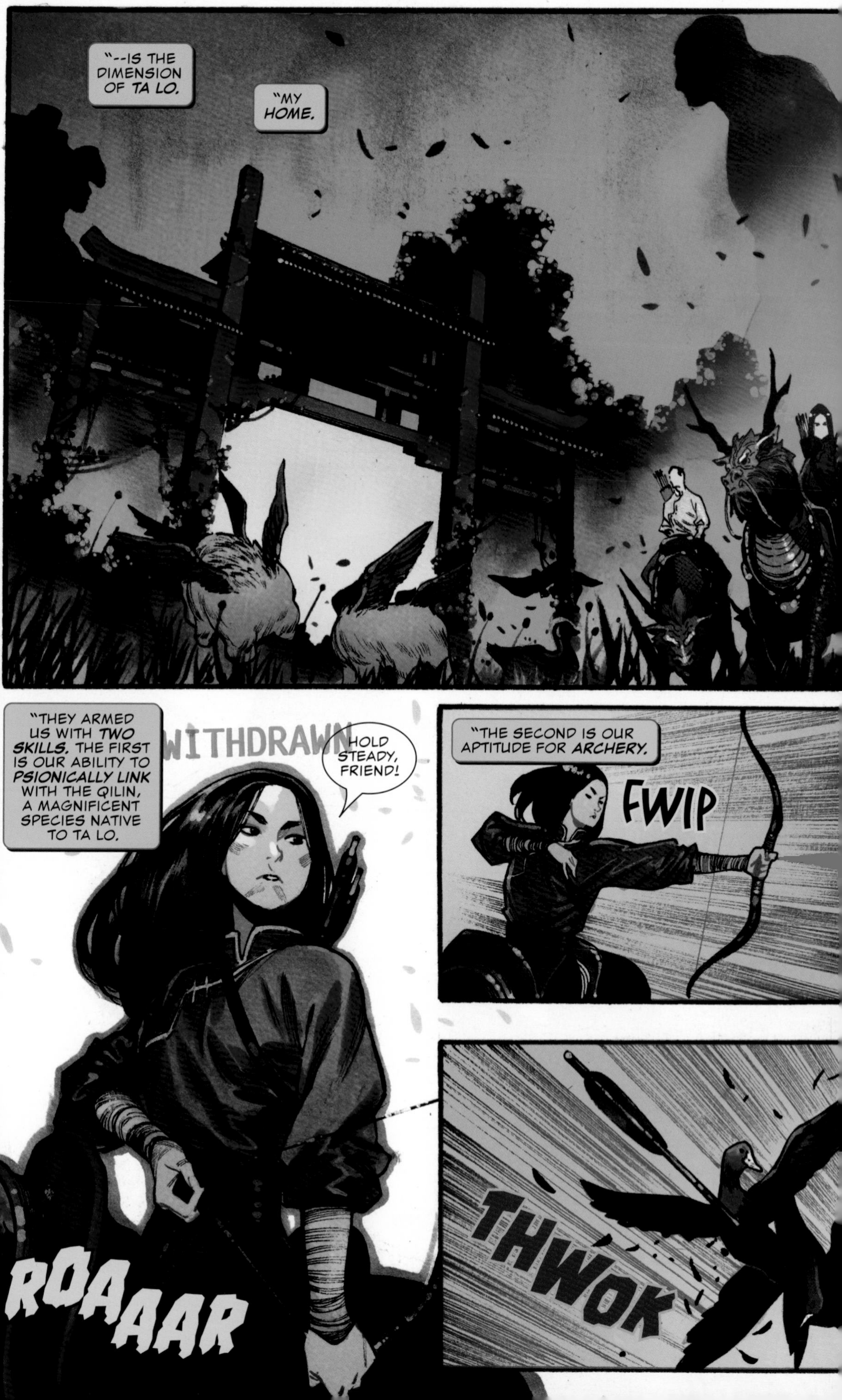
"--IS THE DIMENSION OF TA LO.
"MY HOME.
"THEY ARMED US WITH TWO SKILLS. THE FIRST IS OUR ABILITY TO PSIONICALLY LINK WITH THE QILIN, A MAGNIFICENT SPECIES NATIVE TO TA LO.
HOLD STEADY, FRIEND!
ROAAAR
"THE SECOND IS OUR APTITUDE FOR ARCHERY.
FWIP
THWOK

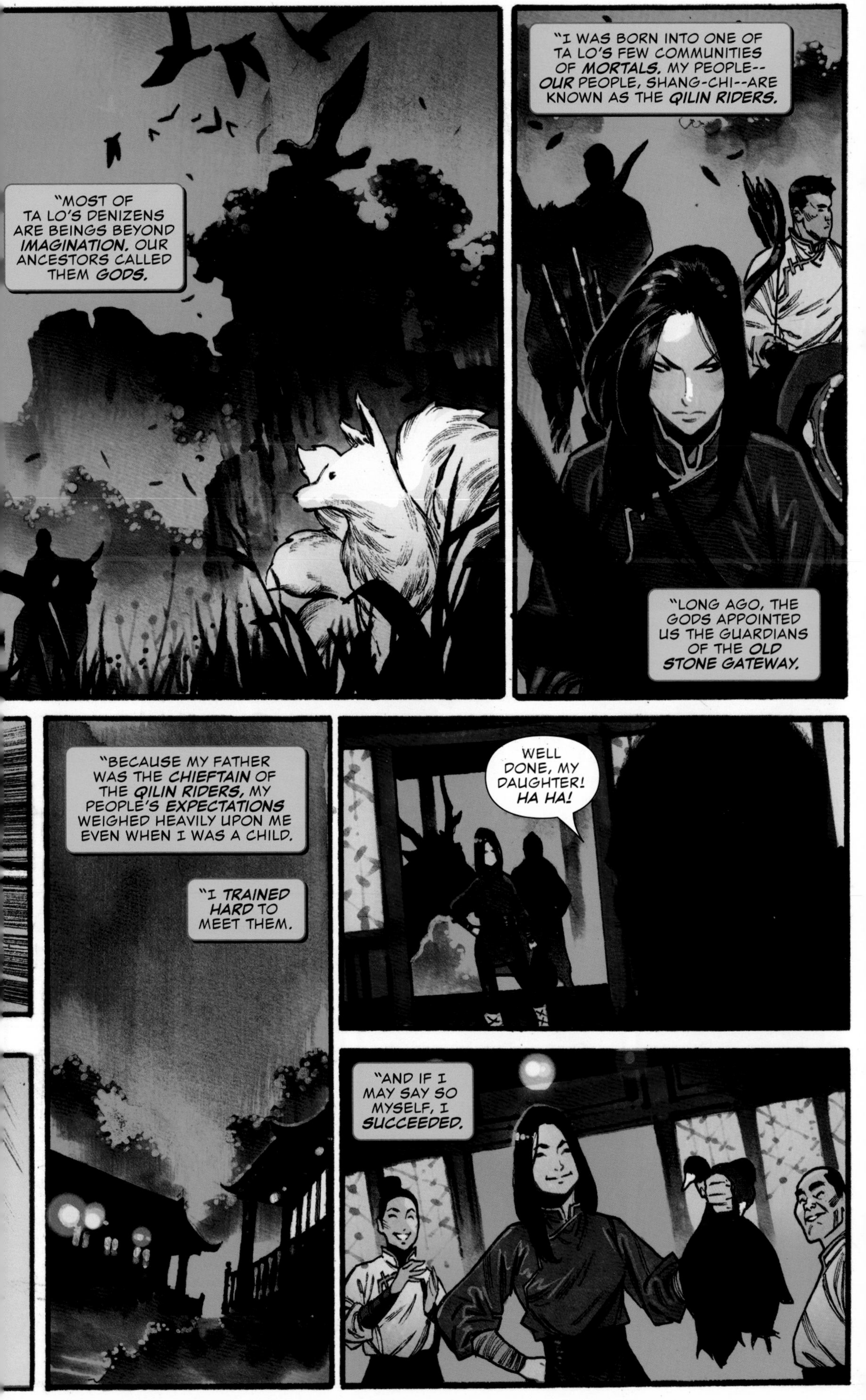

"MOST OF TA LO'S DENIZENS ARE BEINGS BEYOND IMAGINATION. OUR ANCESTORS CALLED THEM GODS.
"I WAS BORN INTO ONE OF TA LO'S FEW COMMUNITIES OF MORTALS. MY PEOPLE--OUR PEOPLE, SHANG-CHI--ARE KNOWN AS THE QILIN RIDERS.
"LONG AGO, THE GODS APPOINTED US THE GUARDIANS OF THE OLD STONE GATEWAY.
"BECAUSE MY FATHER WAS THE CHIEFTAIN OF THE QILIN RIDERS, MY PEOPLE'S EXPECTATIONS WEIGHED HEAVILY UPON ME EVEN WHEN I WAS A CHILD.
"I TRAINED HARD TO MEET THEM.
WELL DONE, MY DAUGHTER! HA HA!
"AND IF I MAY SAY SO MYSELF, I SUCCEEDED.

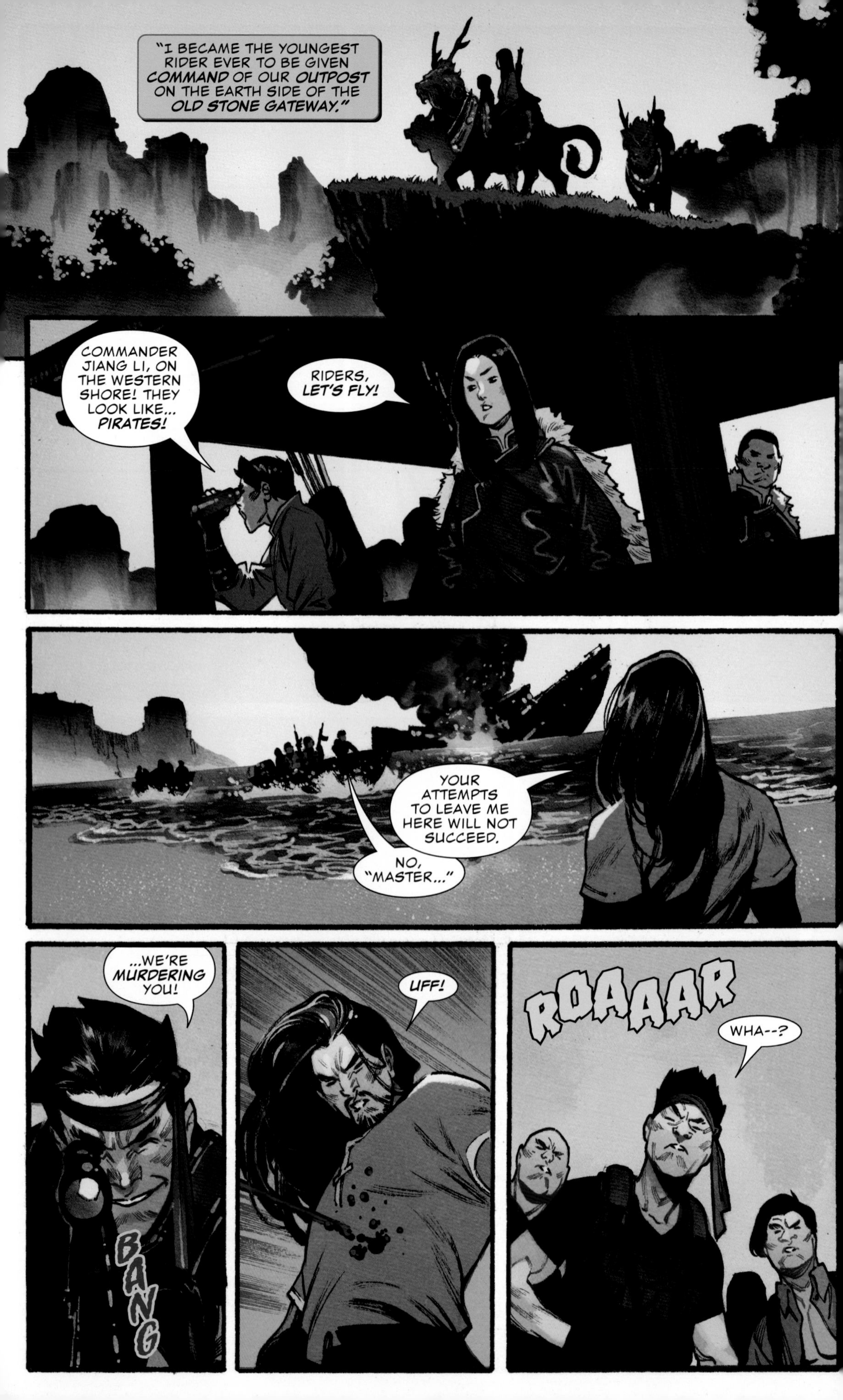
"I BECAME THE YOUNGEST RIDER EVER TO BE GIVEN COMMAND OF OUR OUTPOST ON THE EARTH SIDE OF THE OLD STONE GATEWAY."
COMMANDER JIANG LI, ON THE WESTERN SHORE! THEY LOOK LIKE... PIRATES!
RIDERS, LET'S FLY!
YOUR ATTEMPTS TO LEAVE ME HERE WILL NOT SUCCEED.
NO, "MASTER..."
...WE'RE MURDERING YOU!
BANG
UFF!
ROAAAR
WHA--?

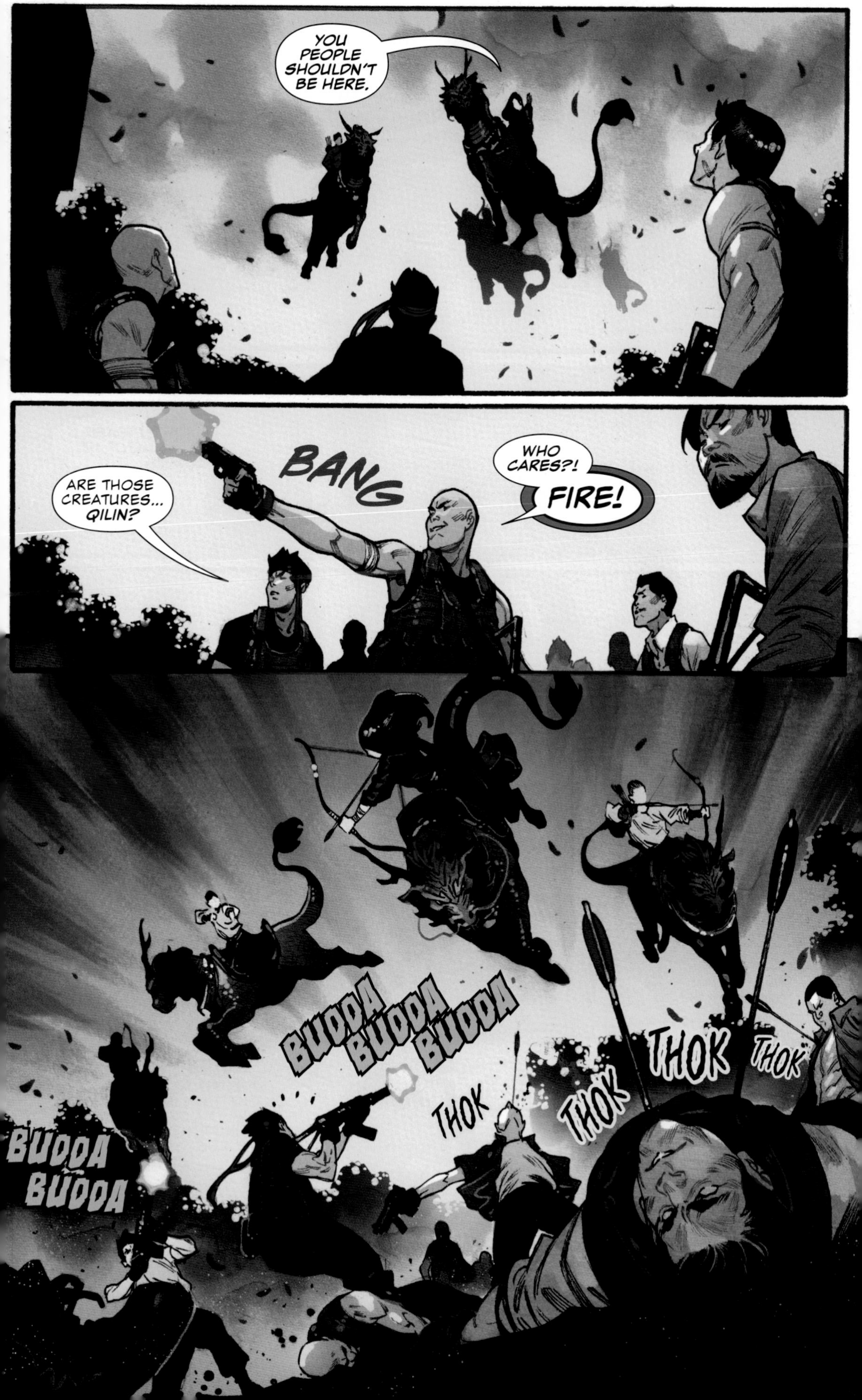
YOU PEOPLE SHOULDN'T BE HERE.
ARE THOSE CREATURES... QILIN?
BANG
WHO CARES?!
FIRE!
BUDDA BUDDA BUDDA
BUDDA BUDDA
THOK
THOK
THOK
THOK

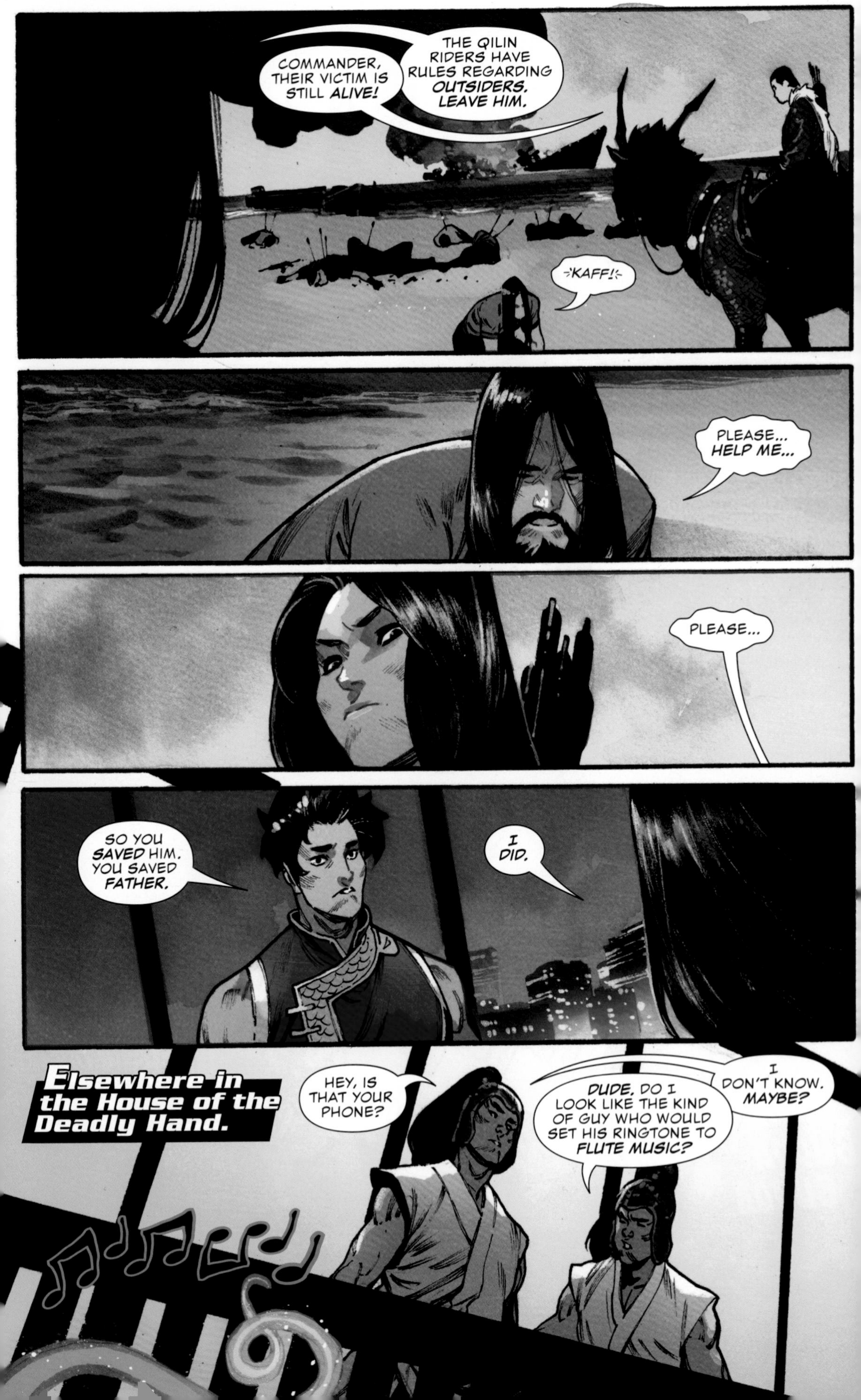
COMMANDER, THEIR VICTIM IS STILL ALIVE!
THE QILIN RIDERS HAVE RULES REGARDING OUTSIDERS. LEAVE HIM.
KAFF!
PLEASE... HELP ME...
PLEASE...
SO YOU SAVED HIM. YOU SAVED FATHER.
I DID.
Elsewhere in the House of the Deadly Hand.
HEY, IS THAT YOUR PHONE?
I DON'T KNOW. MAYBE?
DUDE. DO I LOOK LIKE THE KIND OF GUY WHO WOULD SET HIS RINGTONE TO FLUTE MUSIC?

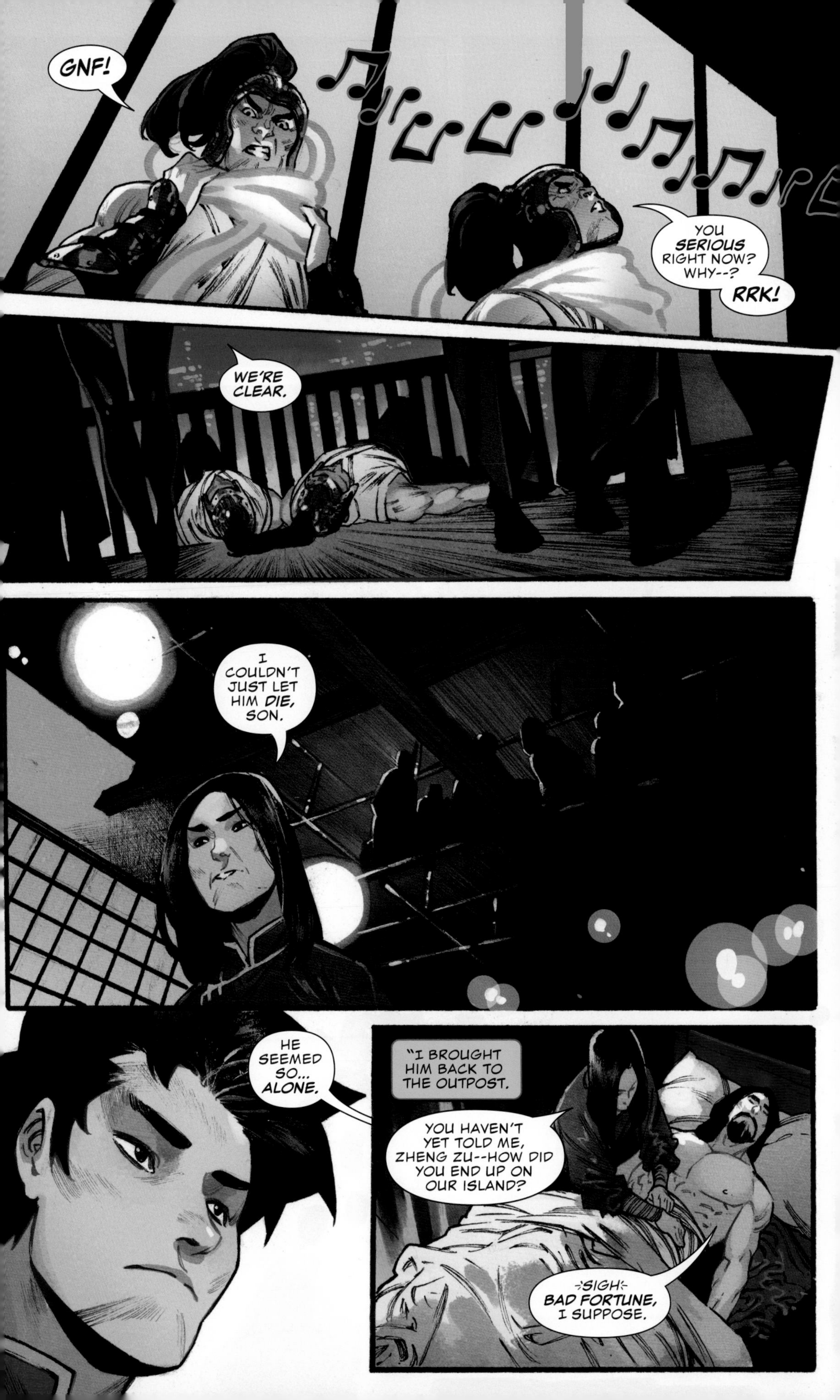
GNF!
YOU SERIOUS RIGHT NOW? WHY--?
RRK!
WE'RE CLEAR.
I COULDN'T JUST LET HIM DIE, SON.
HE SEEMED SO... ALONE.
"I BROUGHT HIM BACK TO THE OUTPOST.
YOU HAVEN'T YET TOLD ME, ZHENG ZU--HOW DID YOU END UP ON OUR ISLAND?
-SIGH- BAD FORTUNE, I SUPPOSE.

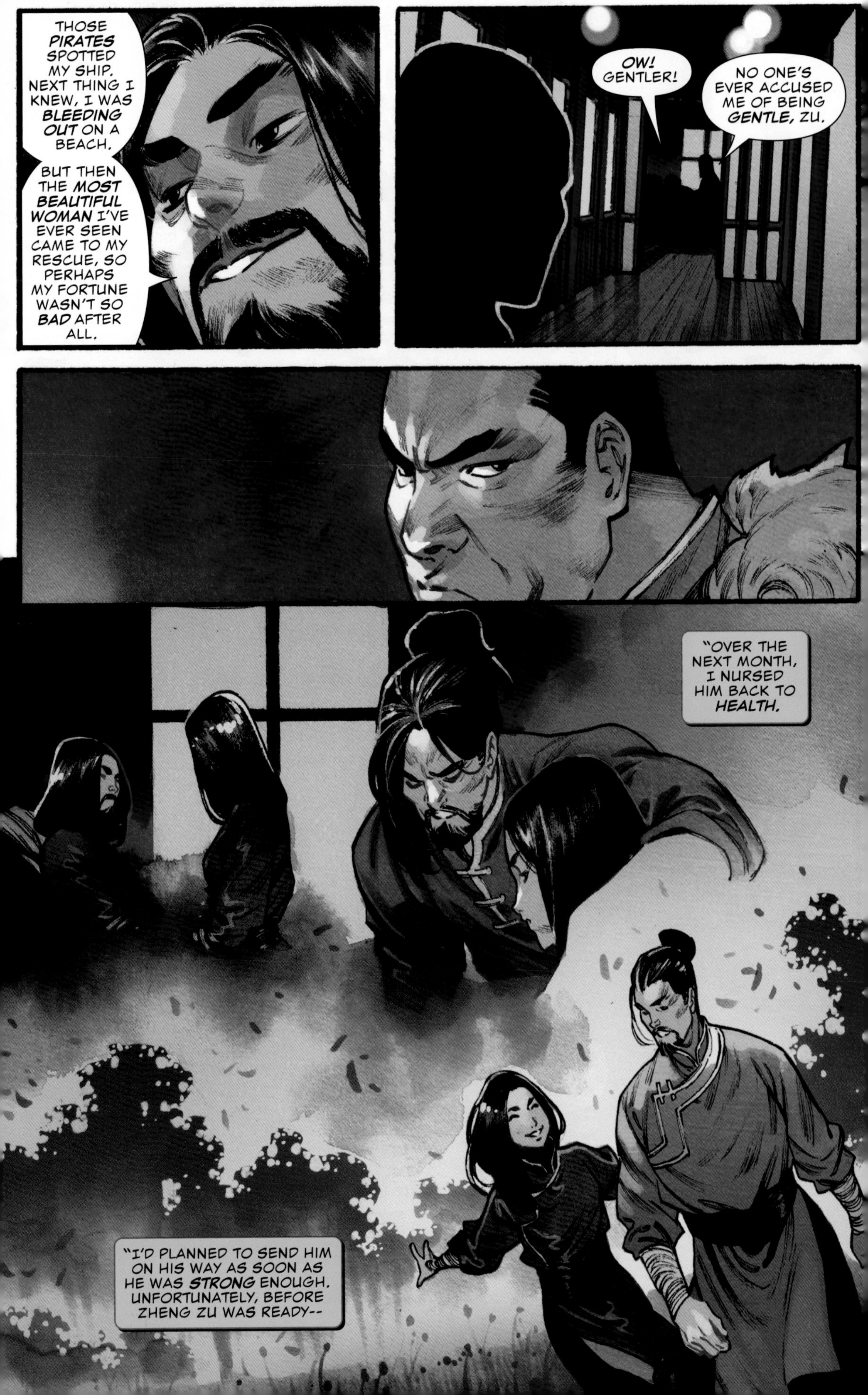
THOSE PIRATES SPOTTED MY SHIP. NEXT THING I KNEW, I WAS BLEEDING OUT ON A BEACH.
BUT THEN THE MOST BEAUTIFUL WOMAN I'VE EVER SEEN CAME TO MY RESCUE, SO PERHAPS MY FORTUNE WASN'T SO BAD AFTER ALL.
OW! GENTLER!
NO ONE'S EVER ACCUSED ME OF BEING GENTLE, ZU.
"OVER THE NEXT MONTH, I NURSED HIM BACK TO HEALTH.
"I'D PLANNED TO SEND HIM ON HIS WAY AS SOON AS HE WAS STRONG ENOUGH. UNFORTUNATELY, BEFORE ZHENG ZU WAS READY--

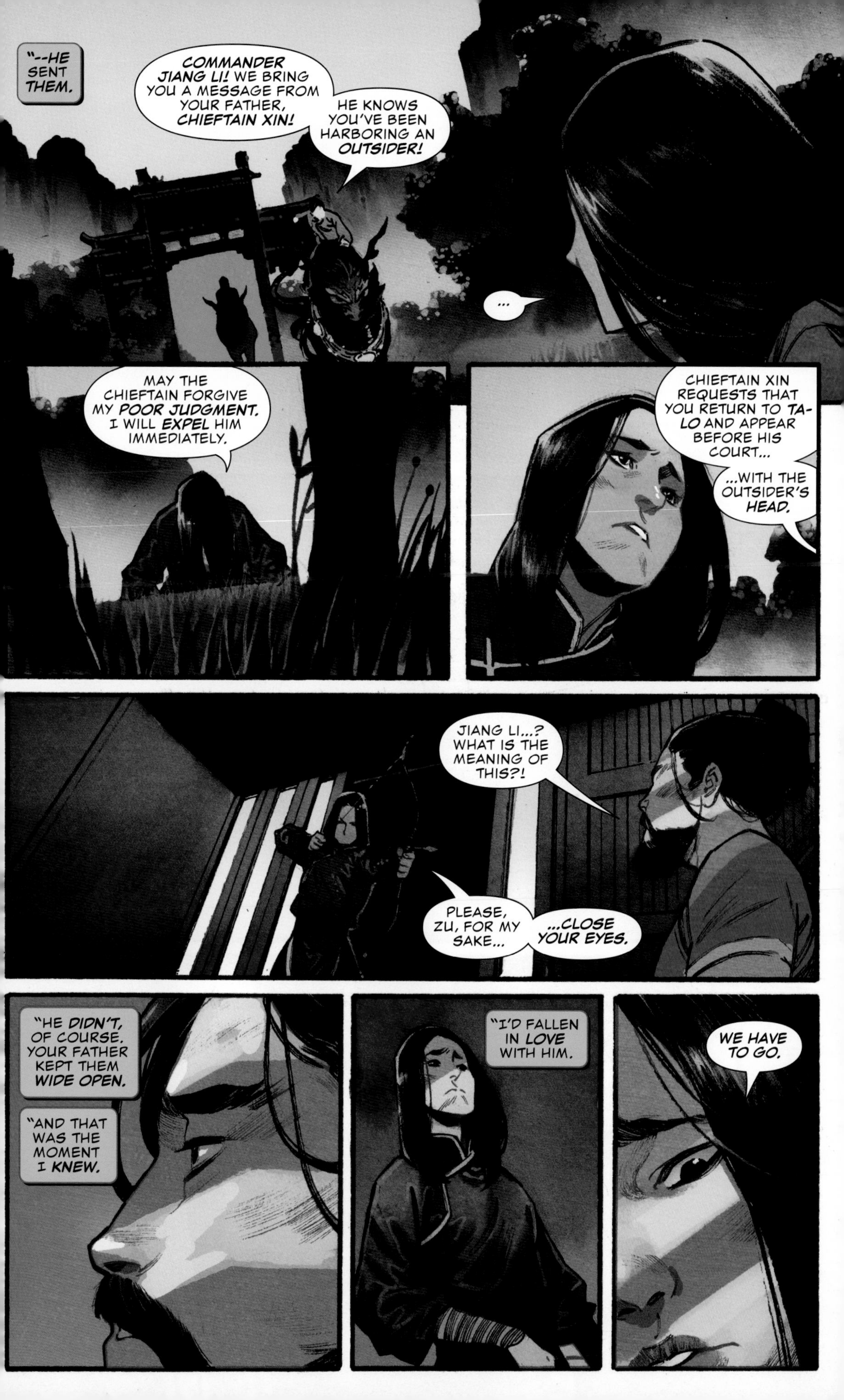
"--HE SENT THEM.
COMMANDER JIANG LI! WE BRING YOU A MESSAGE FROM YOUR FATHER, CHIEFTAIN XIN!
HE KNOWS YOU'VE BEEN HARBORING AN OUTSIDER!
...
MAY THE CHIEFTAIN FORGIVE MY POOR JUDGMENT. I WILL EXPEL HIM IMMEDIATELY.
CHIEFTAIN XIN REQUESTS THAT YOU RETURN TO TA-LO AND APPEAR BEFORE HIS COURT...
...WITH THE OUTSIDER'S HEAD.
JIANG LI...? WHAT IS THE MEANING OF THIS?!
PLEASE, ZU, FOR MY SAKE...
...CLOSE YOUR EYES.
"HE DIDN'T, OF COURSE. YOUR FATHER KEPT THEM WIDE OPEN.
"AND THAT WAS THE MOMENT I KNEW.
"I'D FALLEN IN LOVE WITH HIM.
WE HAVE TO GO.

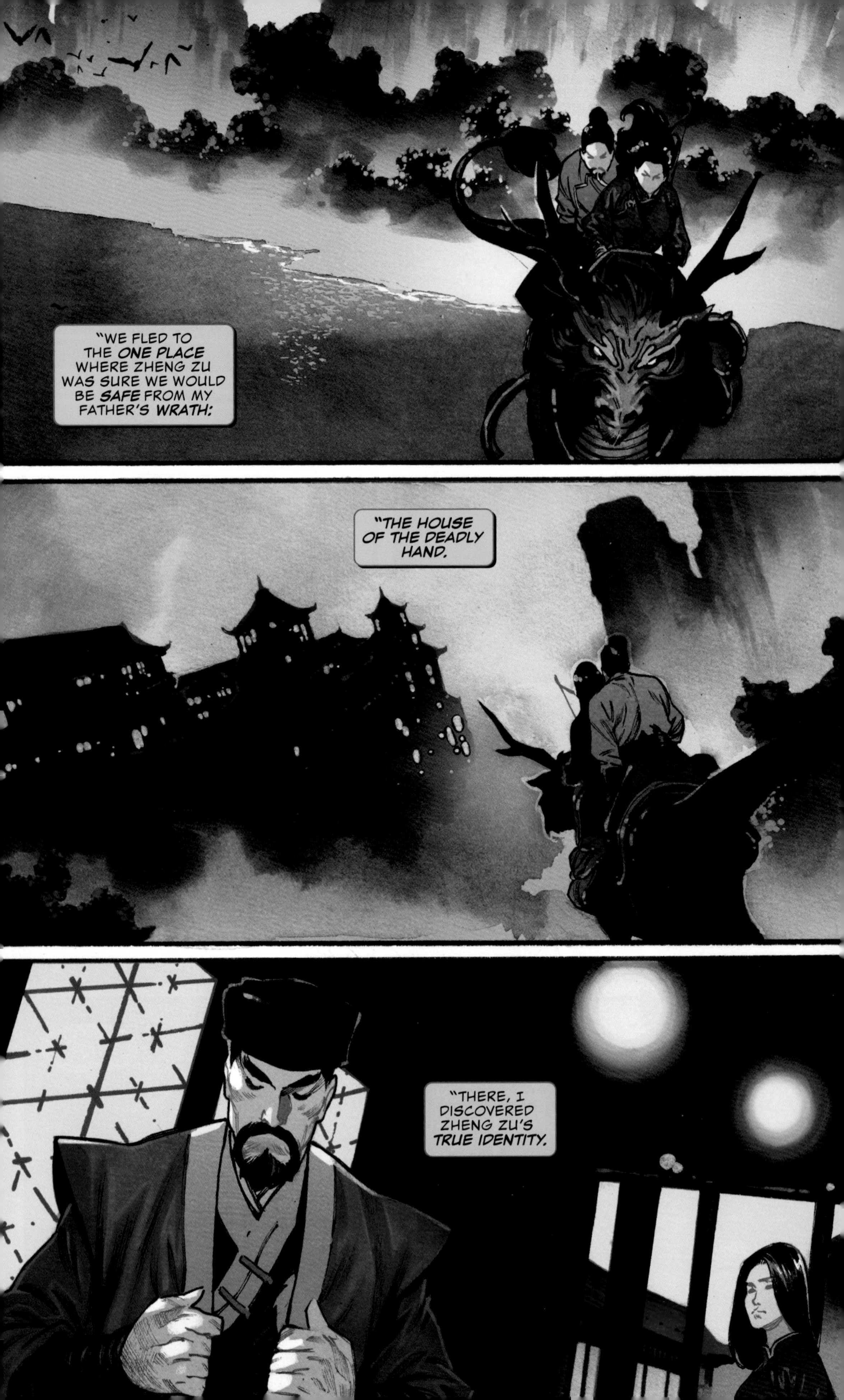
"WE FLED TO THE ONE PLACE WHERE ZHENG ZU WAS SURE WE WOULD BE SAFE FROM MY FATHER'S WRATH:
"THE HOUSE OF THE DEADLY HAND.
"THERE, I DISCOVERED ZHENG ZU'S TRUE IDENTITY.

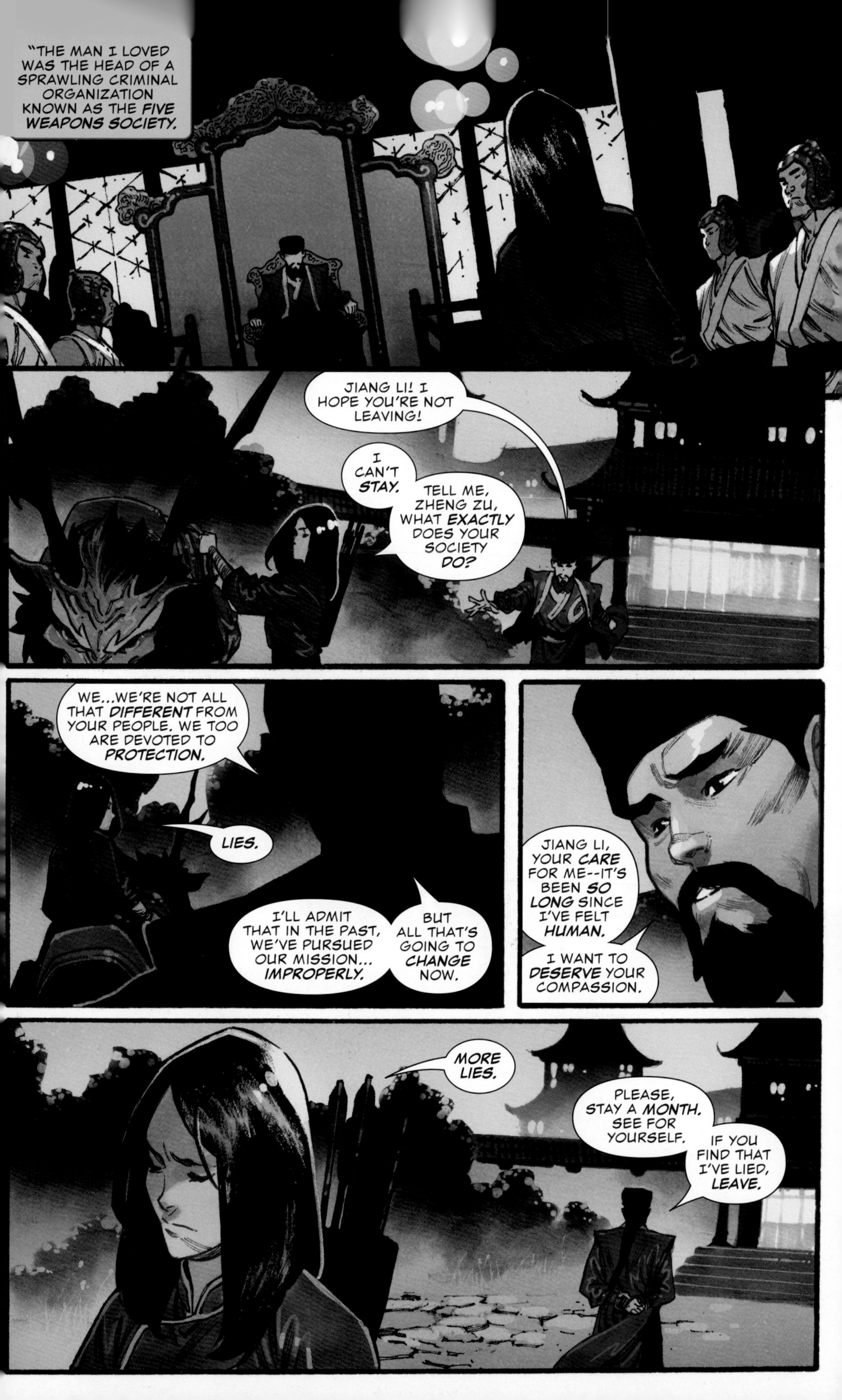

"THE MAN I LOVED WAS THE HEAD OF A SPRAWLING CRIMINAL ORGANIZATION KNOWN AS THE FIVE WEAPONS SOCIETY.
JIANG LI! I HOPE YOU'RE NOT LEAVING!
I CAN'T STAY.
TELL ME, ZHENG ZU, WHAT EXACTLY DOES YOUR SOCIETY DO?
WE...WE'RE NOT ALL THAT DIFFERENT FROM YOUR PEOPLE. WE TOO ARE DEVOTED TO PROTECTION.
LIES.
I'LL ADMIT THAT IN THE PAST, WE'VE PURSUED OUR MISSION... IMPROPERLY.
BUT ALL THAT'S GOING TO CHANGE NOW.
JIANG LI, YOUR CARE FOR ME--IT'S BEEN SO LONG SINCE I'VE FELT HUMAN.
I WANT TO DESERVE YOUR COMPASSION.
MORE LIES.
PLEASE, STAY A MONTH. SEE FOR YOURSELF.
IF YOU FIND THAT I'VE LIED, LEAVE.

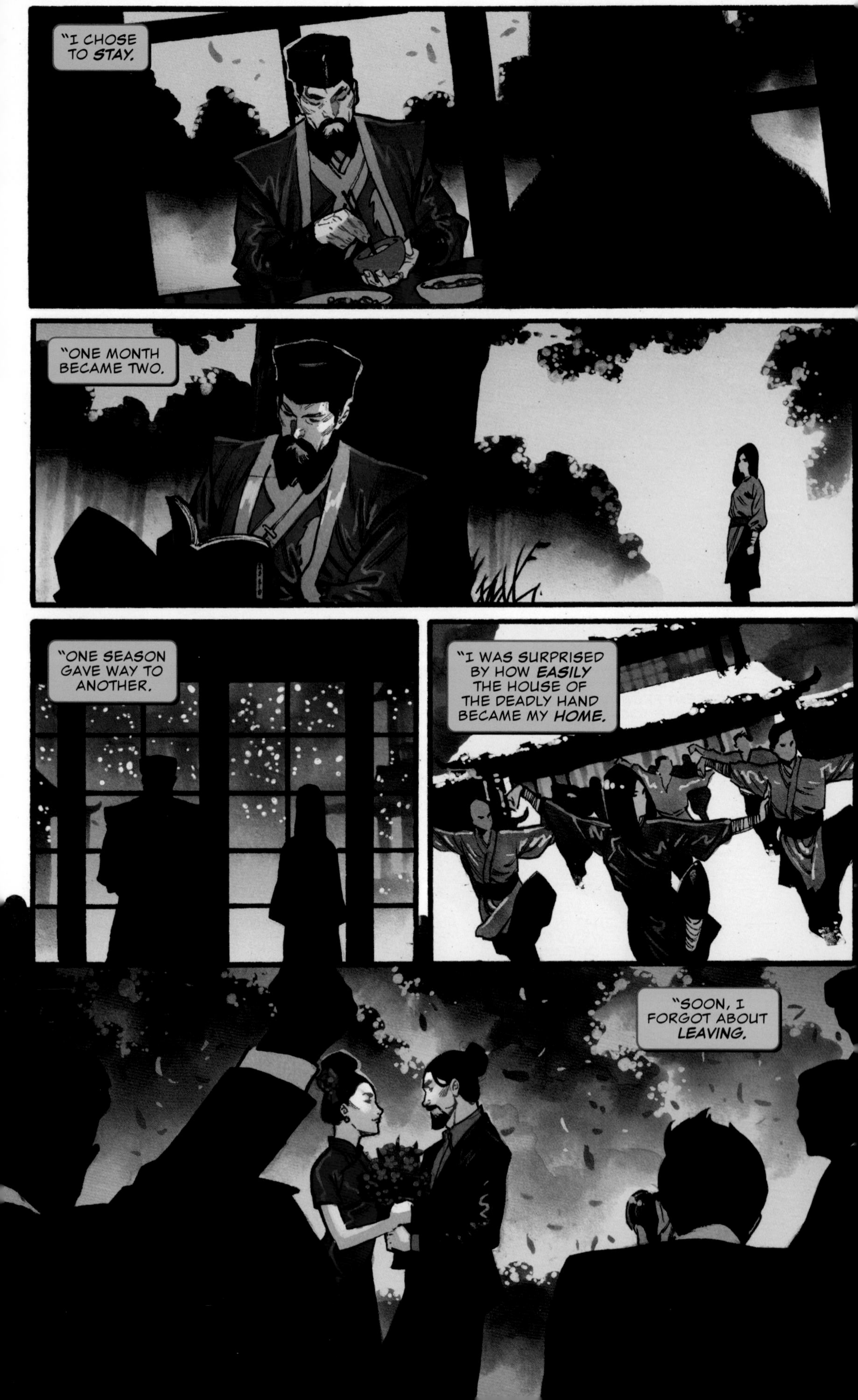
"I CHOSE TO STAY.
"ONE MONTH BECAME TWO.
"ONE SEASON GAVE WAY TO ANOTHER.
"I WAS SURPRISED BY HOW EASILY THE HOUSE OF THE DEADLY HAND BECAME MY HOME.
"SOON, I FORGOT ABOUT LEAVING.

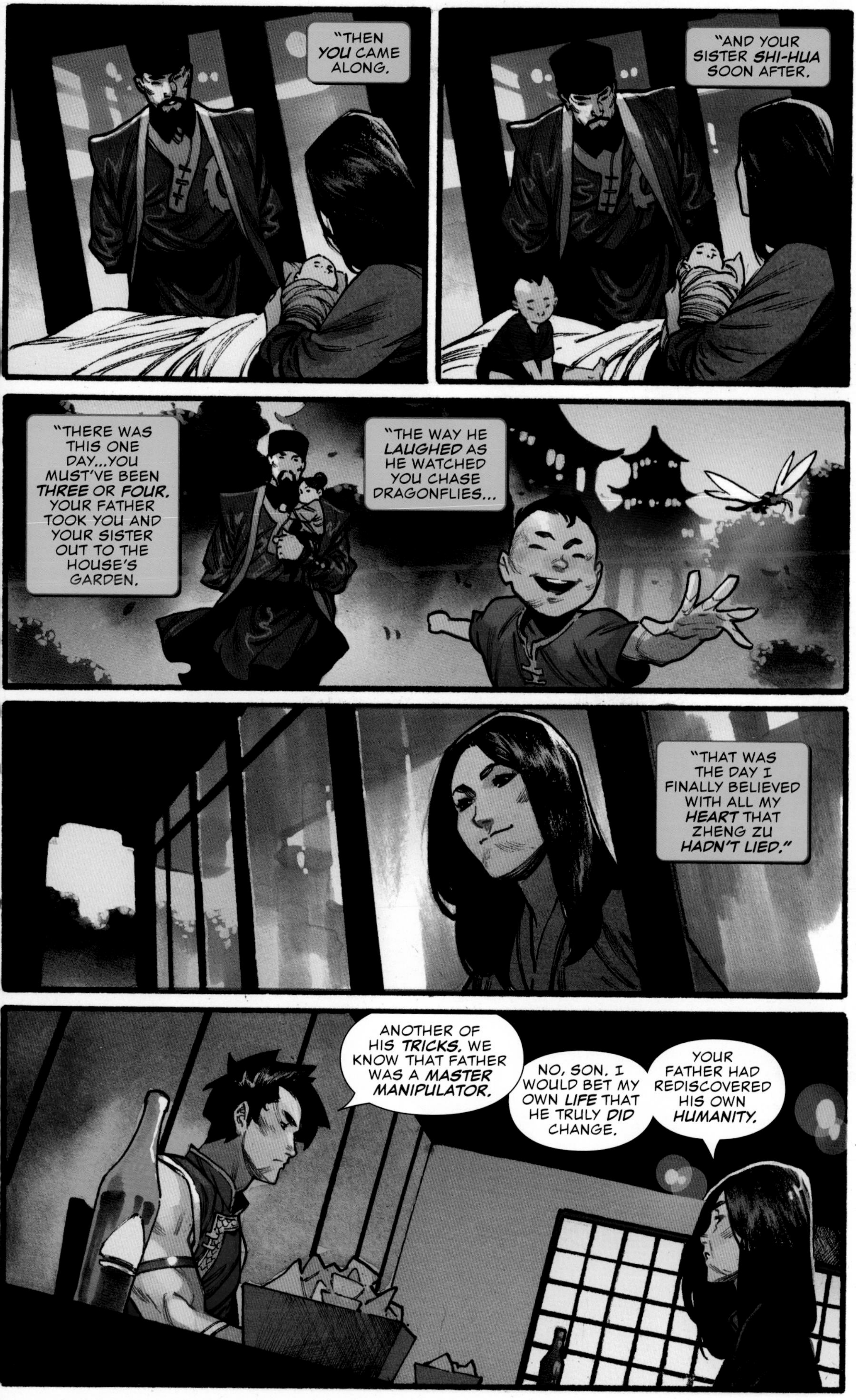
"THEN YOU CAME ALONG.
"AND YOUR SISTER SHI-HUA SOON AFTER.
"THERE WAS THIS ONE DAY...YOU MUST'VE BEEN THREE OR FOUR. YOUR FATHER TOOK YOU AND YOUR SISTER OUT TO THE HOUSE'S GARDEN.
"THE WAY HE LAUGHED AS HE WATCHED YOU CHASE DRAGONFLIES...
"THAT WAS THE DAY I FINALLY BELIEVED WITH ALL MY HEART THAT ZHENG ZU HADN'T LIED."
ANOTHER OF HIS TRICKS. WE KNOW THAT FATHER WAS A MASTER MANIPULATOR.
NO, SON. I WOULD BET MY OWN LIFE THAT HE TRULY DID CHANGE.
YOUR FATHER HAD REDISCOVERED HIS OWN HUMANITY.

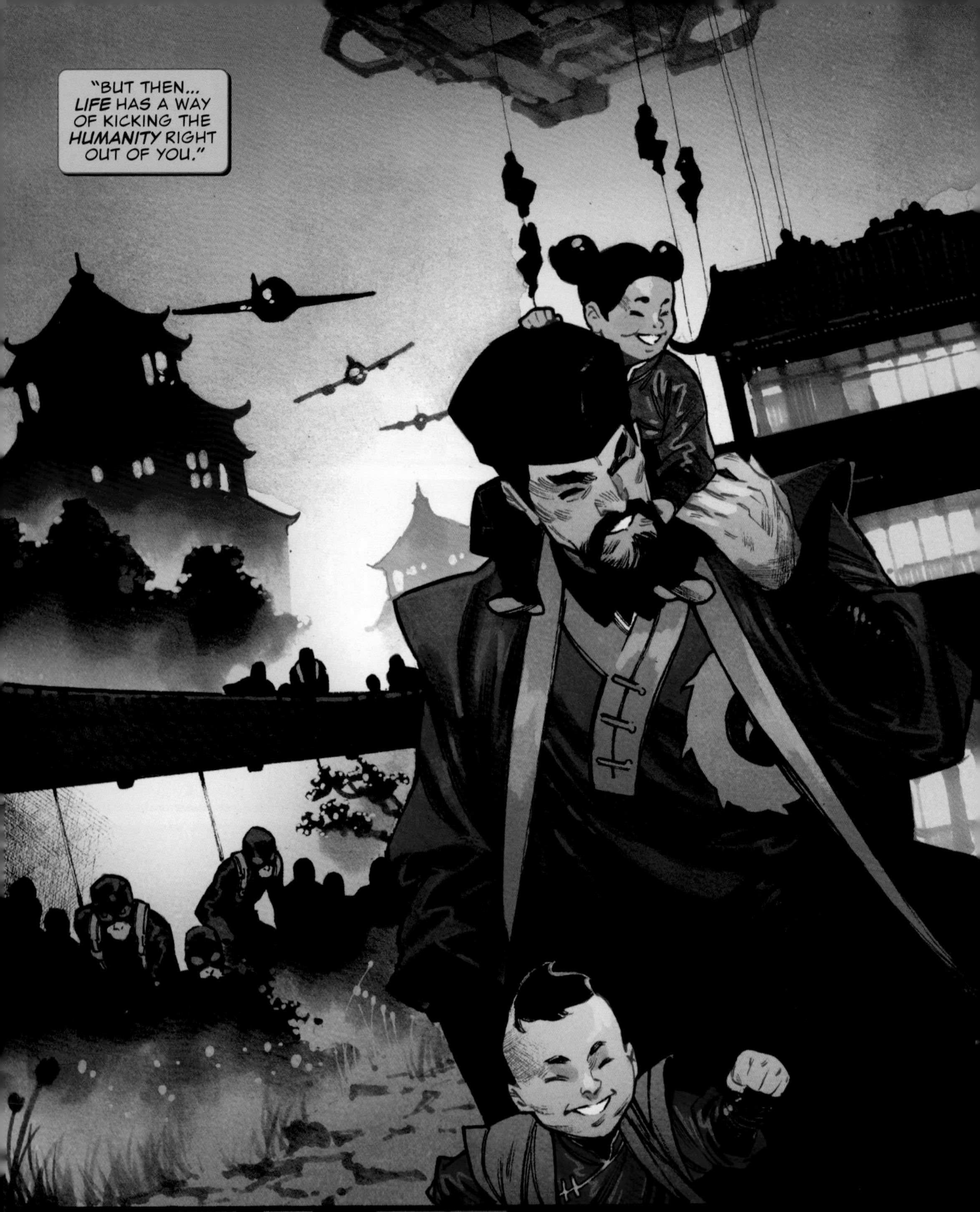
"BUT THEN... *LIFE* HAS A WAY OF KICKING THE *HUMANITY* RIGHT OUT OF YOU."

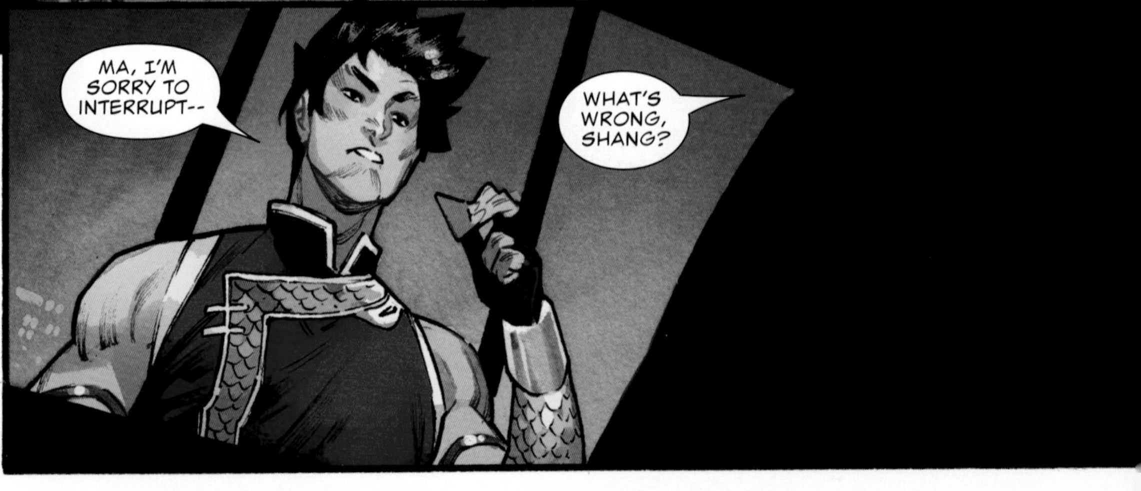
MA, I'M SORRY TO INTERRUPT--
WHAT'S WRONG, SHANG?

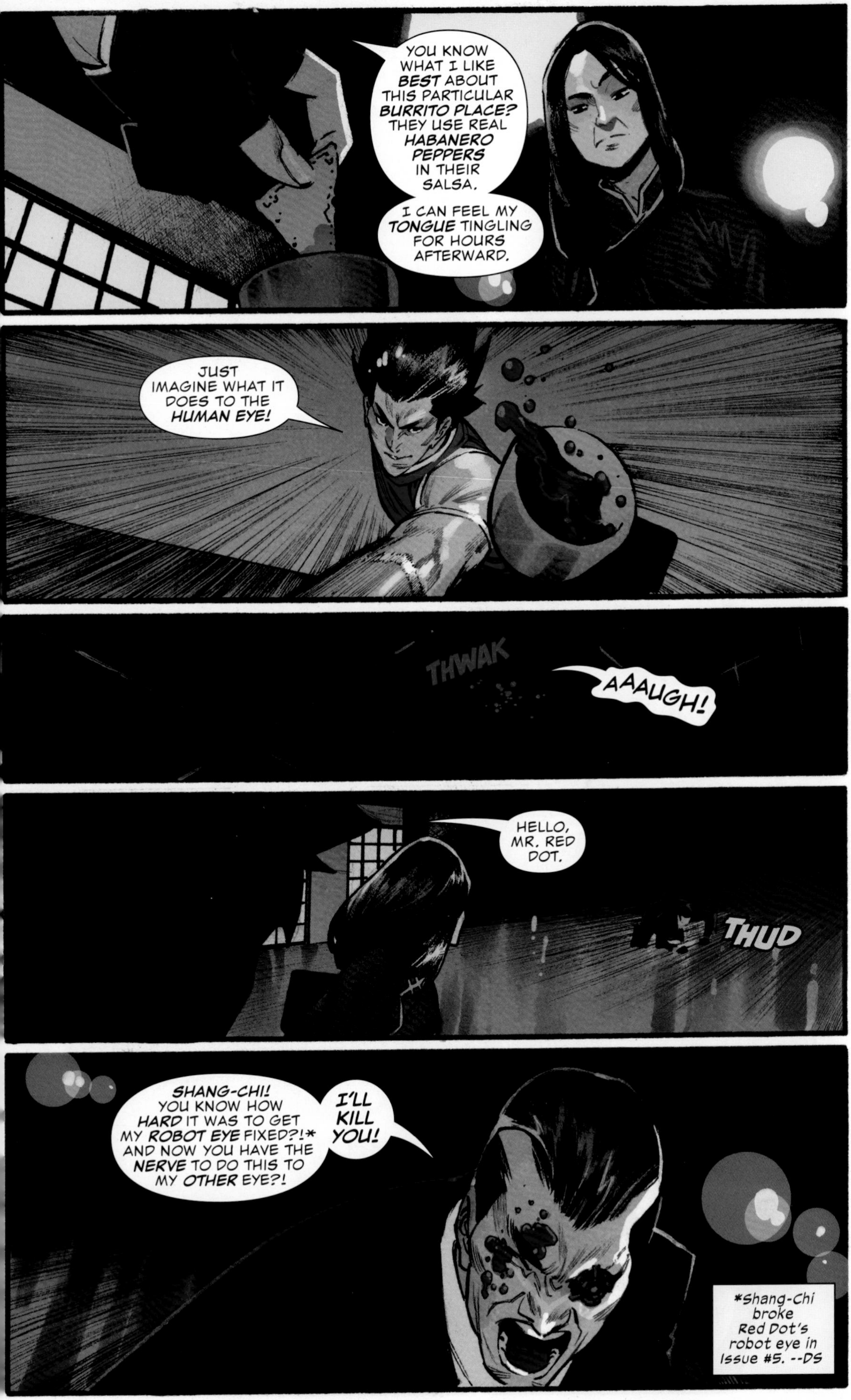
YOU KNOW WHAT I LIKE BEST ABOUT THIS PARTICULAR BURRITO PLACE? THEY USE REAL HABANERO PEPPERS IN THEIR SALSA.
I CAN FEEL MY TONGUE TINGLING FOR HOURS AFTERWARD.
JUST IMAGINE WHAT IT DOES TO THE HUMAN EYE!
THWAK
AAAUGH!
HELLO, MR. RED DOT.
THUD
SHANG-CHI! YOU KNOW HOW HARD IT WAS TO GET MY ROBOT EYE FIXED?!* AND NOW YOU HAVE THE NERVE TO DO THIS TO MY OTHER EYE?!
I'LL KILL YOU!
*Shang-Chi broke Red Dot's robot eye in Issue #5. --DS

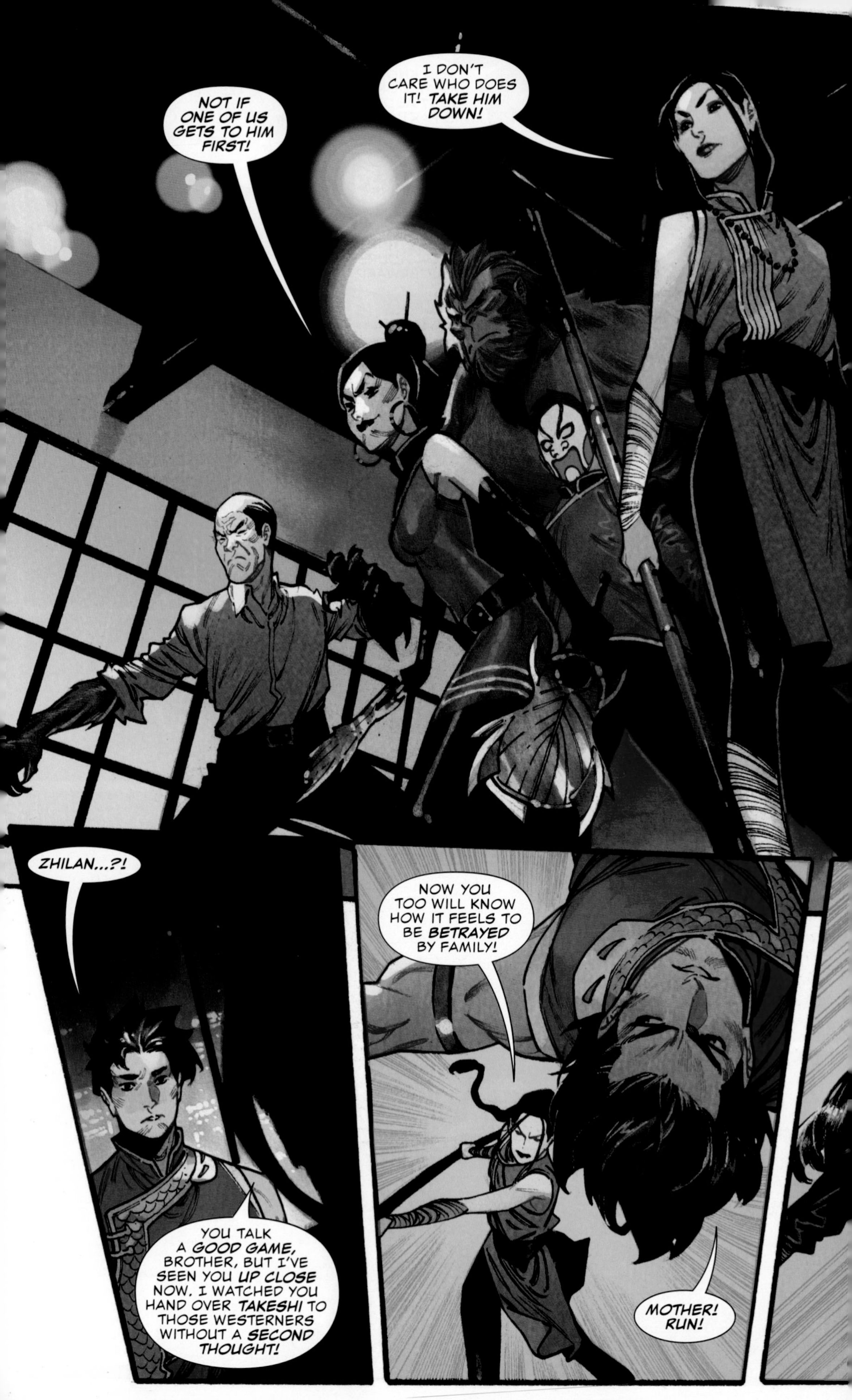
NOT IF ONE OF US GETS TO HIM FIRST!
I DON'T CARE WHO DOES IT! TAKE HIM DOWN!
ZHILAN...?!
YOU TALK A GOOD GAME, BROTHER, BUT I'VE SEEN YOU UP CLOSE NOW. I WATCHED YOU HAND OVER TAKESHI TO THOSE WESTERNERS WITHOUT A SECOND THOUGHT!
NOW YOU TOO WILL KNOW HOW IT FEELS TO BE BETRAYED BY FAMILY!
MOTHER! RUN!

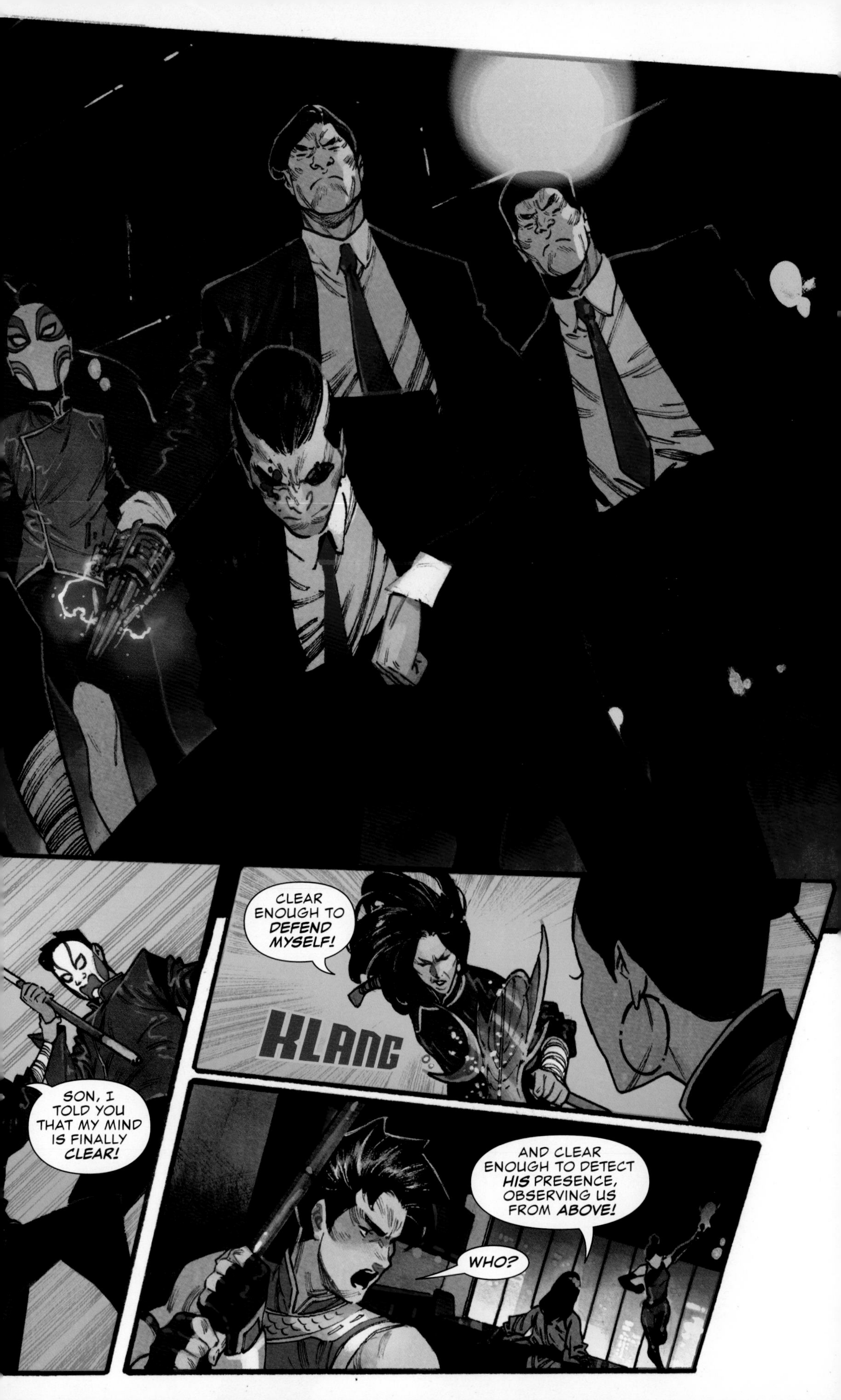
SON, I TOLD YOU THAT MY MIND IS FINALLY CLEAR!
CLEAR ENOUGH TO DEFEND MYSELF!
KLANG
AND CLEAR ENOUGH TO DETECT HIS PRESENCE, OBSERVING US FROM ABOVE!
WHO?

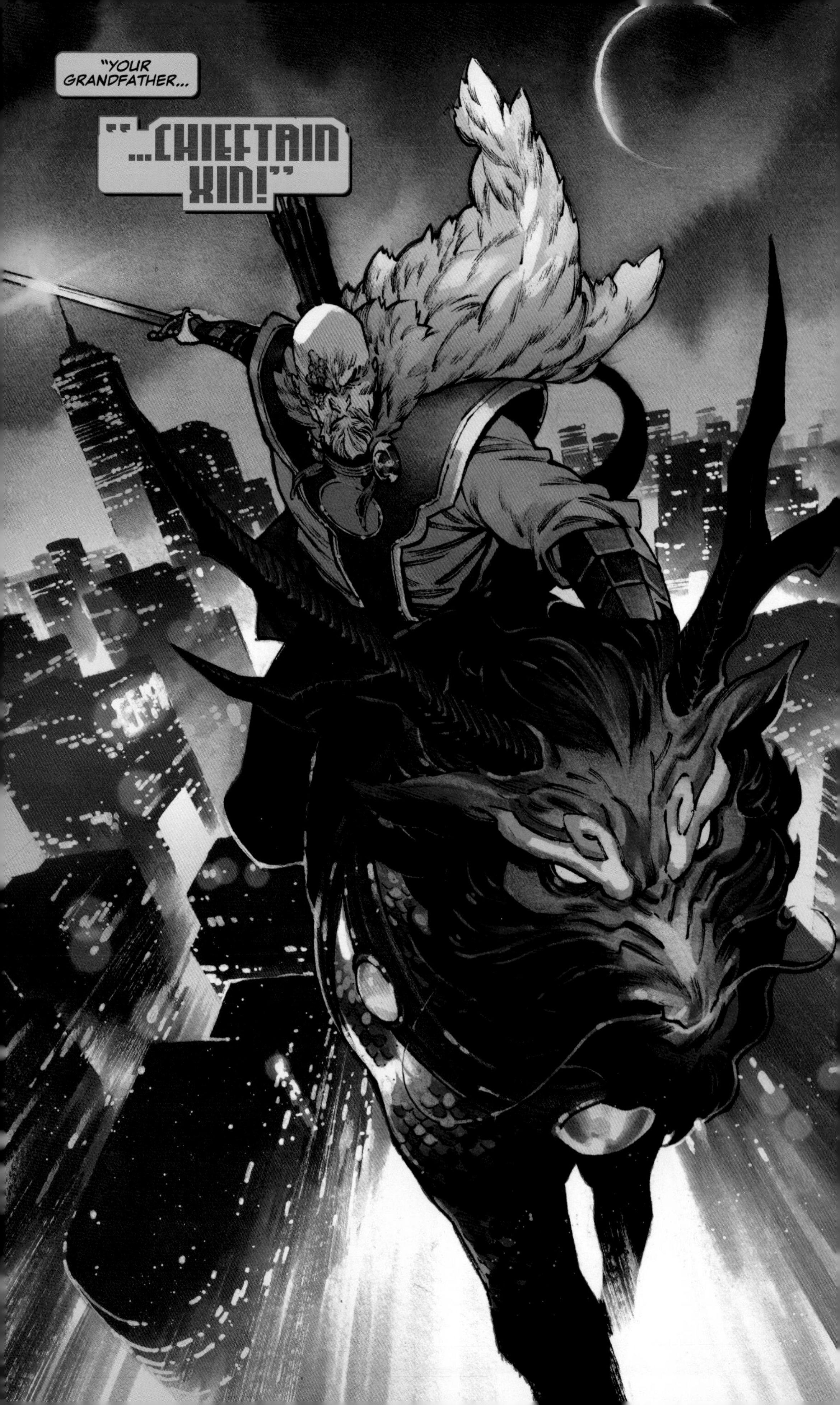
"YOUR GRANDFATHER...
"...CHIEFTAIN XIN!"

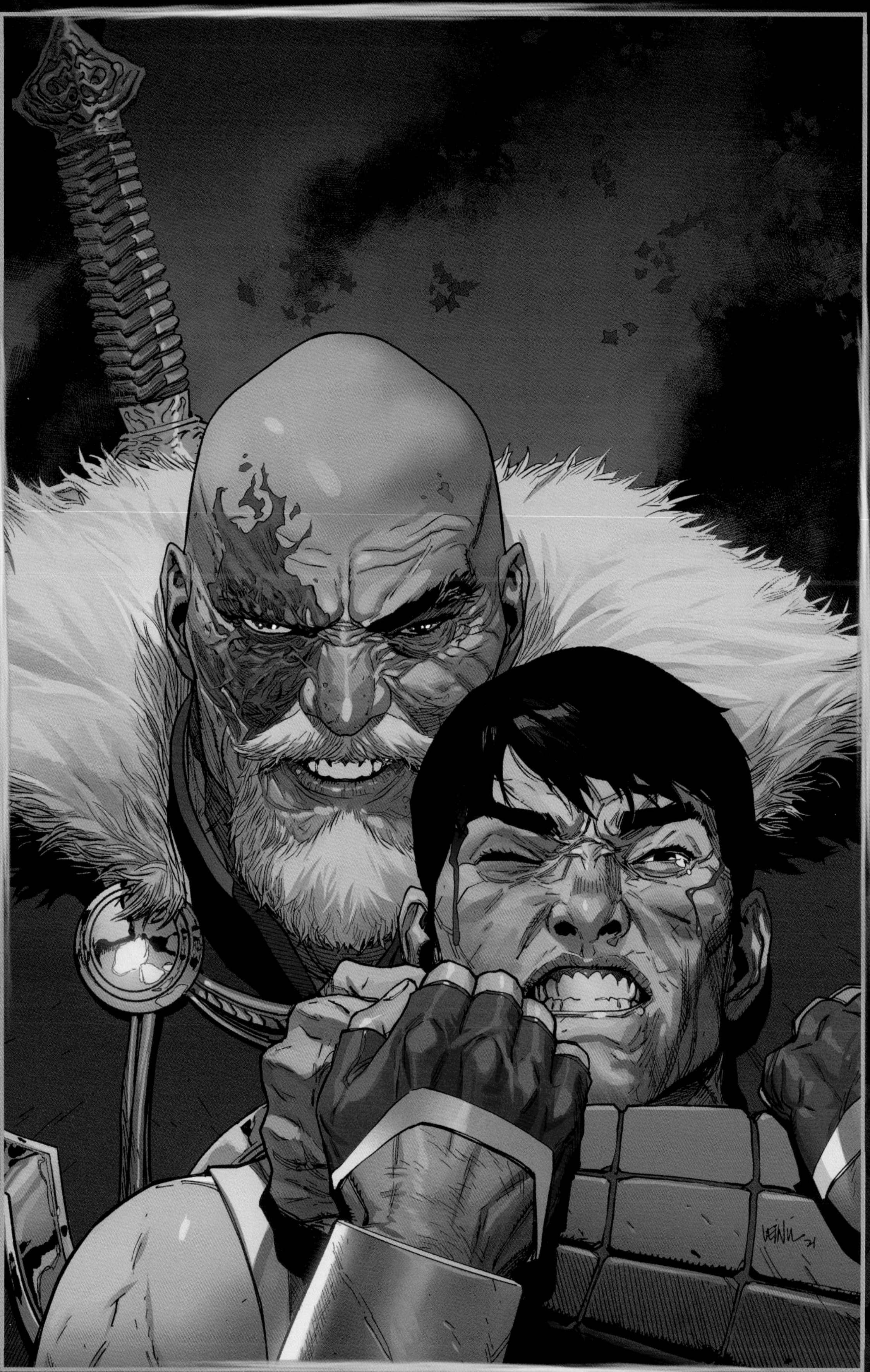

EIGHT

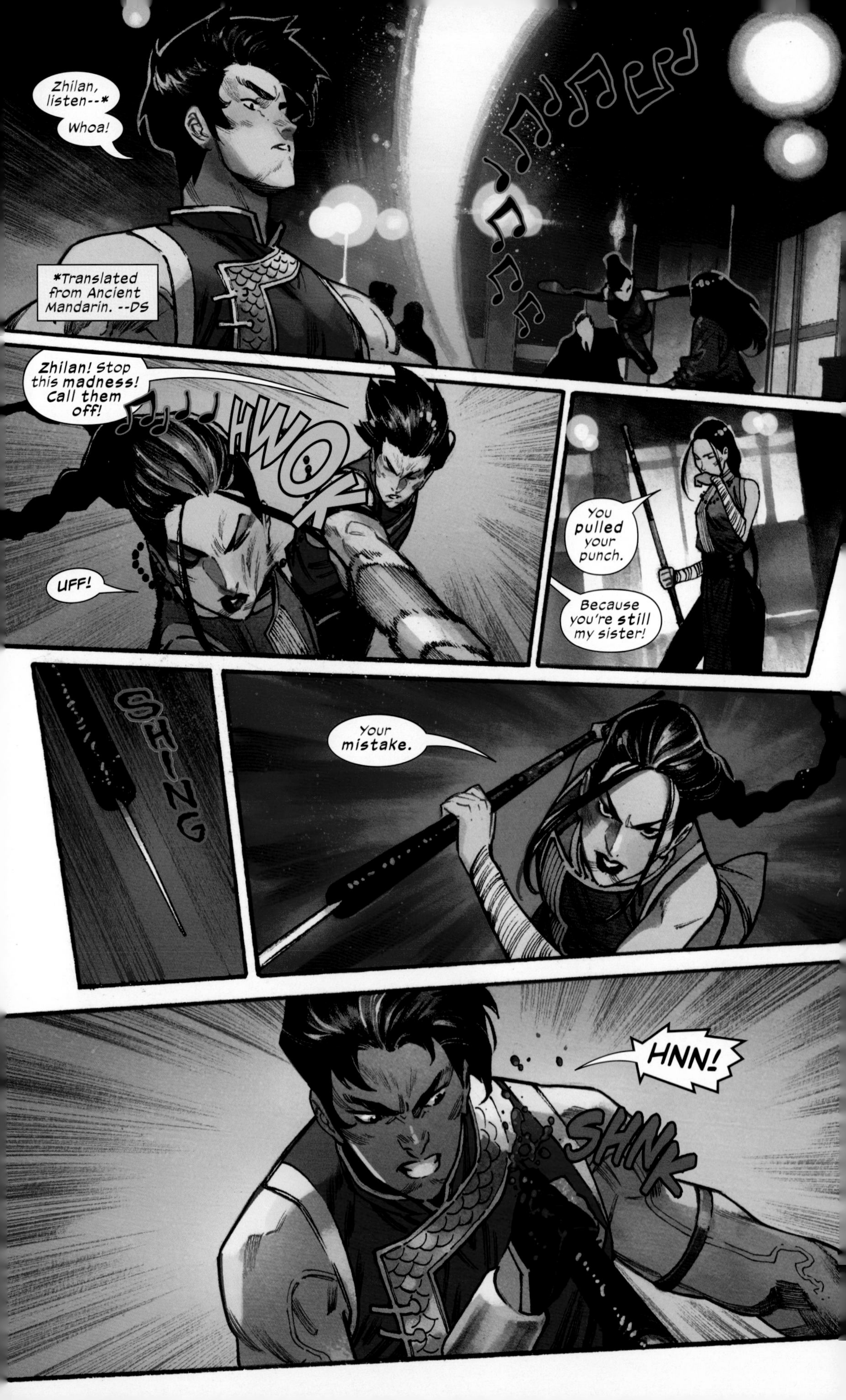

Zhilan, listen--*
Whoa!
*Translated from Ancient Mandarin. --DS
Zhilan! Stop this madness! Call them off!
WOK
UFF!
You pulled your punch.
Because you're still my sister!
SHING
Your mistake.
HNN!
SHNK

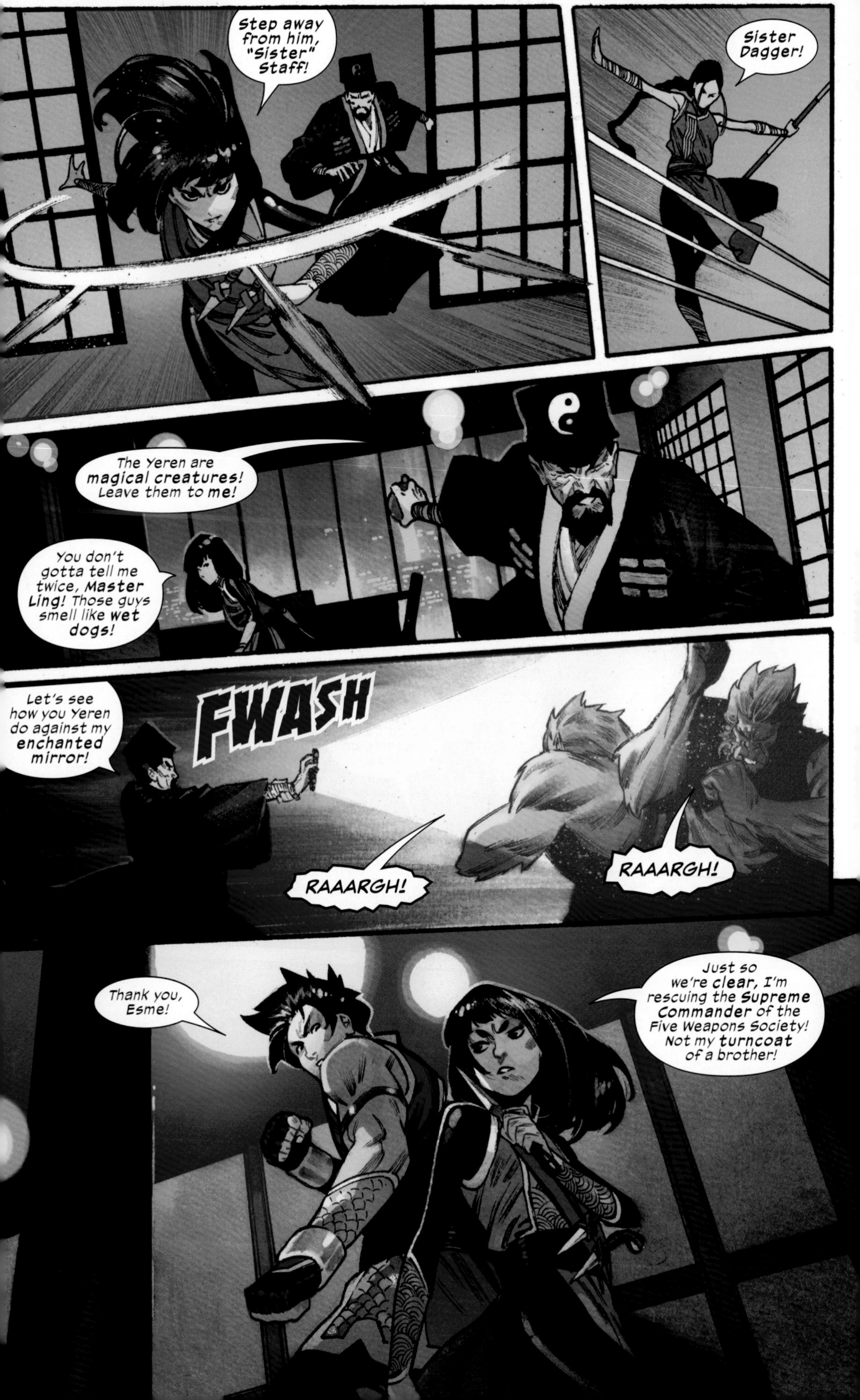
Step away from him, "Sister" Staff!
Sister Dagger!
The Yeren are magical creatures! Leave them to me!
You don't gotta tell me twice, Master Ling! Those guys smell like wet dogs!
Let's see how you Yeren do against my enchanted mirror!
FWASH
RAAARGH!
RAAARGH!
Thank you, Esme!
Just so we're clear, I'm rescuing the Supreme Commander of the Five Weapons Society! Not my turncoat of a brother!

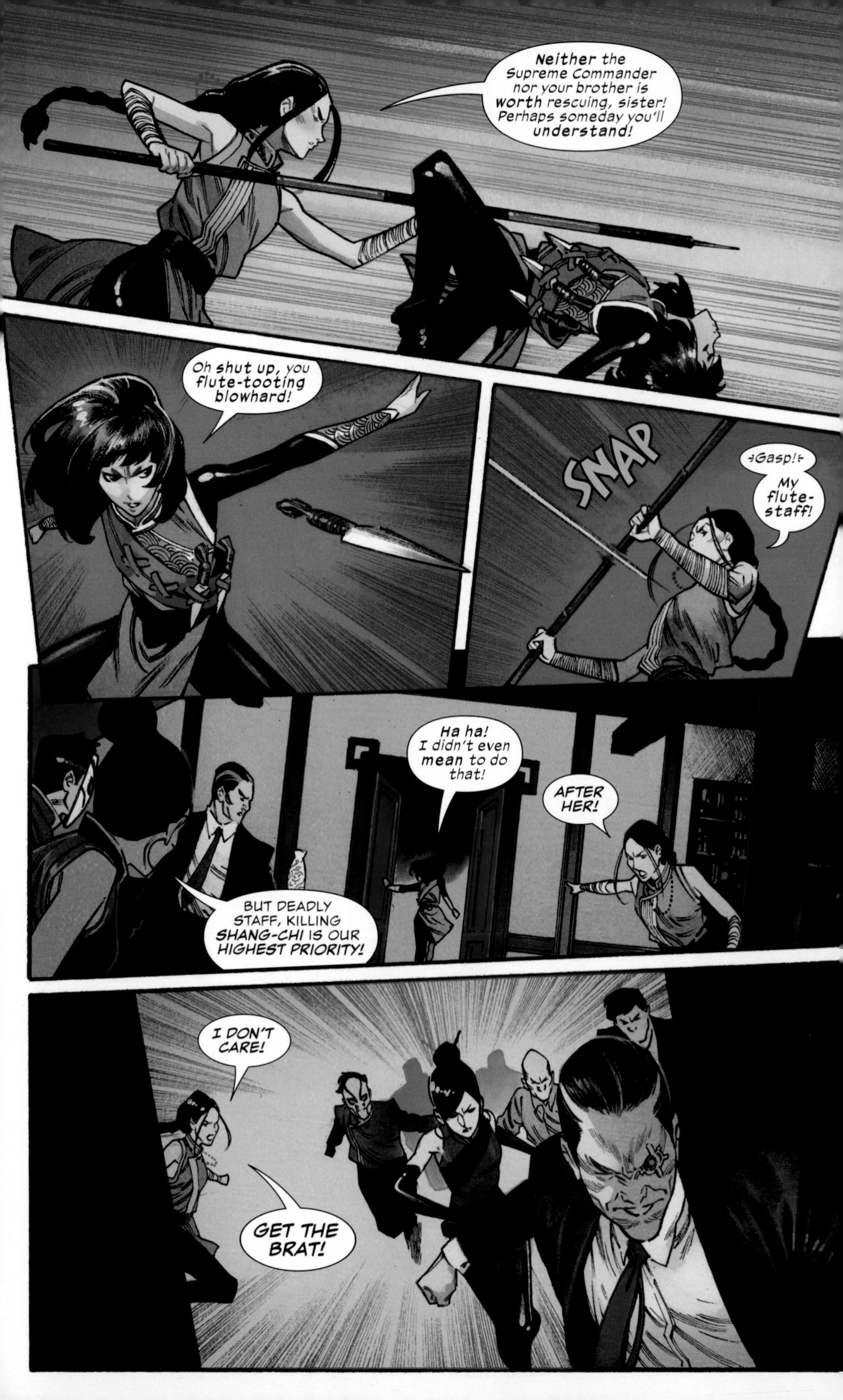
Neither the Supreme Commander nor your brother is worth rescuing, sister! Perhaps someday you'll understand!
Oh shut up, you flute-tooting blowhard!
SNAP
Gasp!
My flute-staff!
Ha ha! I didn't even mean to do that!
AFTER HER!
BUT DEADLY STAFF, KILLING SHANG-CHI IS OUR HIGHEST PRIORITY!
I DON'T CARE!
GET THE BRAT!

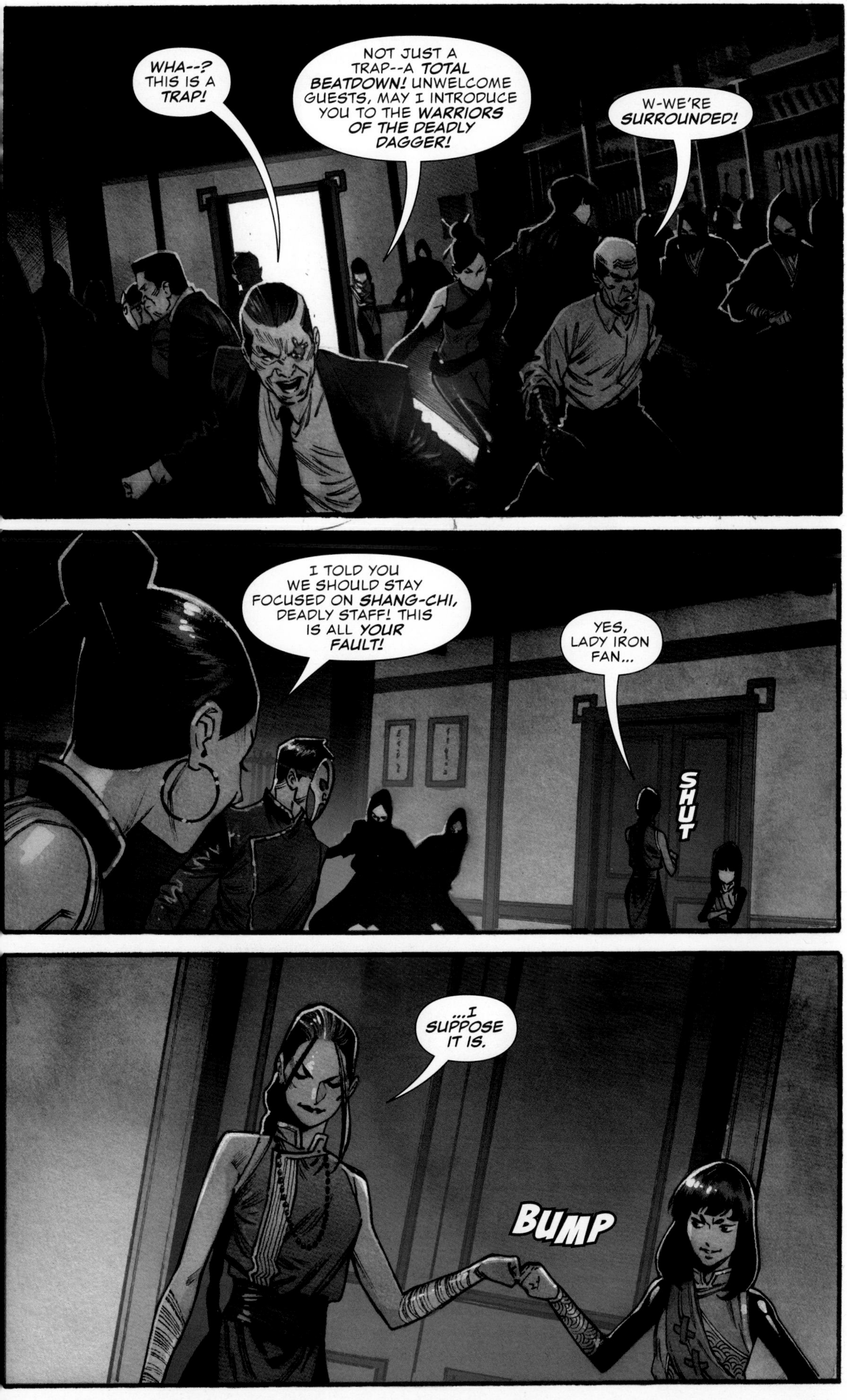
WHA--? THIS IS A TRAP!
NOT JUST A TRAP--A TOTAL BEATDOWN! UNWELCOME GUESTS, MAY I INTRODUCE YOU TO THE WARRIORS OF THE DEADLY DAGGER!
W-WE'RE SURROUNDED!
I TOLD YOU WE SHOULD STAY FOCUSED ON SHANG-CHI, DEADLY STAFF! THIS IS ALL YOUR FAULT!
YES, LADY IRON FAN...
SHUT
...I SUPPOSE IT IS.
BUMP

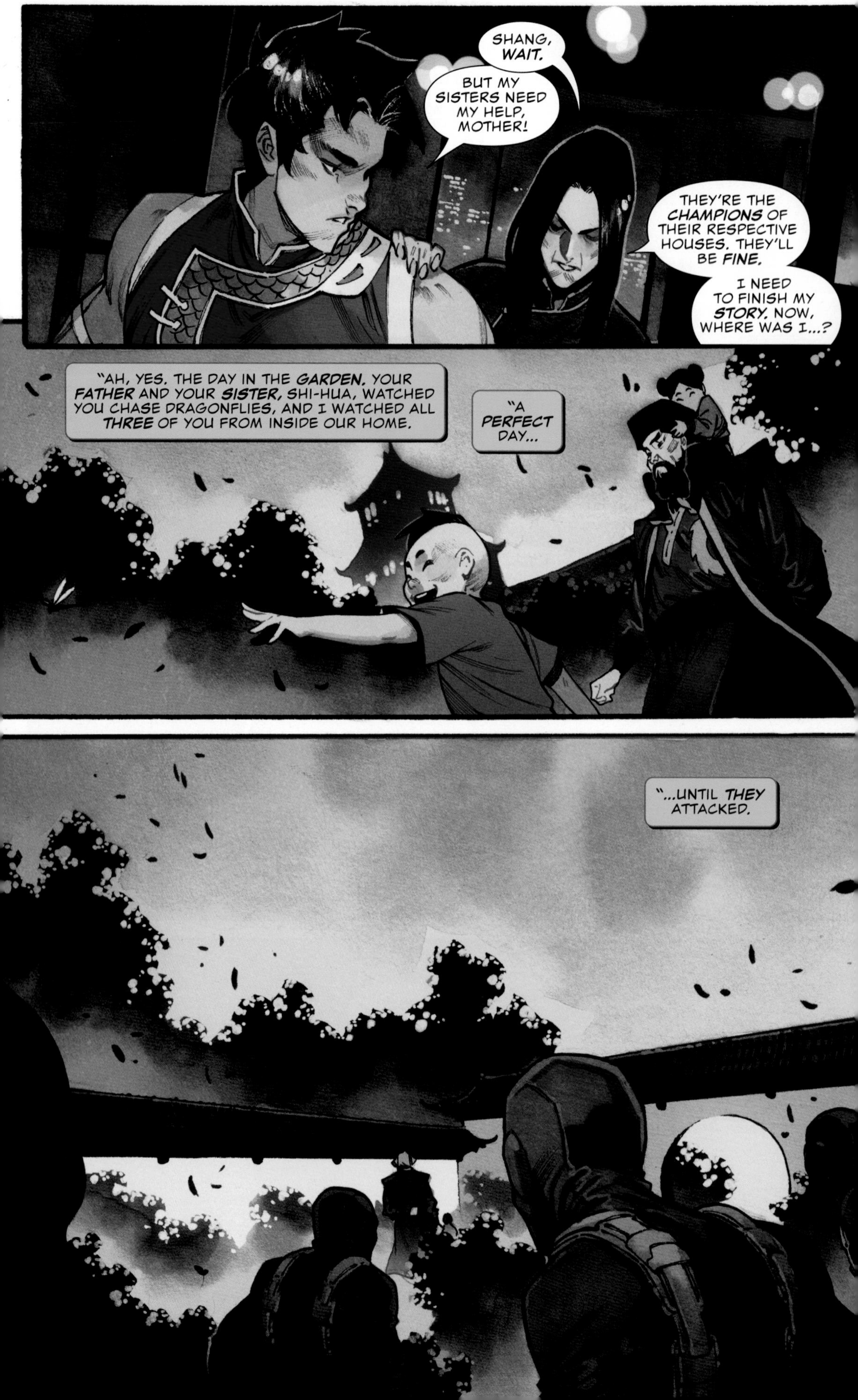
SHANG, WAIT.
BUT MY SISTERS NEED MY HELP, MOTHER!
THEY'RE THE CHAMPIONS OF THEIR RESPECTIVE HOUSES. THEY'LL BE FINE.
I NEED TO FINISH MY STORY. NOW, WHERE WAS I...?
"AH, YES. THE DAY IN THE GARDEN. YOUR FATHER AND YOUR SISTER, SHI-HUA, WATCHED YOU CHASE DRAGONFLIES, AND I WATCHED ALL THREE OF YOU FROM INSIDE OUR HOME.
"A PERFECT DAY...
"...UNTIL THEY ATTACKED.

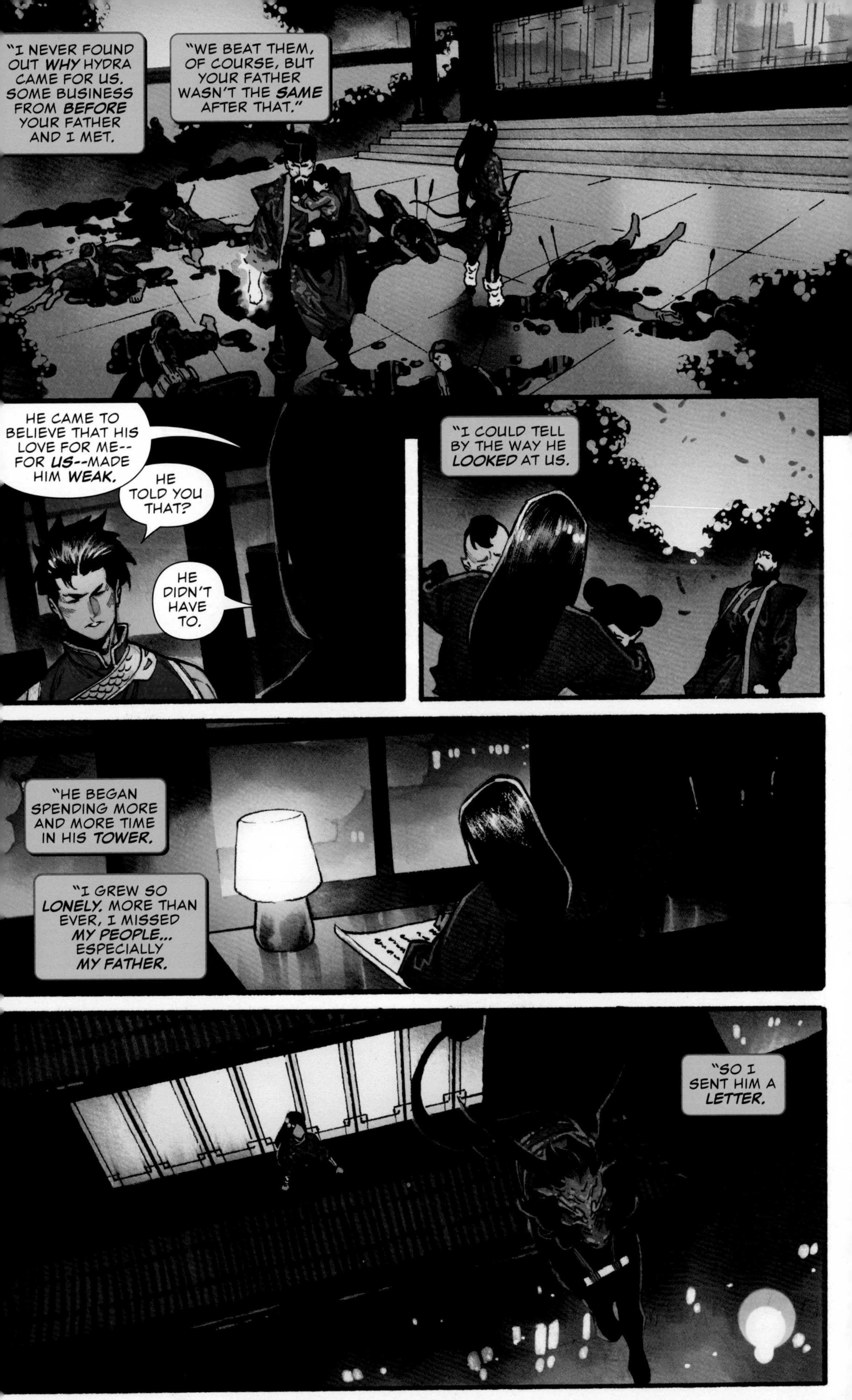

"I NEVER FOUND OUT WHY HYDRA CAME FOR US. SOME BUSINESS FROM BEFORE YOUR FATHER AND I MET.
"WE BEAT THEM, OF COURSE, BUT YOUR FATHER WASN'T THE SAME AFTER THAT."
HE CAME TO BELIEVE THAT HIS LOVE FOR ME--FOR US--MADE HIM WEAK.
HE TOLD YOU THAT?
HE DIDN'T HAVE TO.
"I COULD TELL BY THE WAY HE LOOKED AT US.
"HE BEGAN SPENDING MORE AND MORE TIME IN HIS TOWER.
"I GREW SO LONELY. MORE THAN EVER, I MISSED MY PEOPLE... ESPECIALLY MY FATHER.
"SO I SENT HIM A LETTER.

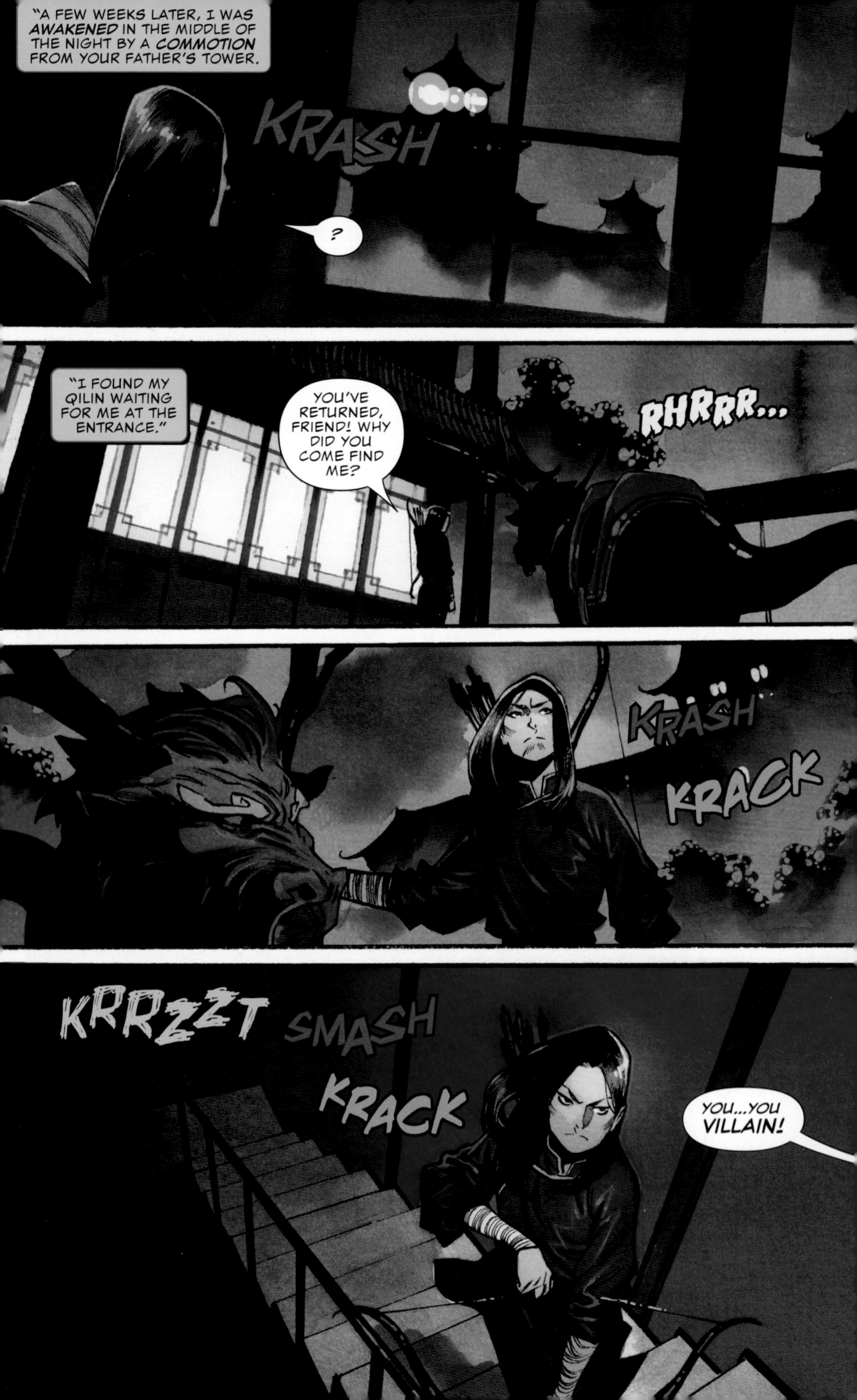
"A FEW WEEKS LATER, I WAS AWAKENED IN THE MIDDLE OF THE NIGHT BY A COMMOTION FROM YOUR FATHER'S TOWER.
KRASSH
?
"I FOUND MY QILIN WAITING FOR ME AT THE ENTRANCE."
YOU'VE RETURNED, FRIEND! WHY DID YOU COME FIND ME?
RHRRR...
KRASH
KRACK
KRRZZT
SMASH
KRACK
YOU...YOU VILLAIN!

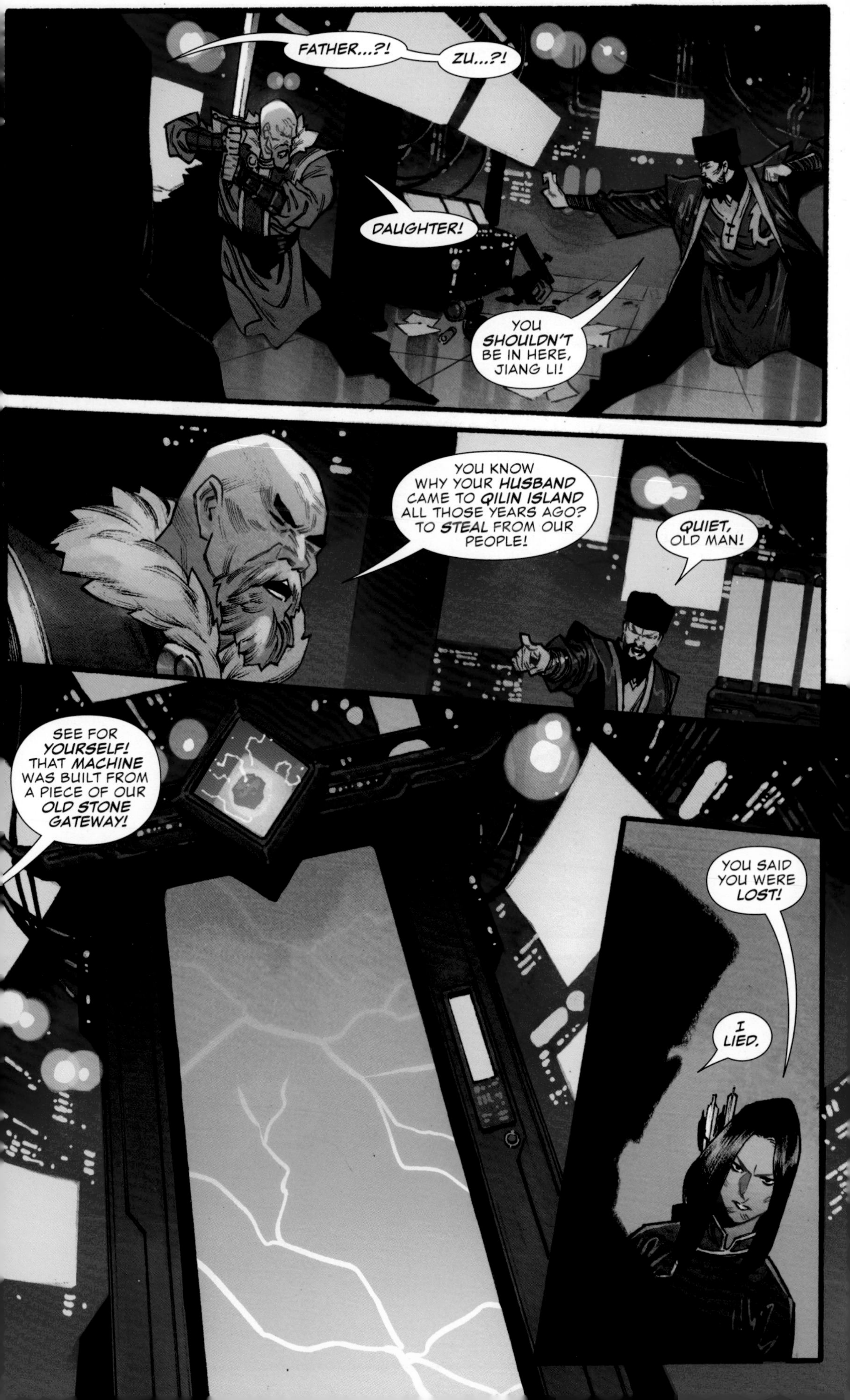
FATHER...?!
ZU...?!
DAUGHTER!
YOU SHOULDN'T BE IN HERE, JIANG LI!
YOU KNOW WHY YOUR HUSBAND CAME TO QILIN ISLAND ALL THOSE YEARS AGO? TO STEAL FROM OUR PEOPLE!
QUIET, OLD MAN!
SEE FOR YOURSELF! THAT MACHINE WAS BUILT FROM A PIECE OF OUR OLD STONE GATEWAY!
YOU SAID YOU WERE LOST!
I LIED.

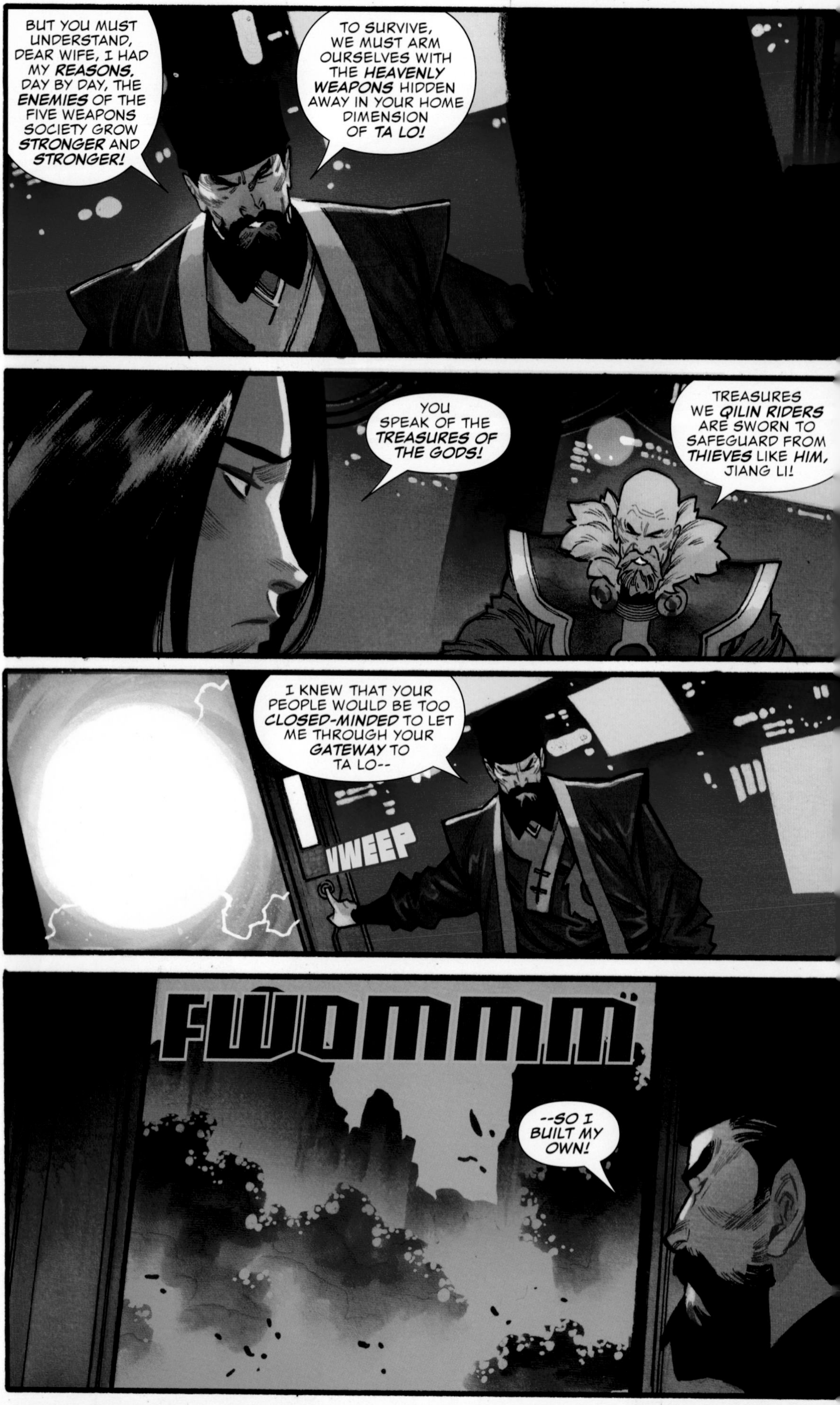
BUT YOU MUST UNDERSTAND, DEAR WIFE, I HAD MY REASONS. DAY BY DAY, THE ENEMIES OF THE FIVE WEAPONS SOCIETY GROW STRONGER AND STRONGER!
TO SURVIVE, WE MUST ARM OURSELVES WITH THE HEAVENLY WEAPONS HIDDEN AWAY IN YOUR HOME DIMENSION OF TA LO!
YOU SPEAK OF THE TREASURES OF THE GODS!
TREASURES WE QILIN RIDERS ARE SWORN TO SAFEGUARD FROM THIEVES LIKE HIM, JIANG LI!
I KNEW THAT YOUR PEOPLE WOULD BE TOO CLOSED-MINDED TO LET ME THROUGH YOUR GATEWAY TO TA LO--
VWEEP
FWOMMM
--SO I BUILT MY OWN!

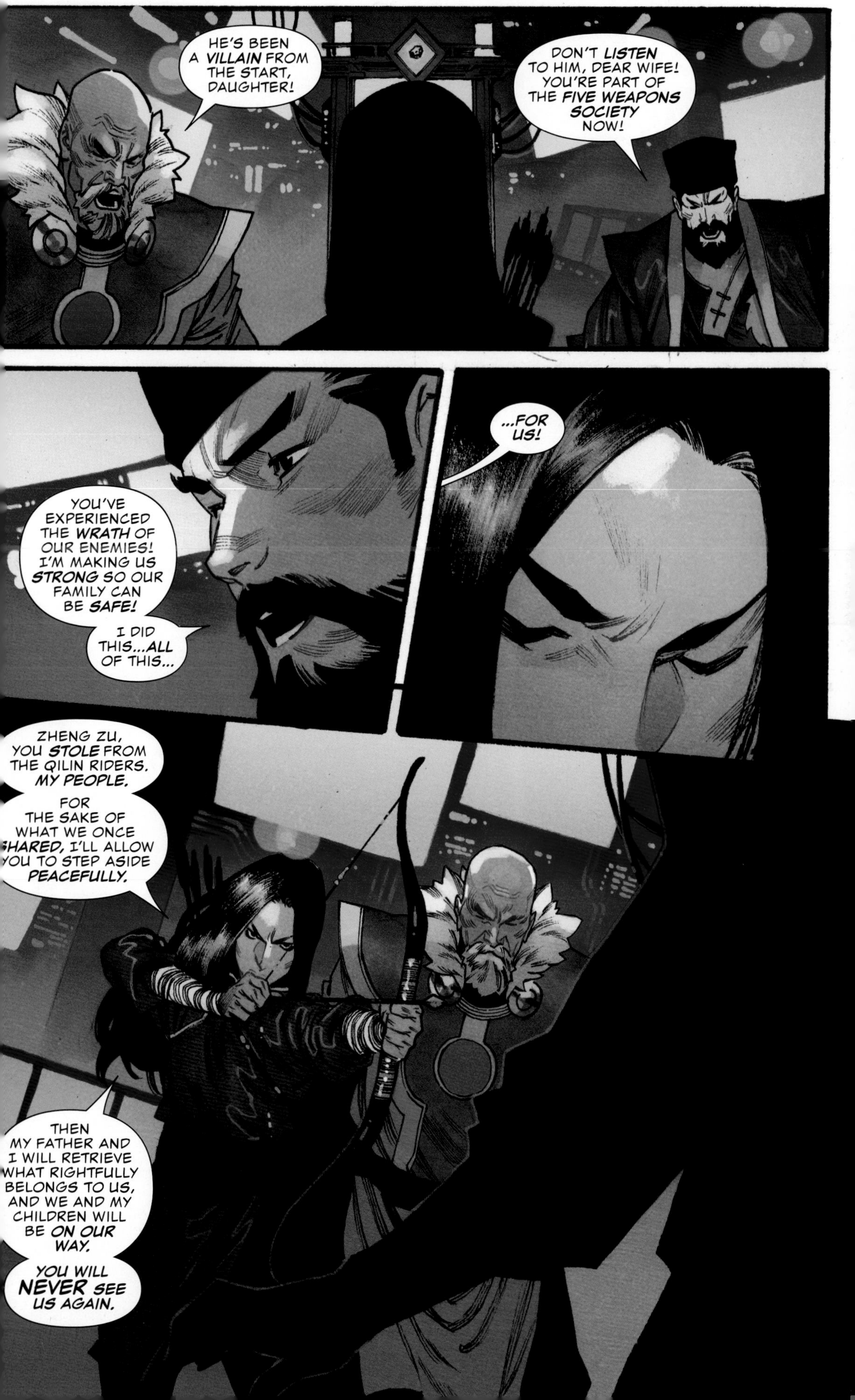
HE'S BEEN A VILLAIN FROM THE START, DAUGHTER!
DON'T LISTEN TO HIM, DEAR WIFE! YOU'RE PART OF THE FIVE WEAPONS SOCIETY NOW!
YOU'VE EXPERIENCED THE WRATH OF OUR ENEMIES! I'M MAKING US STRONG SO OUR FAMILY CAN BE SAFE!
I DID THIS...ALL OF THIS...
...FOR US!
ZHENG ZU, YOU STOLE FROM THE QILIN RIDERS. MY PEOPLE.
FOR THE SAKE OF WHAT WE ONCE SHARED, I'LL ALLOW YOU TO STEP ASIDE PEACEFULLY.
THEN MY FATHER AND I WILL RETRIEVE WHAT RIGHTFULLY BELONGS TO US, AND WE AND MY CHILDREN WILL BE ON OUR WAY.
YOU WILL NEVER SEE US AGAIN.

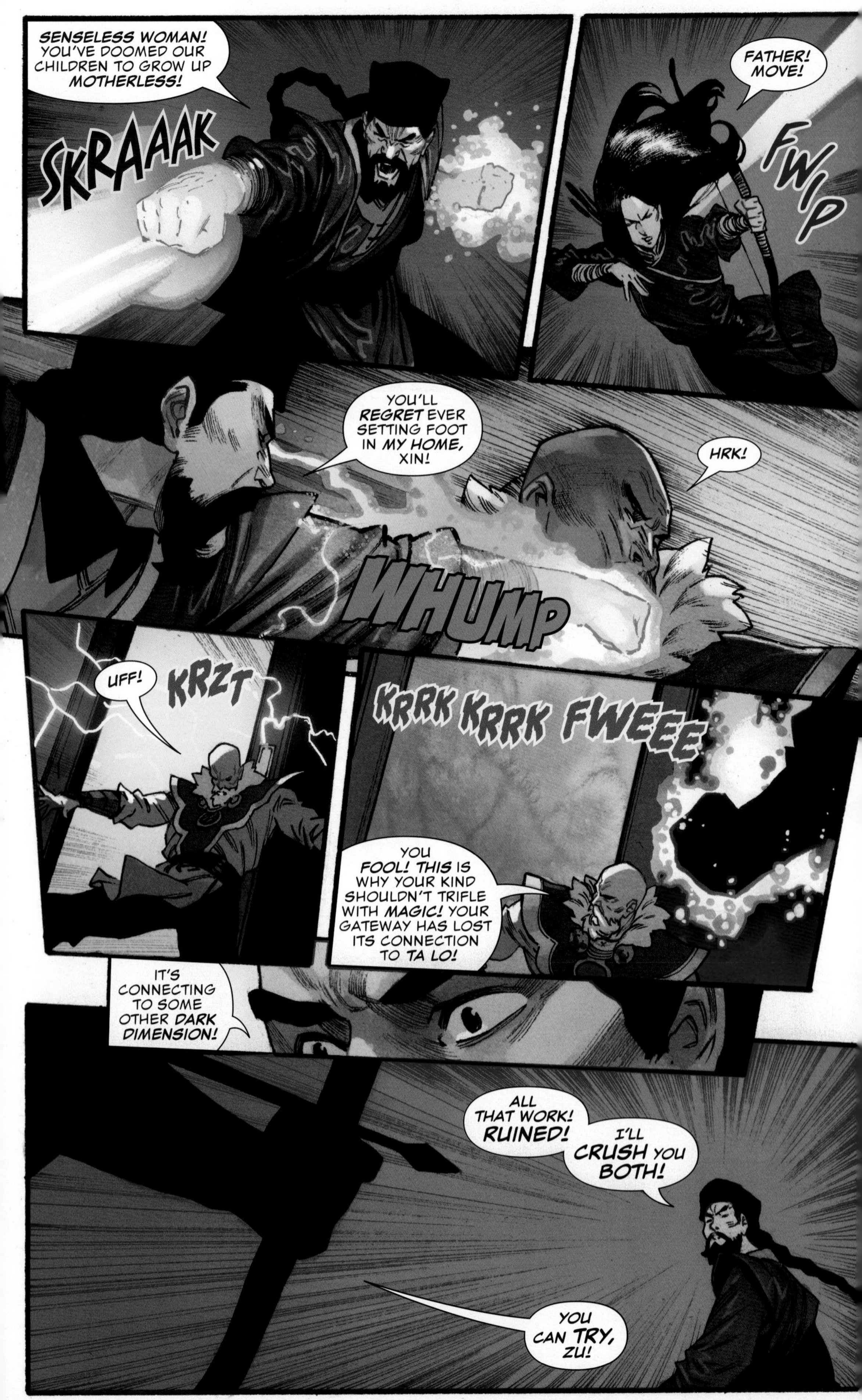

SENSELESS WOMAN! YOU'VE DOOMED OUR CHILDREN TO GROW UP MOTHERLESS!
SKRAAAK
FATHER! MOVE!
FWIP
YOU'LL REGRET EVER SETTING FOOT IN MY HOME, XIN!
HRK!
WHUMP
UFF!
KRZT
KRRK KRRK FWEEE
YOU FOOL! THIS IS WHY YOUR KIND SHOULDN'T TRIFLE WITH MAGIC! YOUR GATEWAY HAS LOST ITS CONNECTION TO TA LO!
IT'S CONNECTING TO SOME OTHER DARK DIMENSION!
ALL THAT WORK! RUINED!
I'LL CRUSH YOU BOTH!
YOU CAN TRY, ZU!

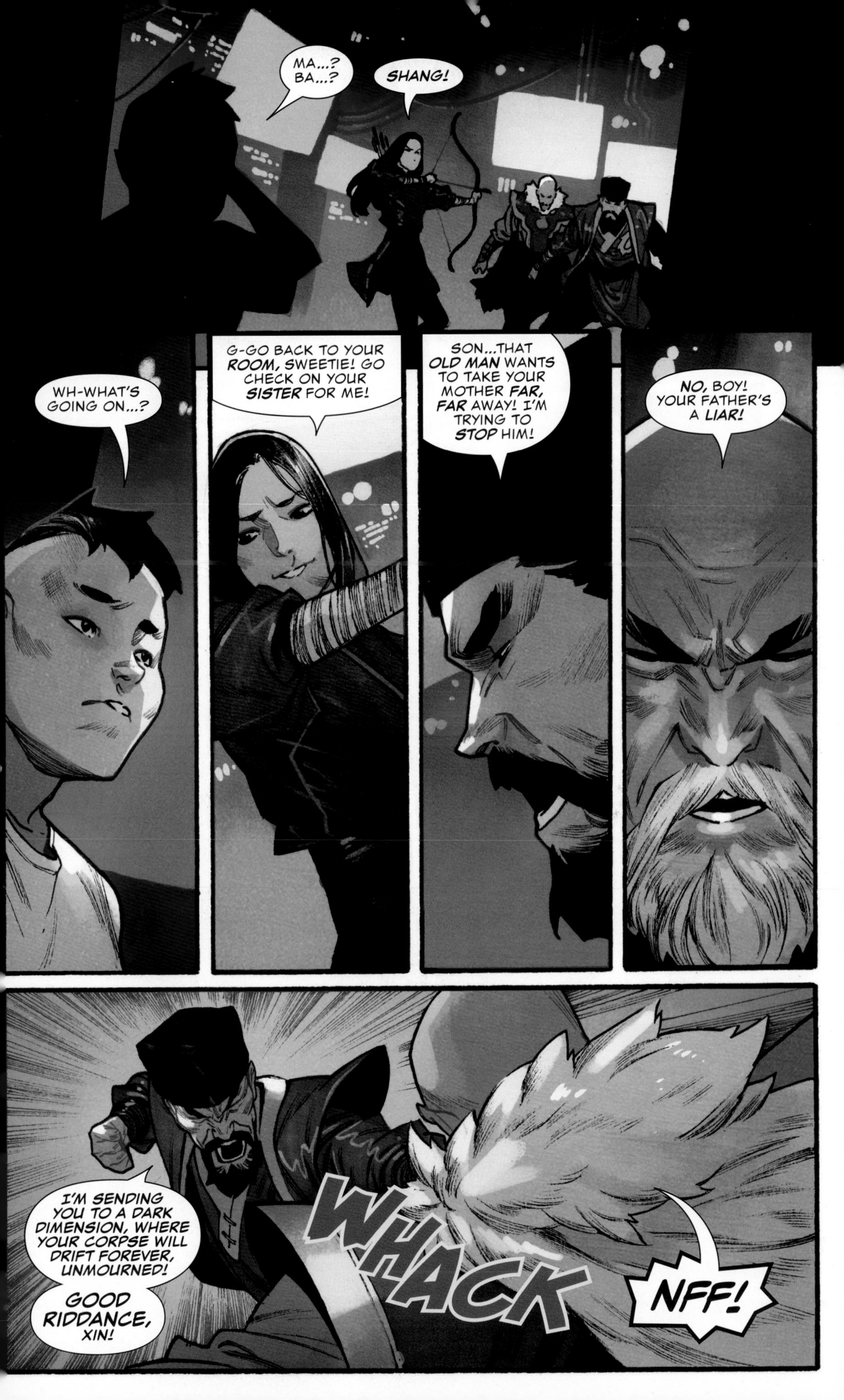
MA...? BA...?
SHANG!
WH-WHAT'S GOING ON...?
G-GO BACK TO YOUR ROOM, SWEETIE! GO CHECK ON YOUR SISTER FOR ME!
SON...THAT OLD MAN WANTS TO TAKE YOUR MOTHER FAR, FAR AWAY! I'M TRYING TO STOP HIM!
NO, BOY! YOUR FATHER'S A LIAR!
I'M SENDING YOU TO A DARK DIMENSION, WHERE YOUR CORPSE WILL DRIFT FOREVER, UNMOURNED!
GOOD RIDDANCE, XIN!
WHACK
NFF!

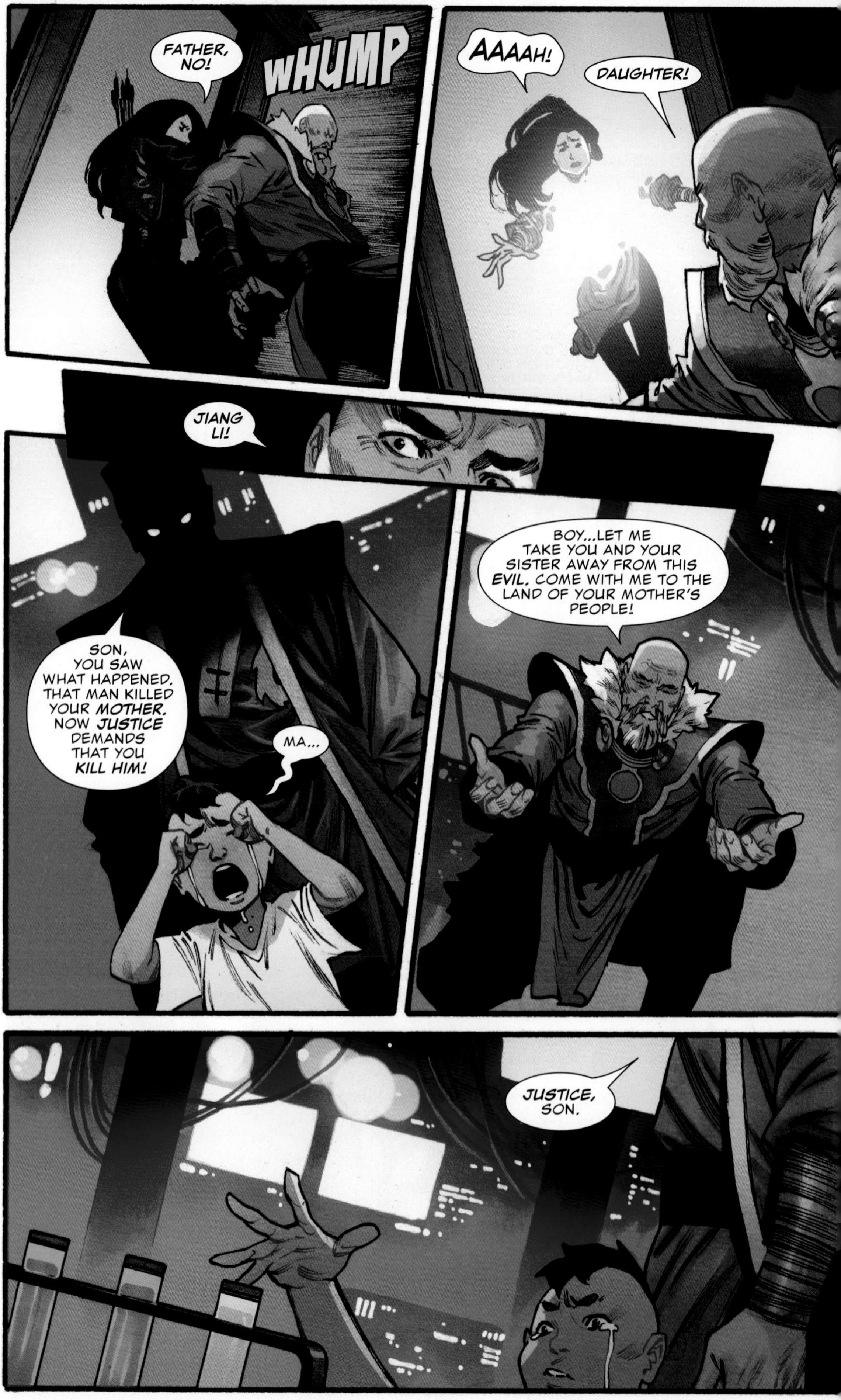
FATHER, NO!
WHUMP
AAAAH!
DAUGHTER!
JIANG LI!
SON, YOU SAW WHAT HAPPENED. THAT MAN KILLED YOUR MOTHER. NOW JUSTICE DEMANDS THAT YOU KILL HIM!
MA...
BOY...LET ME TAKE YOU AND YOUR SISTER AWAY FROM THIS EVIL. COME WITH ME TO THE LAND OF YOUR MOTHER'S PEOPLE!
JUSTICE, SON.

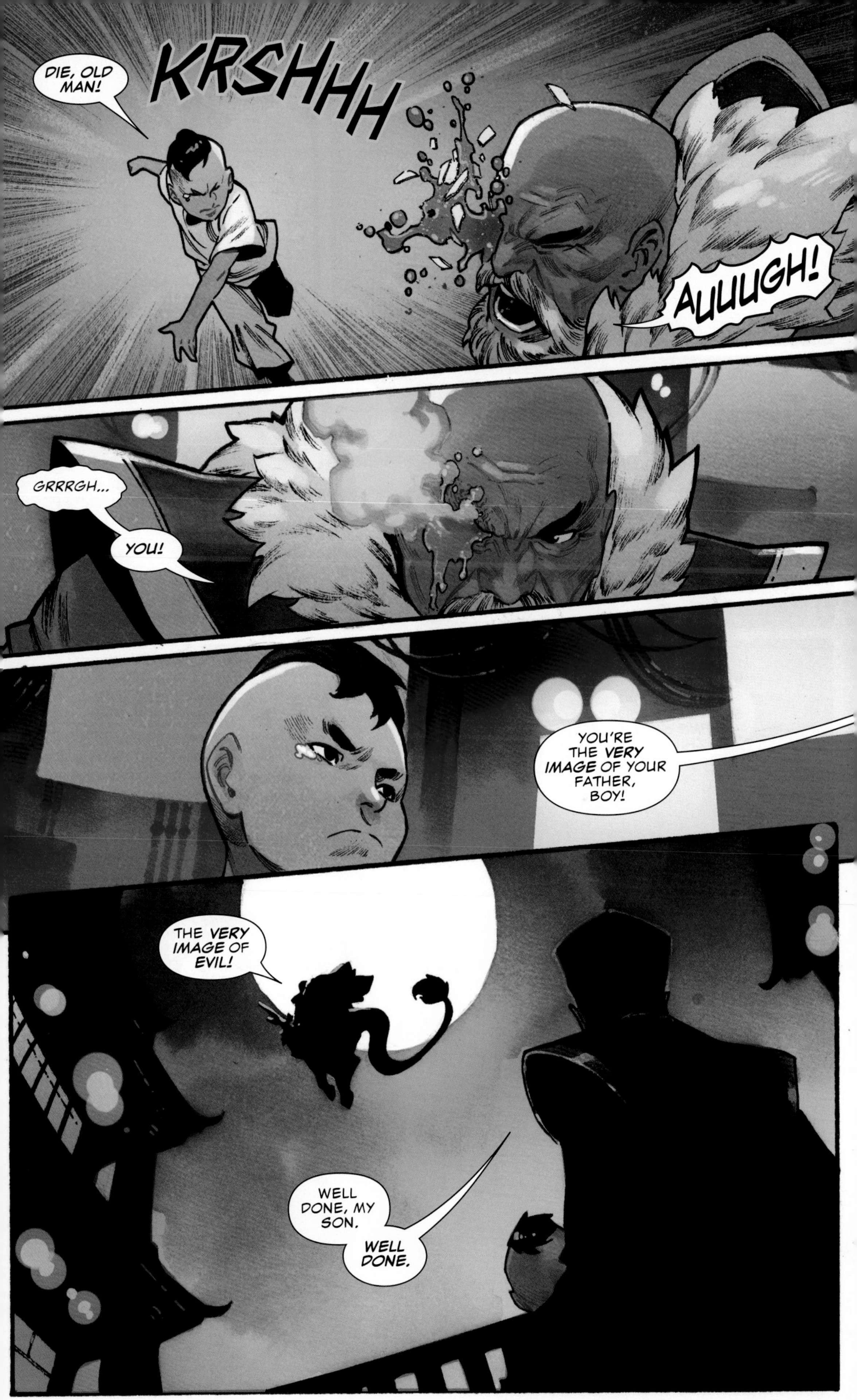
DIE, OLD MAN!
KRSHHH
AUUUGH!
GRRRGH...
YOU!
YOU'RE THE VERY IMAGE OF YOUR FATHER, BOY!
THE VERY IMAGE OF EVIL!
WELL DONE, MY SON.
WELL DONE.

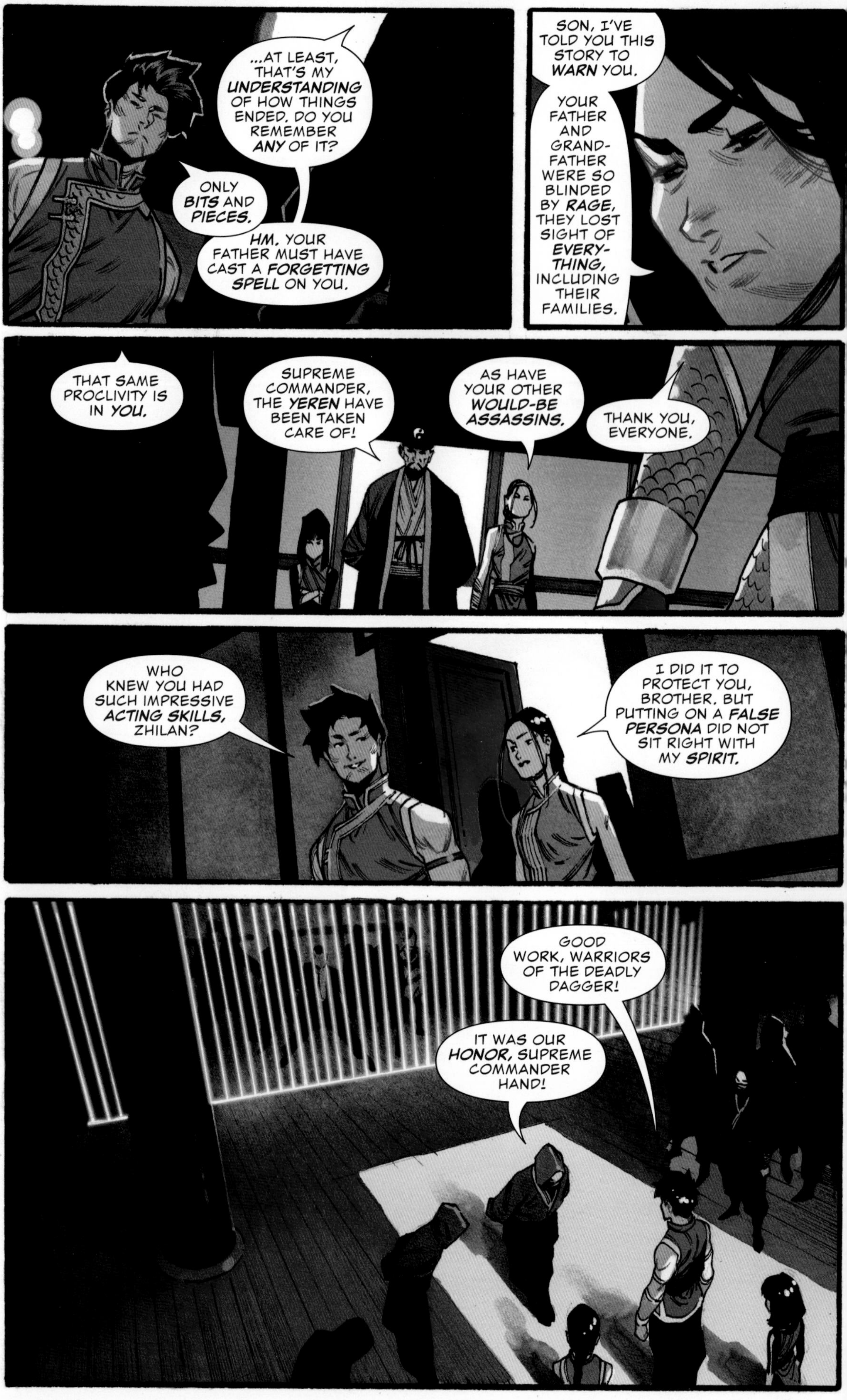
...AT LEAST, THAT'S MY UNDERSTANDING OF HOW THINGS ENDED. DO YOU REMEMBER ANY OF IT?
ONLY BITS AND PIECES.
HM. YOUR FATHER MUST HAVE CAST A FORGETTING SPELL ON YOU.
SON, I'VE TOLD YOU THIS STORY TO WARN YOU.
YOUR FATHER AND GRAND-FATHER WERE SO BLINDED BY RAGE, THEY LOST SIGHT OF EVERY-THING, INCLUDING THEIR FAMILIES.
THAT SAME PROCLIVITY IS IN YOU.
SUPREME COMMANDER, THE YEREN HAVE BEEN TAKEN CARE OF!
AS HAVE YOUR OTHER WOULD-BE ASSASSINS.
THANK YOU, EVERYONE.
WHO KNEW YOU HAD SUCH IMPRESSIVE ACTING SKILLS, ZHILAN?
I DID IT TO PROTECT YOU, BROTHER. BUT PUTTING ON A FALSE PERSONA DID NOT SIT RIGHT WITH MY SPIRIT.
GOOD WORK, WARRIORS OF THE DEADLY DAGGER!
IT WAS OUR HONOR, SUPREME COMMANDER HAND!

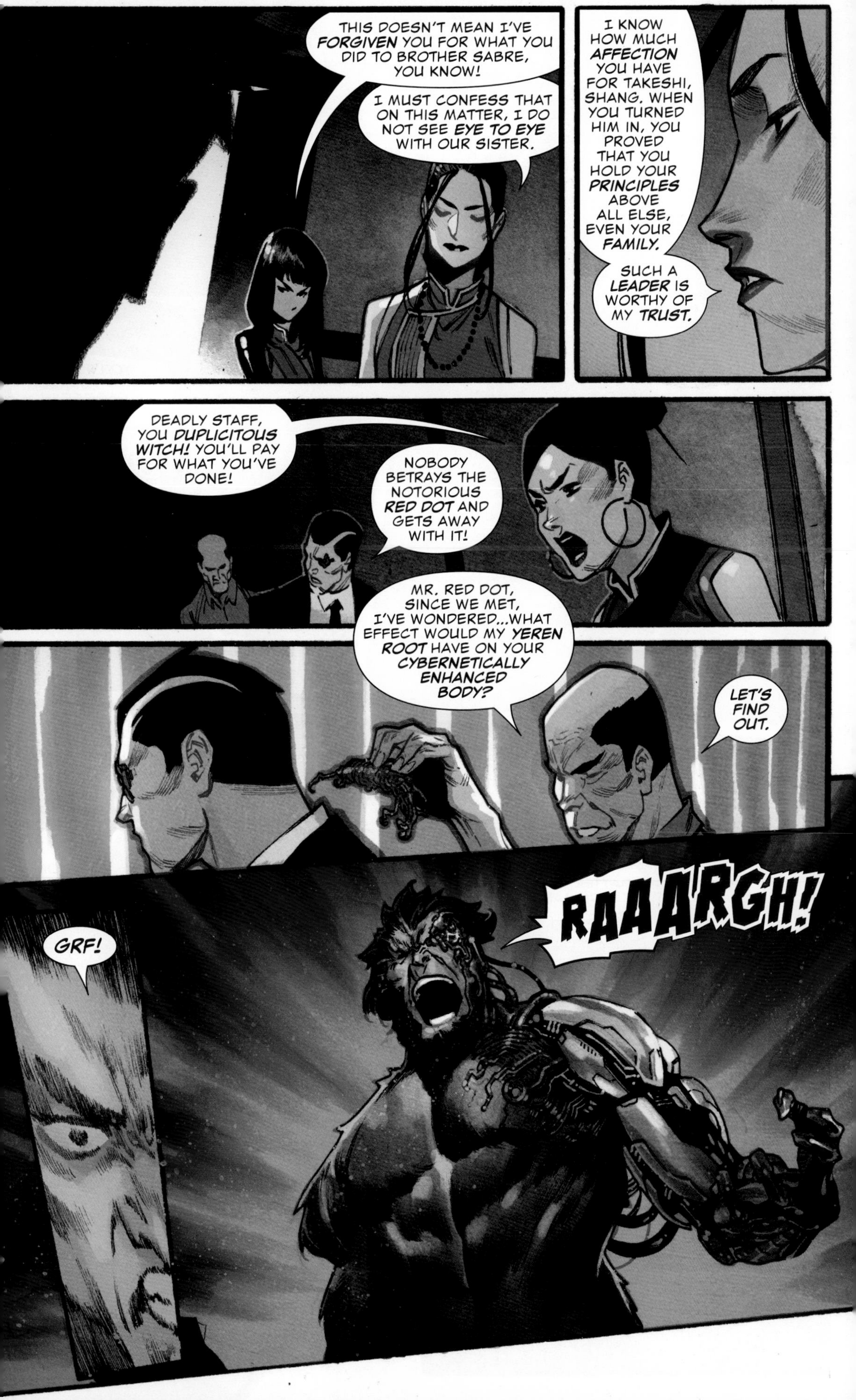

THIS DOESN'T MEAN I'VE FORGIVEN YOU FOR WHAT YOU DID TO BROTHER SABRE, YOU KNOW!
I MUST CONFESS THAT ON THIS MATTER, I DO NOT SEE EYE TO EYE WITH OUR SISTER.
I KNOW HOW MUCH AFFECTION YOU HAVE FOR TAKESHI, SHANG. WHEN YOU TURNED HIM IN, YOU PROVED THAT YOU HOLD YOUR PRINCIPLES ABOVE ALL ELSE, EVEN YOUR FAMILY.
SUCH A LEADER IS WORTHY OF MY TRUST.
DEADLY STAFF, YOU DUPLICITOUS WITCH! YOU'LL PAY FOR WHAT YOU'VE DONE!
NOBODY BETRAYS THE NOTORIOUS RED DOT AND GETS AWAY WITH IT!
MR. RED DOT, SINCE WE MET, I'VE WONDERED...WHAT EFFECT WOULD MY YEREN ROOT HAVE ON YOUR CYBERNETICALLY ENHANCED BODY?
LET'S FIND OUT.
RAAARGH!
GRF!

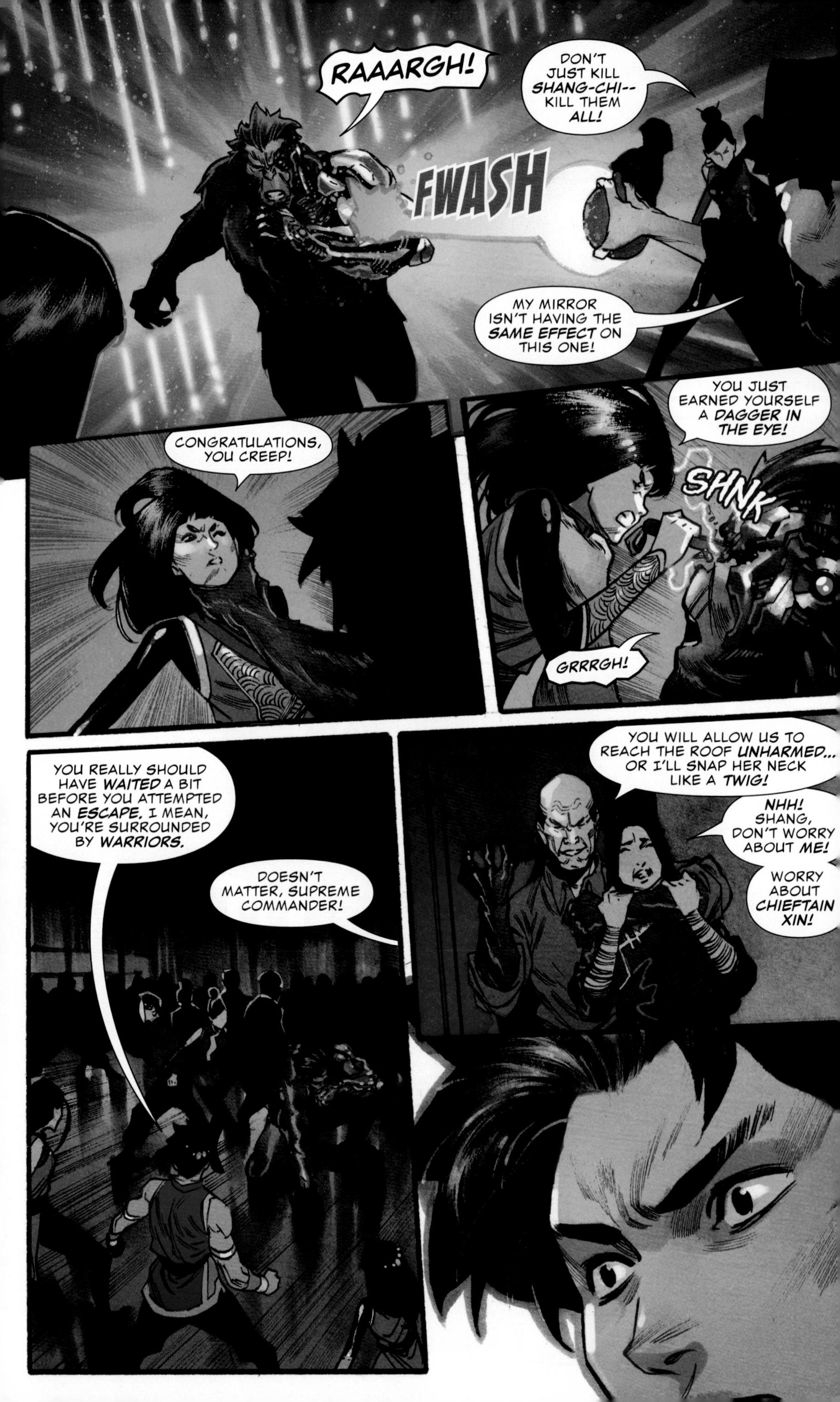
RAAARGH!
DON'T JUST KILL SHANG-CHI-- KILL THEM ALL!
FWASH
MY MIRROR ISN'T HAVING THE SAME EFFECT ON THIS ONE!
CONGRATULATIONS, YOU CREEP!
YOU JUST EARNED YOURSELF A DAGGER IN THE EYE!
SHNK
GRRRGH!
YOU REALLY SHOULD HAVE WAITED A BIT BEFORE YOU ATTEMPTED AN ESCAPE. I MEAN, YOU'RE SURROUNDED BY WARRIORS.
DOESN'T MATTER, SUPREME COMMANDER!
YOU WILL ALLOW US TO REACH THE ROOF UNHARMED... OR I'LL SNAP HER NECK LIKE A TWIG!
NHH! SHANG, DON'T WORRY ABOUT ME!
WORRY ABOUT CHIEFTAIN XIN!

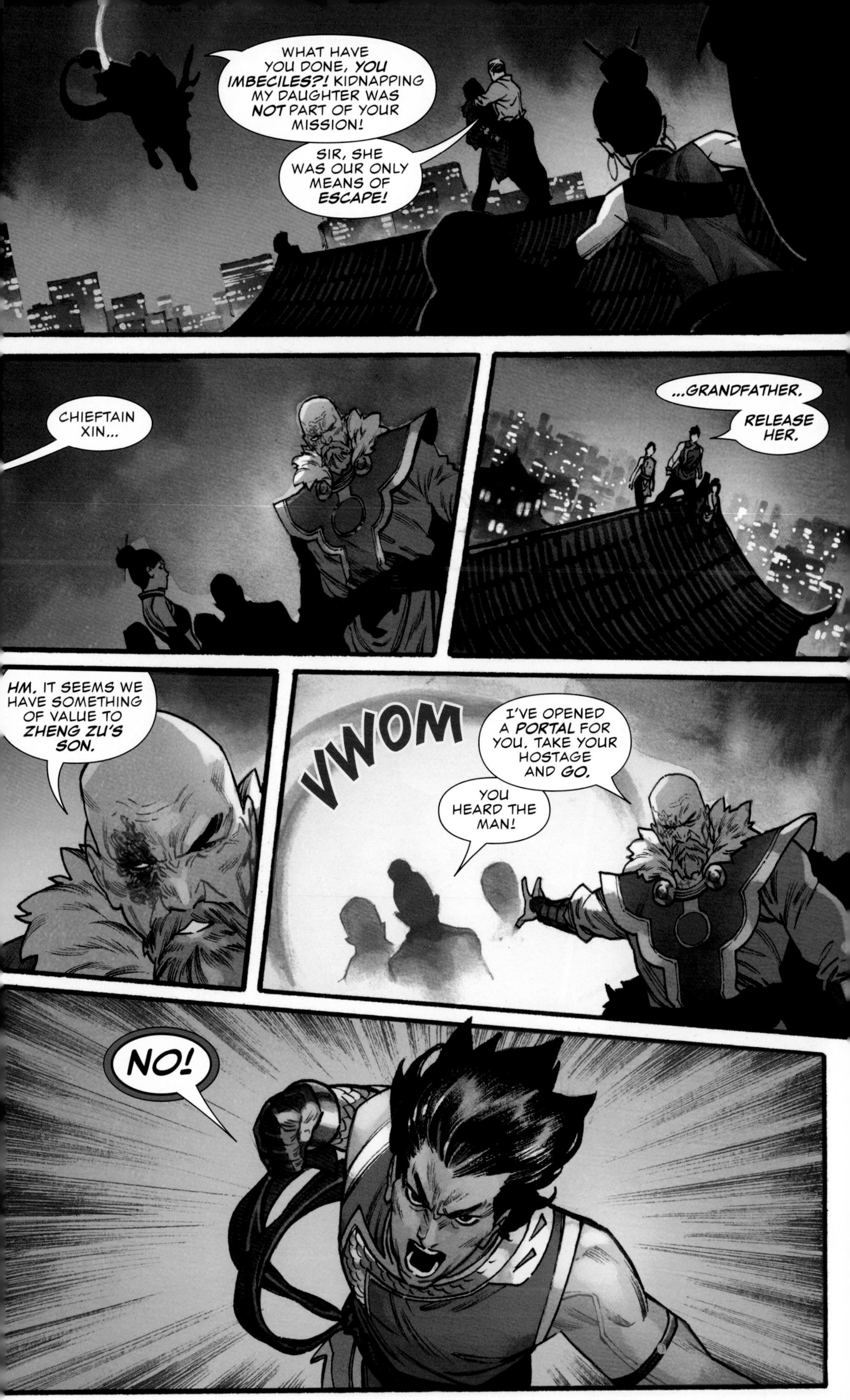
WHAT HAVE YOU DONE, YOU IMBECILES?! KIDNAPPING MY DAUGHTER WAS NOT PART OF YOUR MISSION!
SIR, SHE WAS OUR ONLY MEANS OF ESCAPE!
CHIEFTAIN XIN...
...GRANDFATHER.
RELEASE HER.
HM. IT SEEMS WE HAVE SOMETHING OF VALUE TO ZHENG ZU'S SON.
VWOM
I'VE OPENED A PORTAL FOR YOU. TAKE YOUR HOSTAGE AND GO.
YOU HEARD THE MAN!
NO!

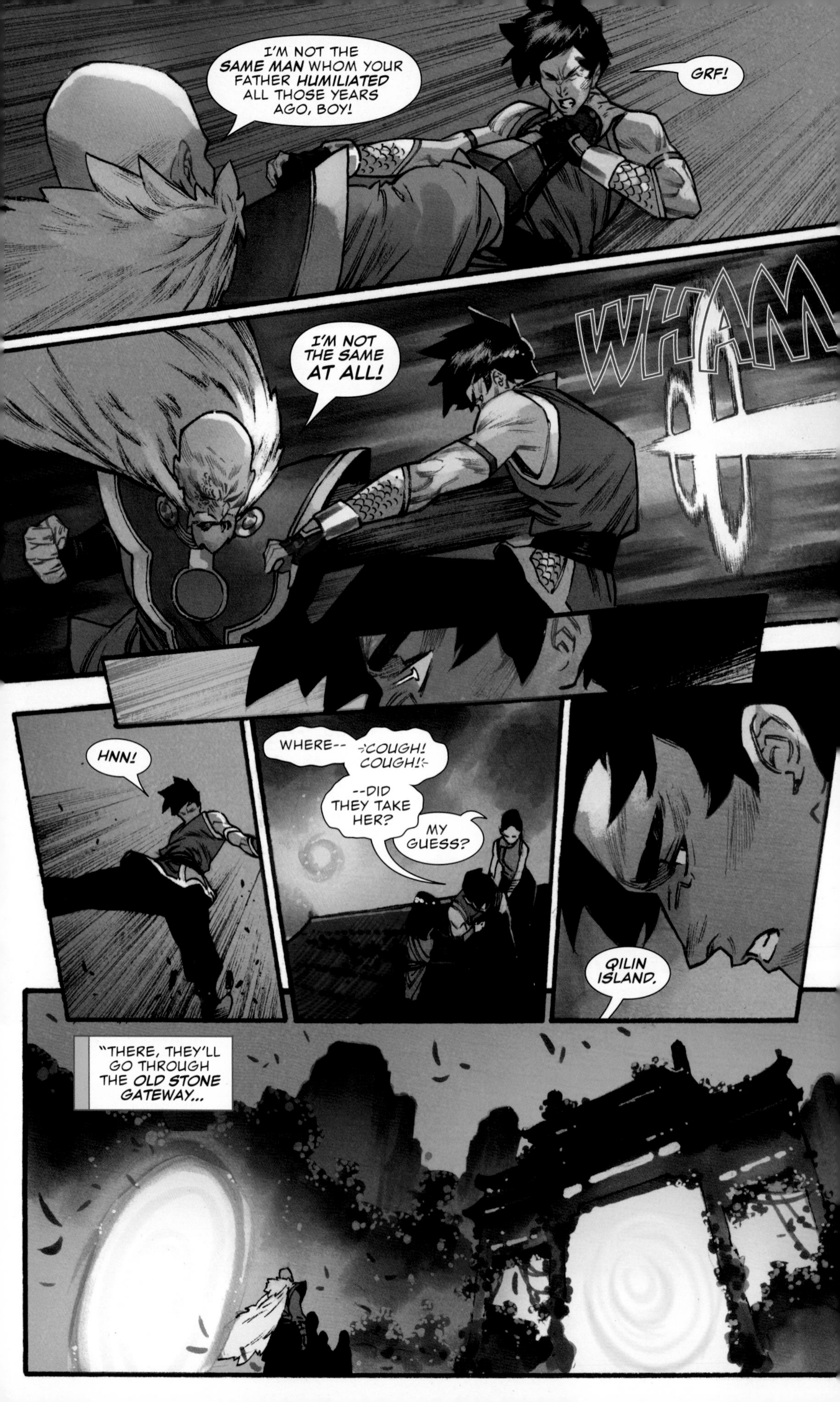
I'M NOT THE SAME MAN WHOM YOUR FATHER HUMILIATED ALL THOSE YEARS AGO, BOY!
GRF!
WHAM
I'M NOT THE SAME AT ALL!
HNN!
WHERE--
COUGH! COUGH!
--DID THEY TAKE HER?
MY GUESS?
QILIN ISLAND.
"THERE, THEY'LL GO THROUGH THE OLD STONE GATEWAY...

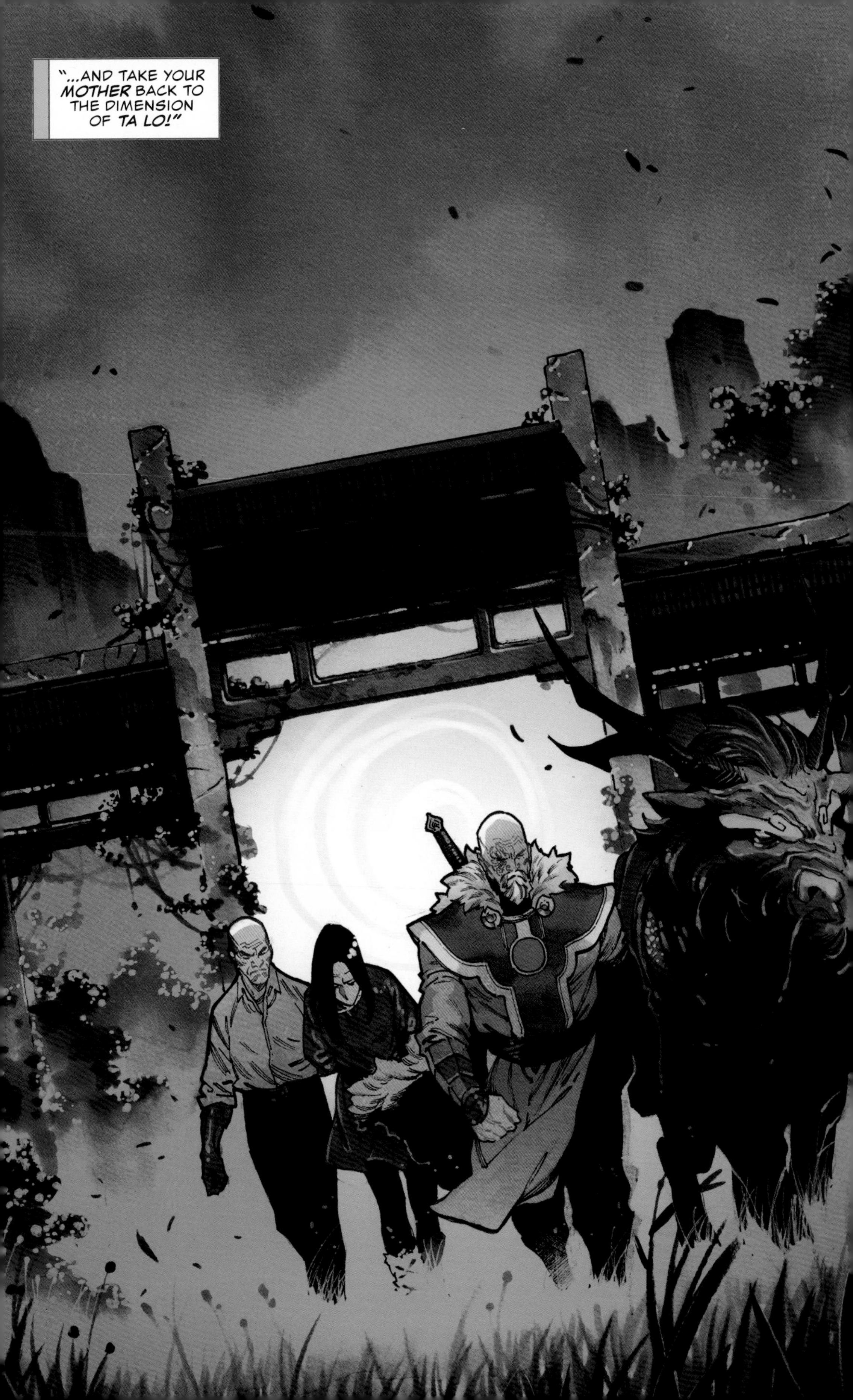
"...AND TAKE YOUR MOTHER BACK TO THE DIMENSION OF TA LO!"

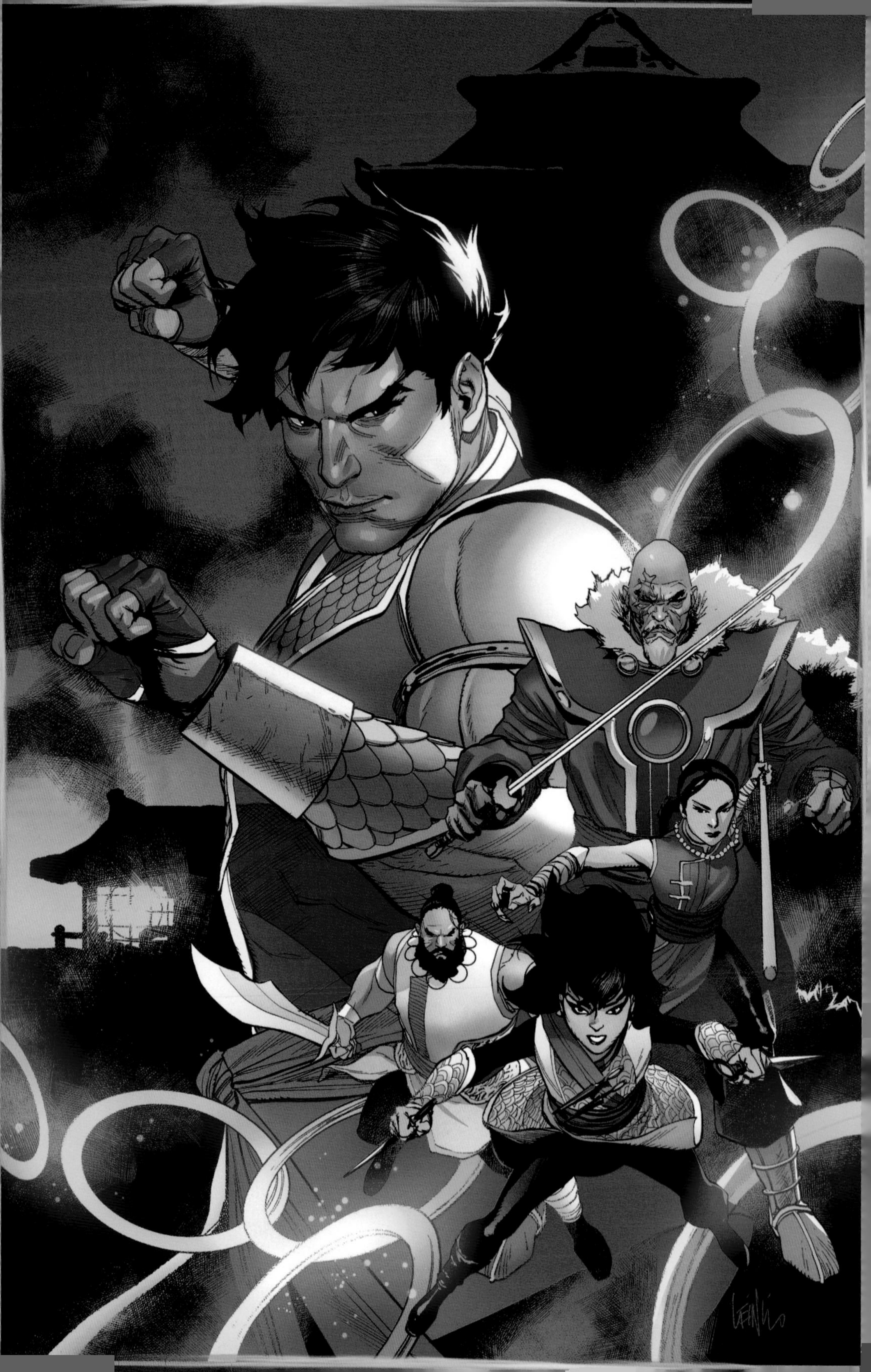

NE

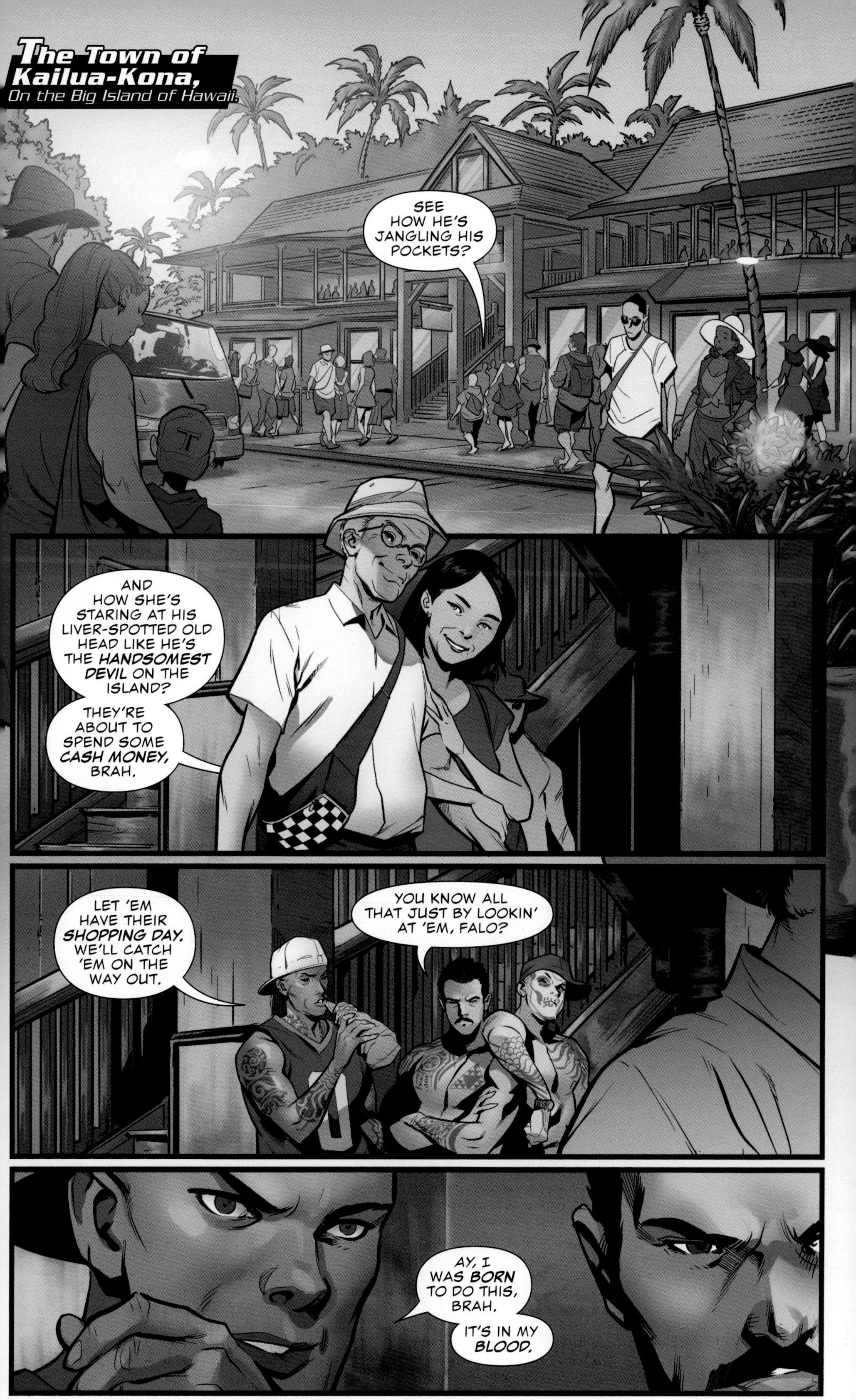
The Town of Kailua-Kona,
On the Big Island of Hawaii.
SEE HOW HE'S JANGLING HIS POCKETS?
AND HOW SHE'S STARING AT HIS LIVER-SPOTTED OLD HEAD LIKE HE'S THE HANDSOMEST DEVIL ON THE ISLAND?
THEY'RE ABOUT TO SPEND SOME CASH MONEY, BRAH.
LET 'EM HAVE THEIR SHOPPING DAY. WE'LL CATCH 'EM ON THE WAY OUT.
YOU KNOW ALL THAT JUST BY LOOKIN' AT 'EM, FALO?
AY, I WAS BORN TO DO THIS, BRAH.
IT'S IN MY BLOOD.

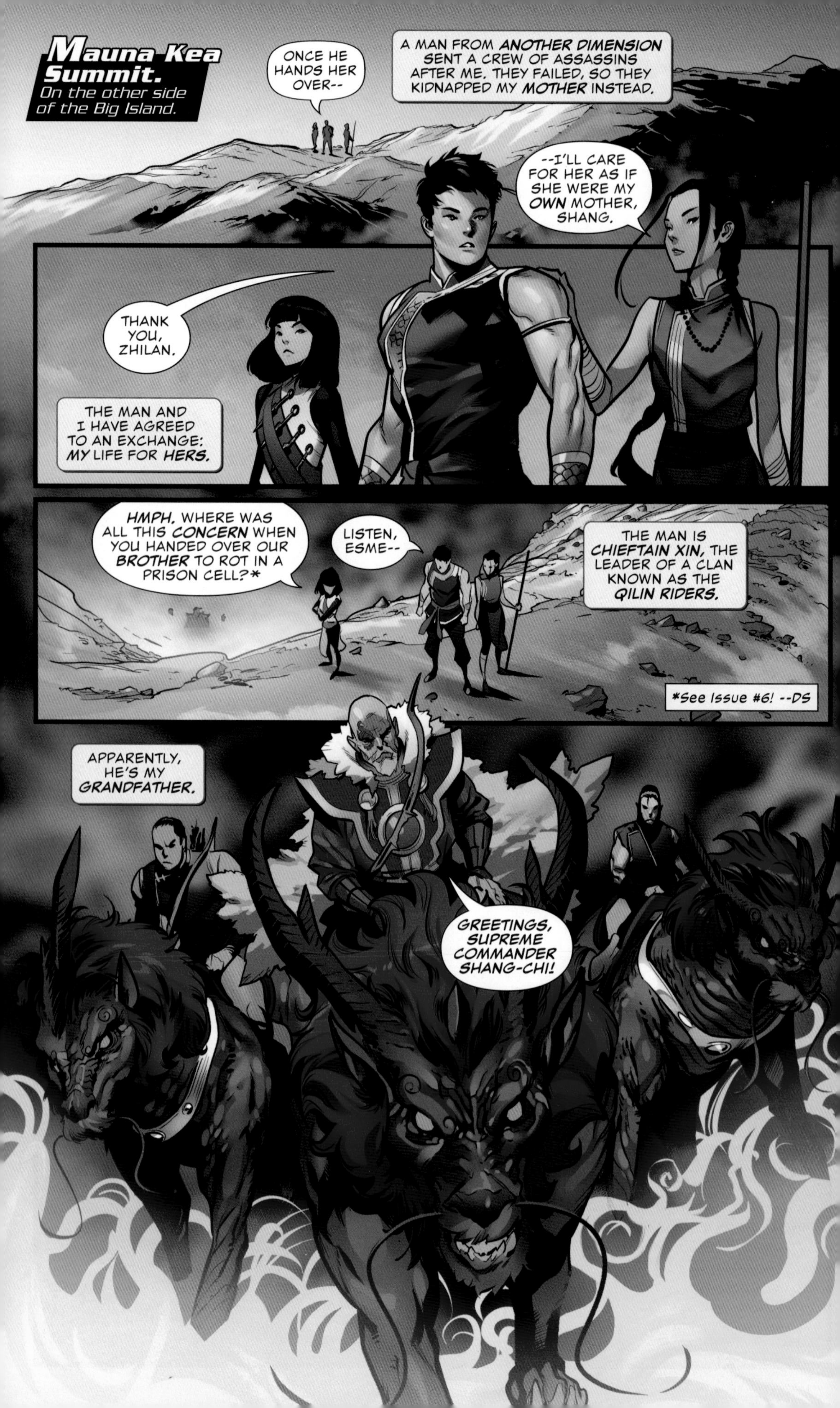

Mauna Kea Summit.
On the other side of the Big Island.
ONCE HE HANDS HER OVER--
A MAN FROM ANOTHER DIMENSION SENT A CREW OF ASSASSINS AFTER ME. THEY FAILED, SO THEY KIDNAPPED MY MOTHER INSTEAD.
--I'LL CARE FOR HER AS IF SHE WERE MY OWN MOTHER, SHANG.
THANK YOU, ZHILAN.
THE MAN AND I HAVE AGREED TO AN EXCHANGE: MY LIFE FOR HERS.
HMPH. WHERE WAS ALL THIS CONCERN WHEN YOU HANDED OVER OUR BROTHER TO ROT IN A PRISON CELL?*
LISTEN, ESME--
THE MAN IS CHIEFTAIN XIN, THE LEADER OF A CLAN KNOWN AS THE QILIN RIDERS.
*See Issue #6! --DS
APPARENTLY, HE'S MY GRANDFATHER.
GREETINGS, SUPREME COMMANDER SHANG-CHI!

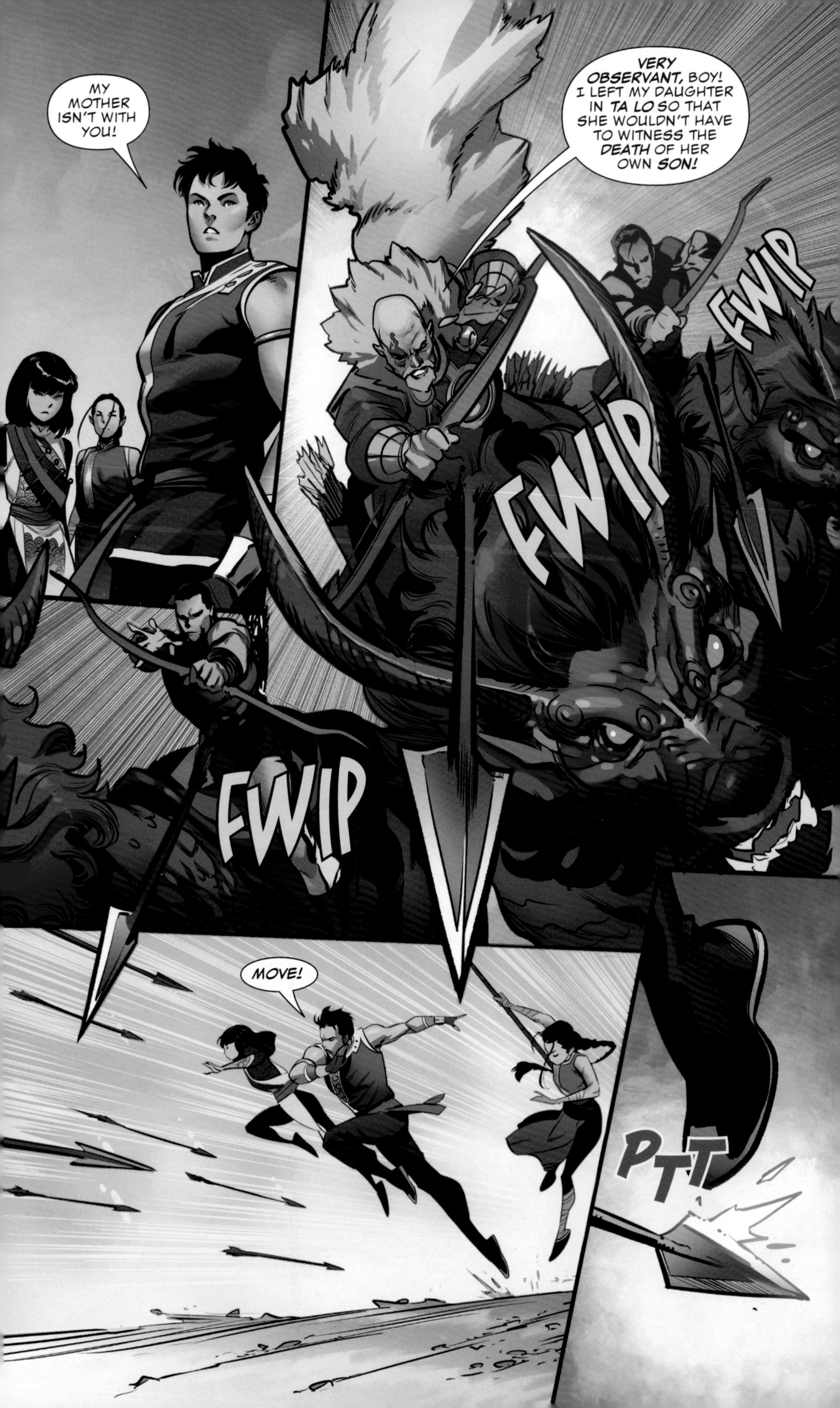

MY MOTHER ISN'T WITH YOU!
VERY OBSERVANT, BOY! I LEFT MY DAUGHTER IN TA LO SO THAT SHE WOULDN'T HAVE TO WITNESS THE DEATH OF HER OWN SON!
FWIP
FWIP
FWIP
MOVE!
PTT

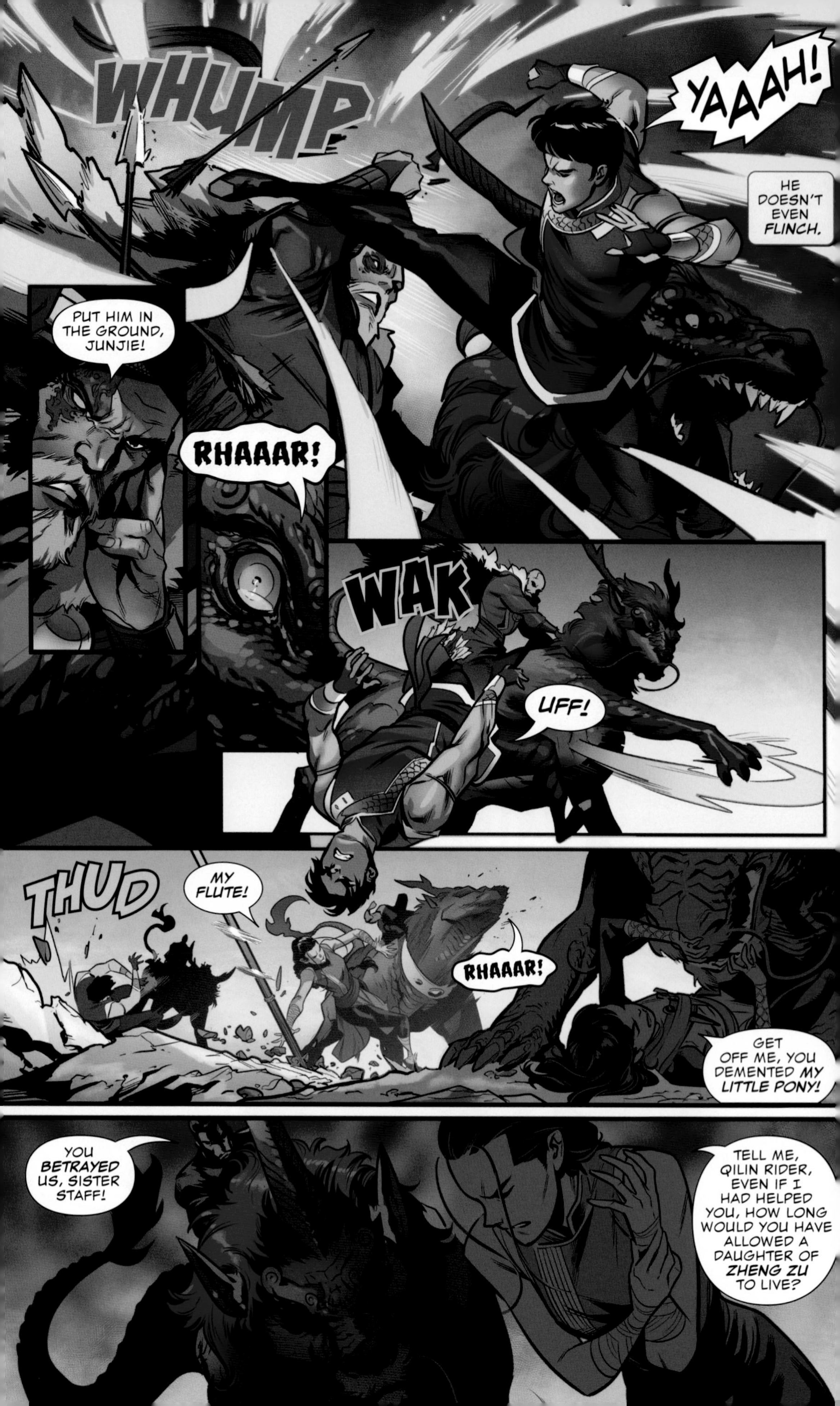
WHUMP
YAAAH!
HE DOESN'T EVEN FLINCH.
PUT HIM IN THE GROUND, JUNJIE!
RHAAAR!
WAK
UFF!
THUD
MY FLUTE!
RHAAAR!
GET OFF ME, YOU DEMENTED MY LITTLE PONY!
YOU BETRAYED US, SISTER STAFF!
TELL ME, QILIN RIDER, EVEN IF I HAD HELPED YOU, HOW LONG WOULD YOU HAVE ALLOWED A DAUGHTER OF ZHENG ZU TO LIVE?

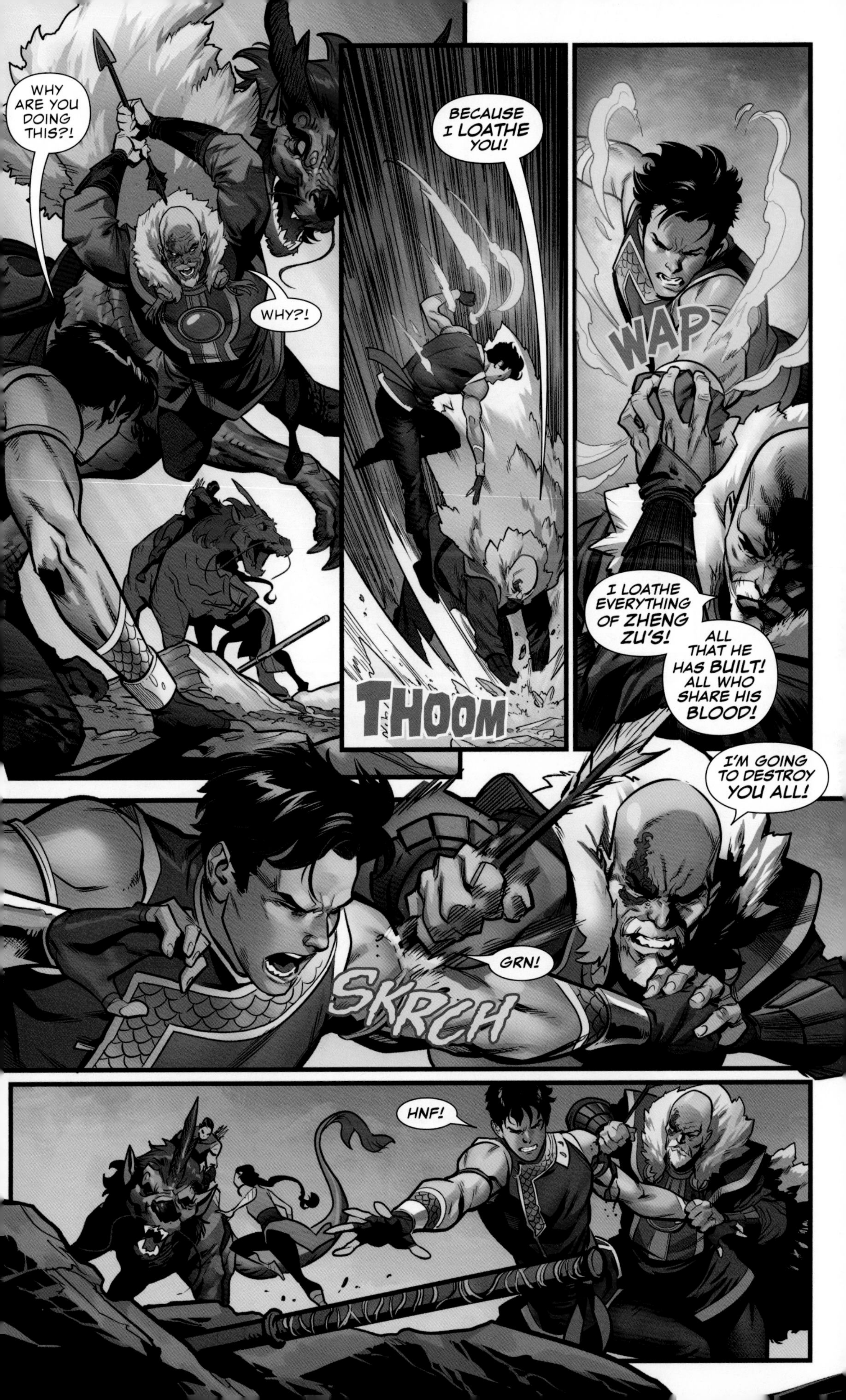
WHY ARE YOU DOING THIS?!
WHY?!
BECAUSE I LOATHE YOU!
THOOM
WAP
I LOATHE EVERYTHING OF ZHENG ZU'S!
ALL THAT HE HAS BUILT! ALL WHO SHARE HIS BLOOD!
I'M GOING TO DESTROY YOU ALL!
GRN!
SKRCH
HNF!

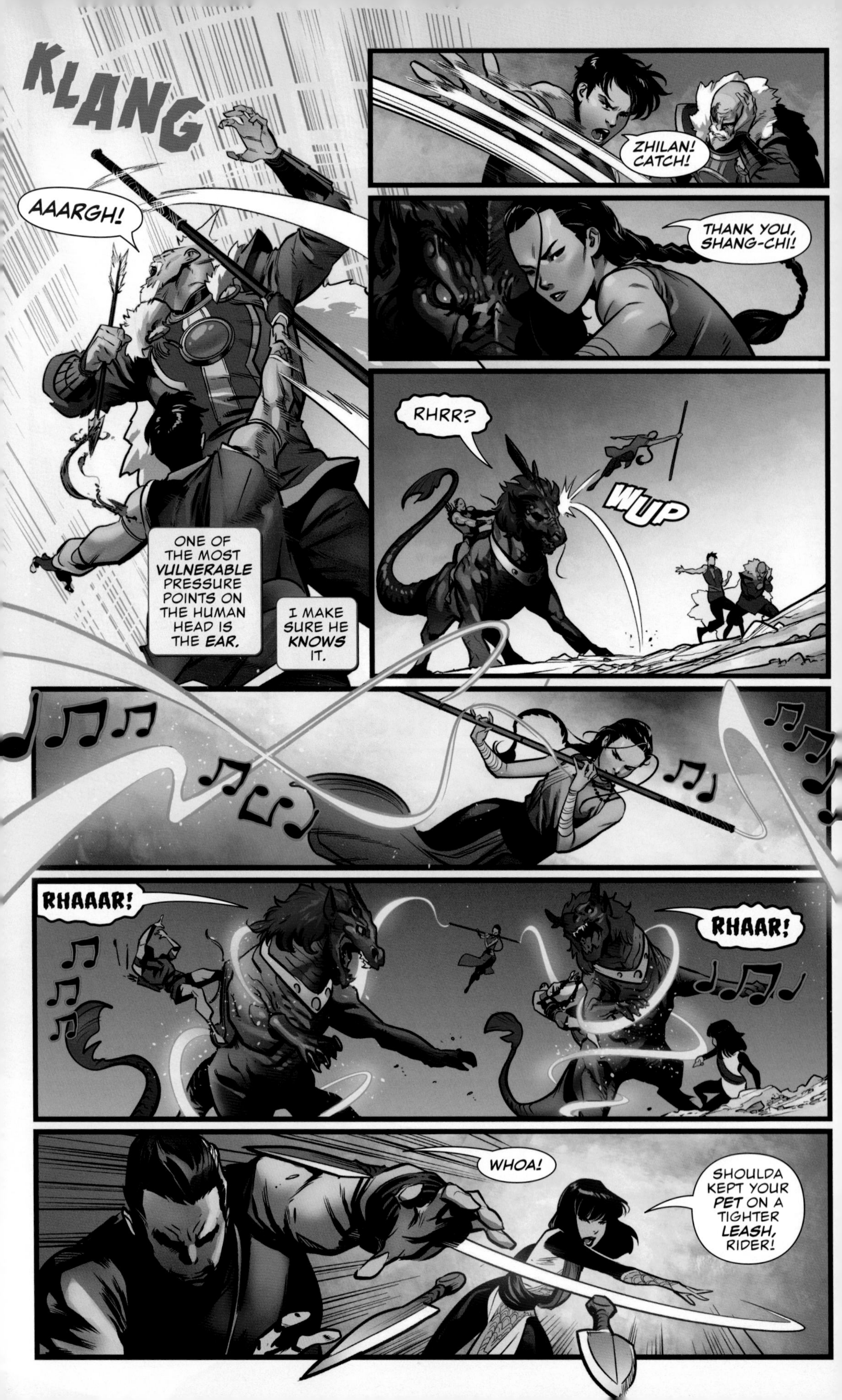
KLANG
AAARGH!
ZHILAN! CATCH!
THANK YOU, SHANG-CHI!
RHRR?
WUP
ONE OF THE MOST VULNERABLE PRESSURE POINTS ON THE HUMAN HEAD IS THE EAR.
I MAKE SURE HE KNOWS IT.
RHAAAR!
RHAAR!
WHOA!
SHOULDA KEPT YOUR PET ON A TIGHTER LEASH, RIDER!

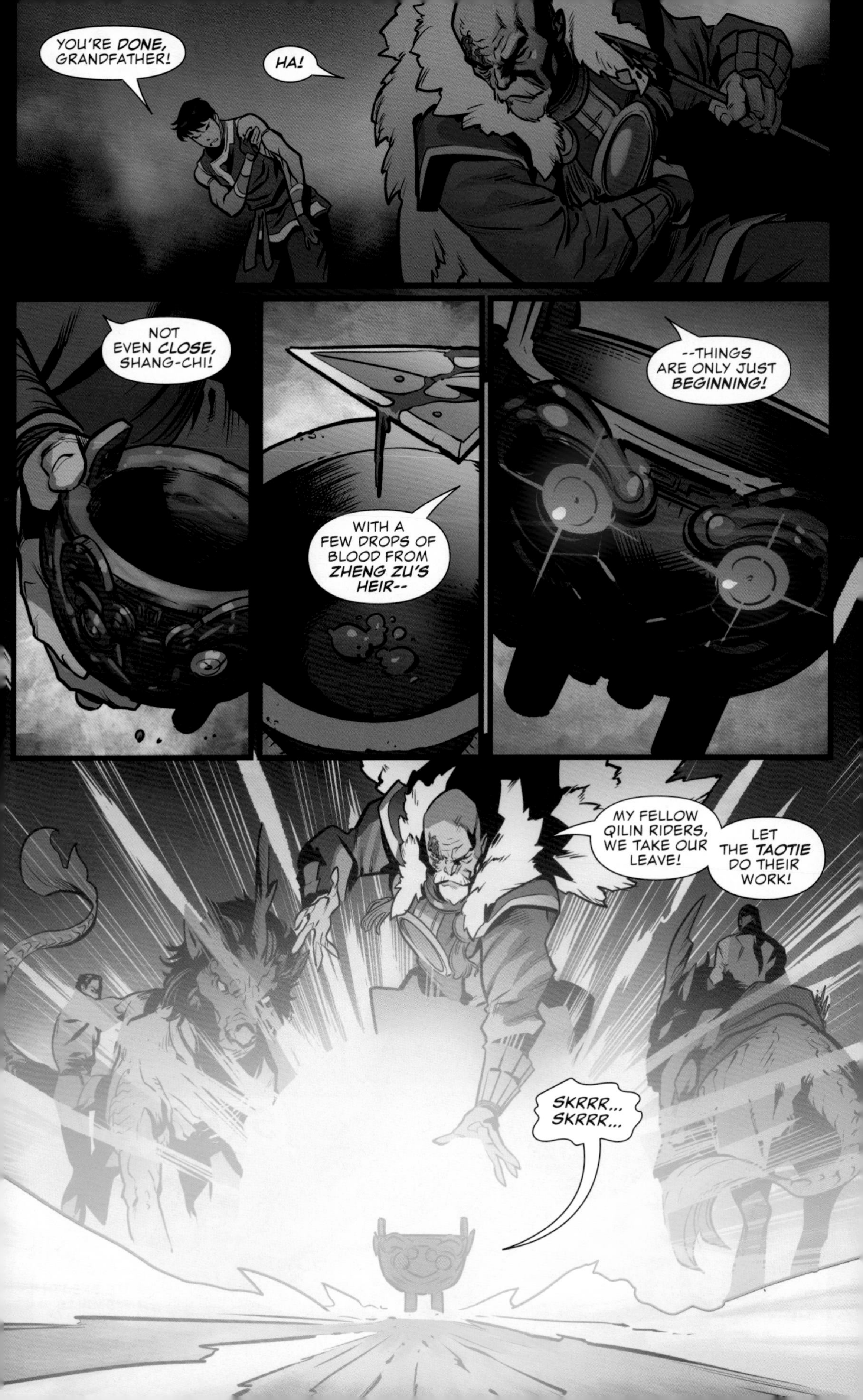
YOU'RE DONE, GRANDFATHER!
HA!
NOT EVEN CLOSE, SHANG-CHI!
WITH A FEW DROPS OF BLOOD FROM ZHENG ZU'S HEIR--
--THINGS ARE ONLY JUST BEGINNING!
MY FELLOW QILIN RIDERS, WE TAKE OUR LEAVE!
LET THE TAOTIE DO THEIR WORK!
SKRRR... SKRRR...

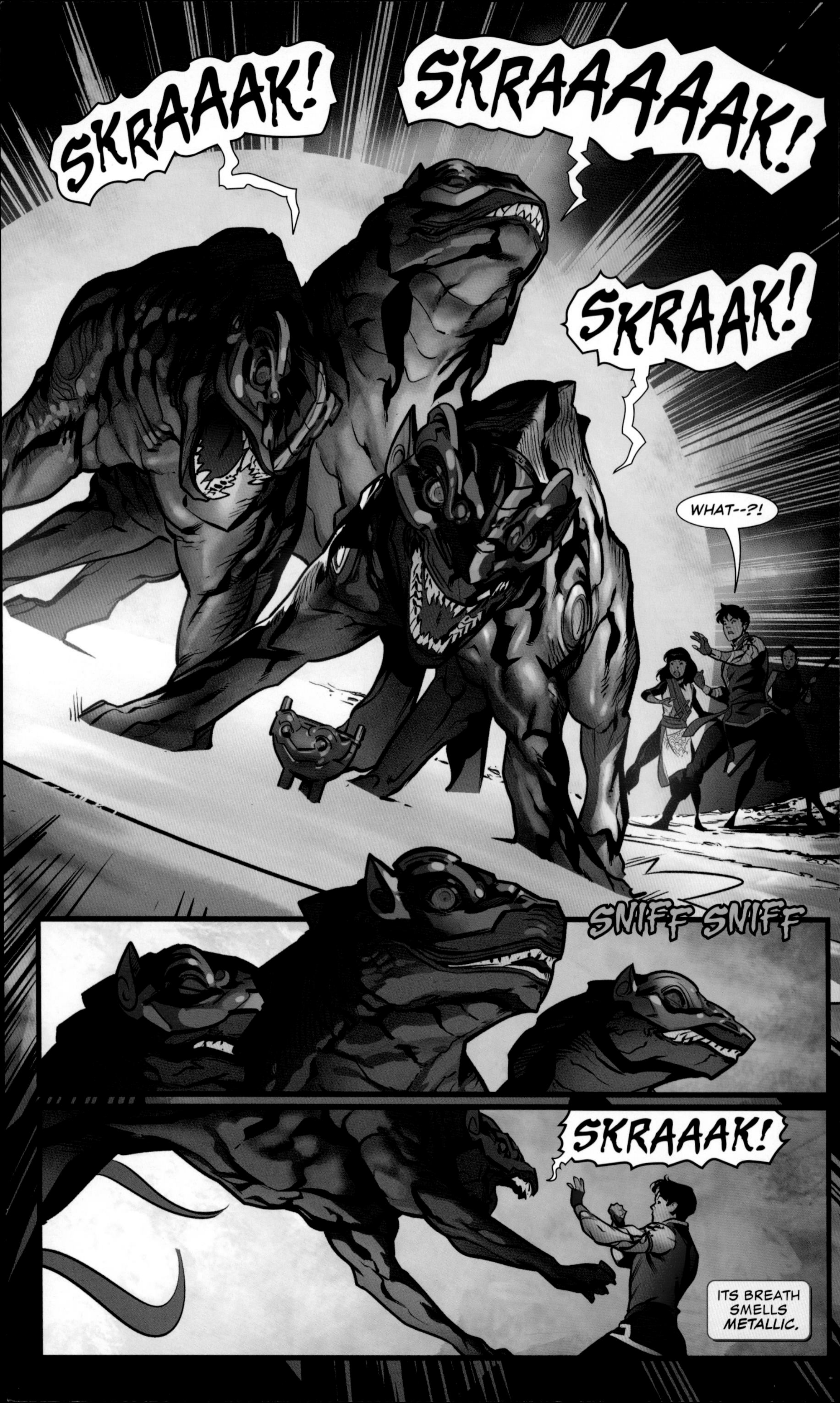
SKRAAAK!
SKRAAAAAAK!
SKRAAK!
WHAT--?!
SNIFF SNIFF
SKRAAAK!
ITS BREATH SMELLS METALLIC.

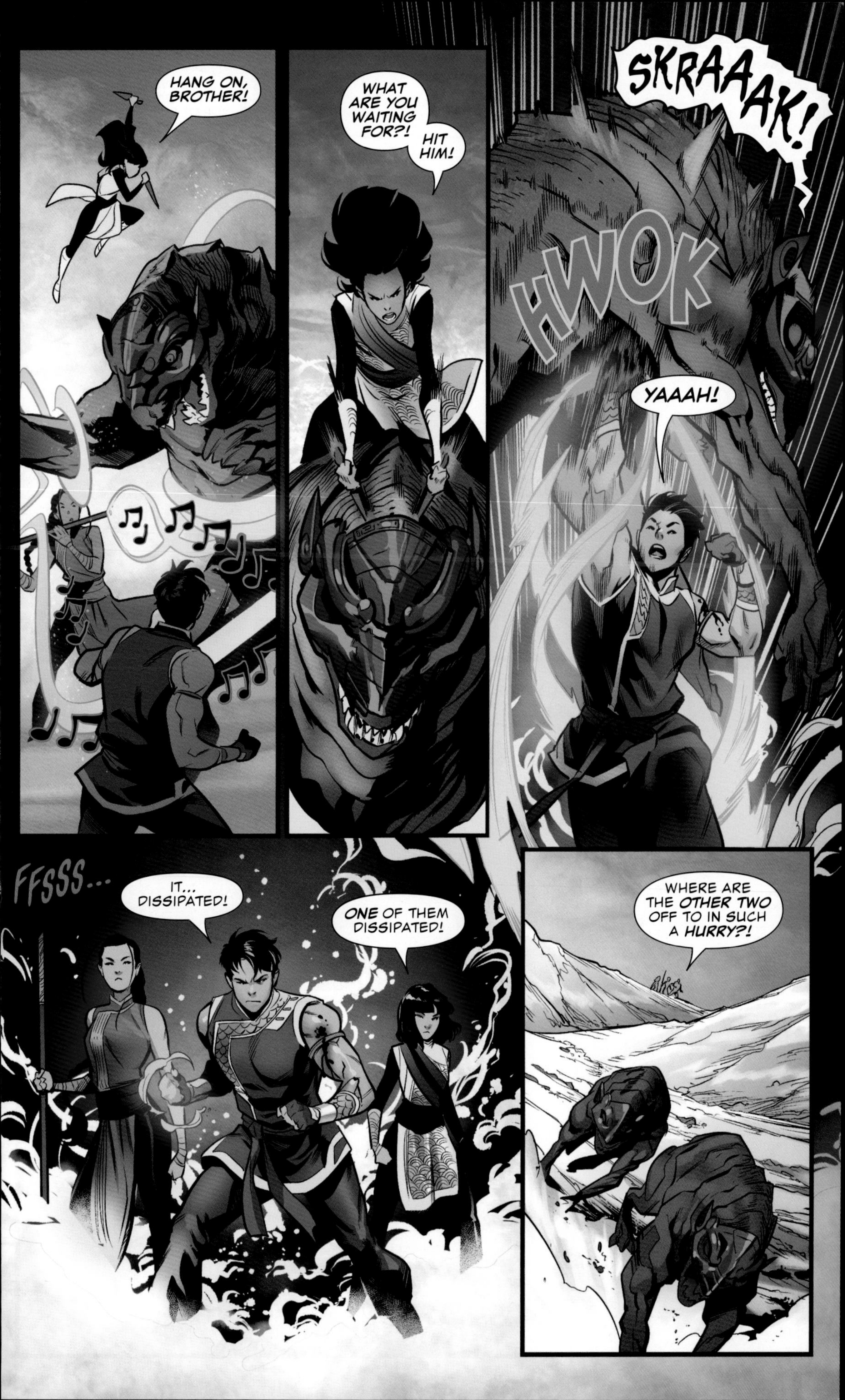
HANG ON, BROTHER!
WHAT ARE YOU WAITING FOR?!
HIT HIM!
SKRAAAAK!
HWOK
YAAAH!
FFSSS...
IT... DISSIPATED!
ONE OF THEM DISSIPATED!
WHERE ARE THE OTHER TWO OFF TO IN SUCH A HURRY?!

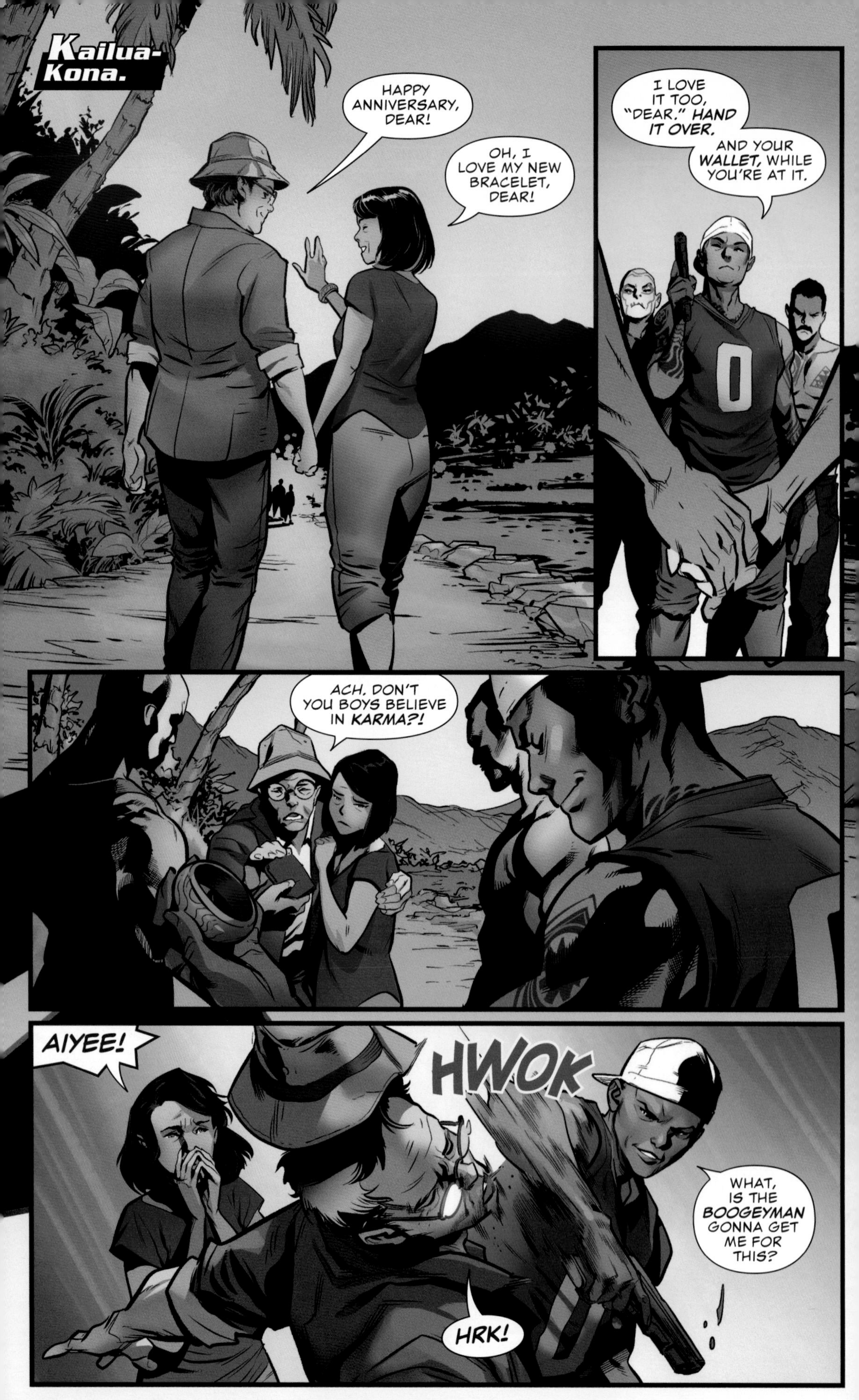
Kailua-Kona.
HAPPY ANNIVERSARY, DEAR!
OH, I LOVE MY NEW BRACELET, DEAR!
I LOVE IT TOO, "DEAR." HAND IT OVER.
AND YOUR WALLET, WHILE YOU'RE AT IT.
0
ACH. DON'T YOU BOYS BELIEVE IN KARMA?!
AIYEE!
HWOK
WHAT, IS THE BOOGEYMAN GONNA GET ME FOR THIS?
HRK!

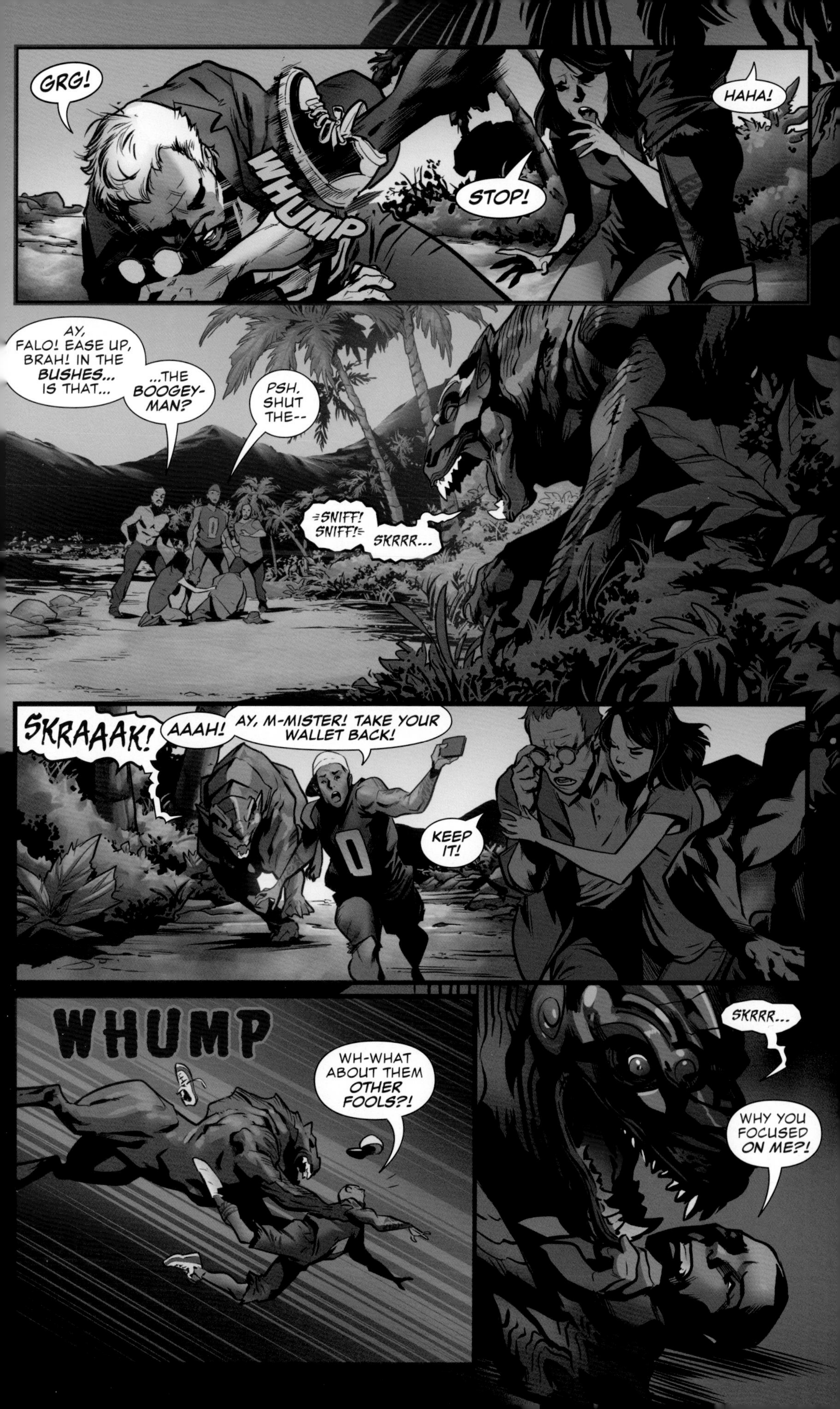
GRG!
WHUMP
STOP!
HAHA!
AY, FALO! EASE UP, BRAH! IN THE BUSHES... IS THAT...
...THE BOOGEY-MAN?
PSH, SHUT THE--
SNIFF! SNIFF!
SKRRR...
SKRAAAK!
AAAH!
AY, M-MISTER! TAKE YOUR WALLET BACK!
KEEP IT!
WHUMP
WH-WHAT ABOUT THEM OTHER FOOLS?!
SKRRR...
WHY YOU FOCUSED ON ME?!

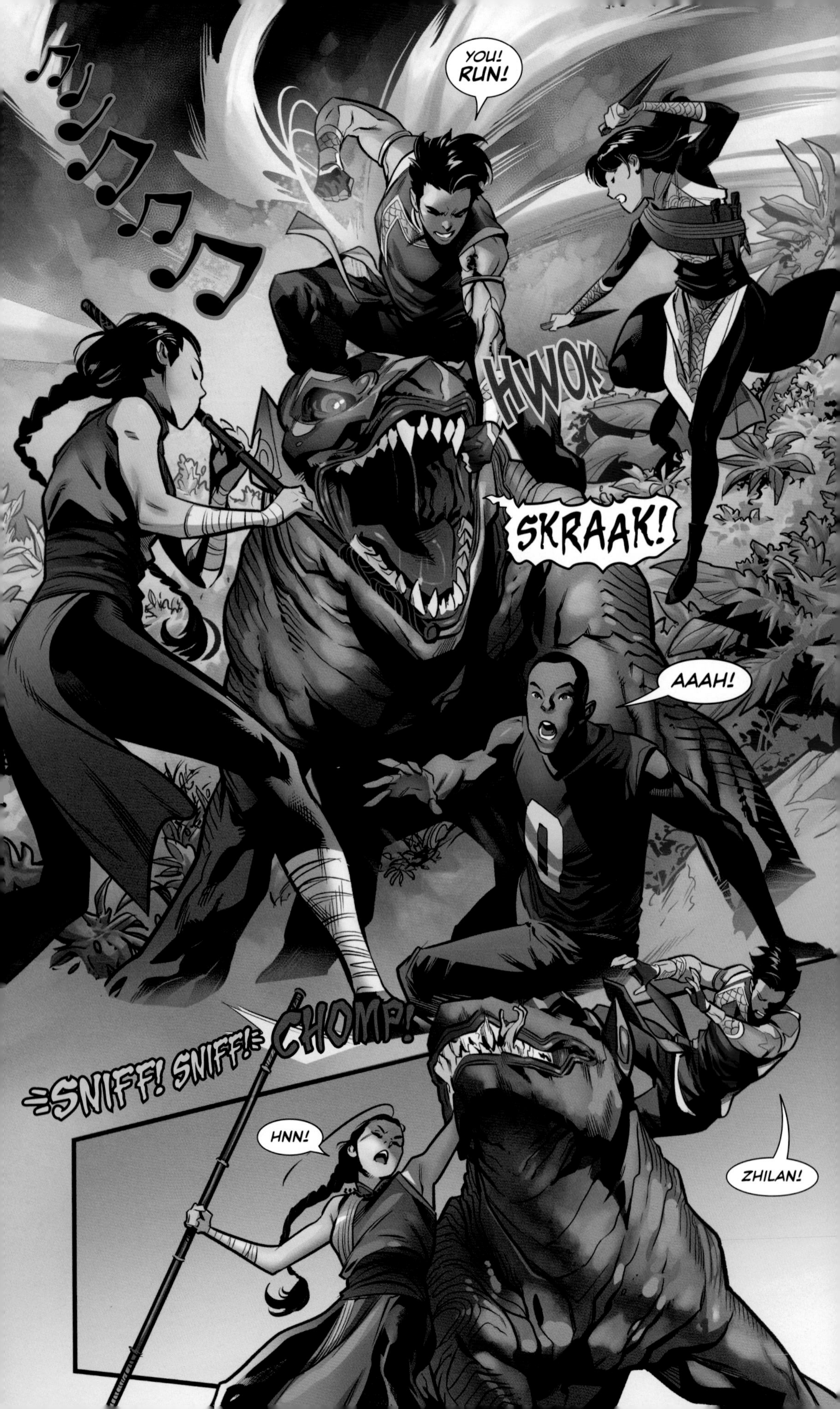
YOU! RUN!
HWOK
SKRAAK!
AAAH!
SNIFF! SNIFF!
CHOMP!
HNN!
ZHILAN!

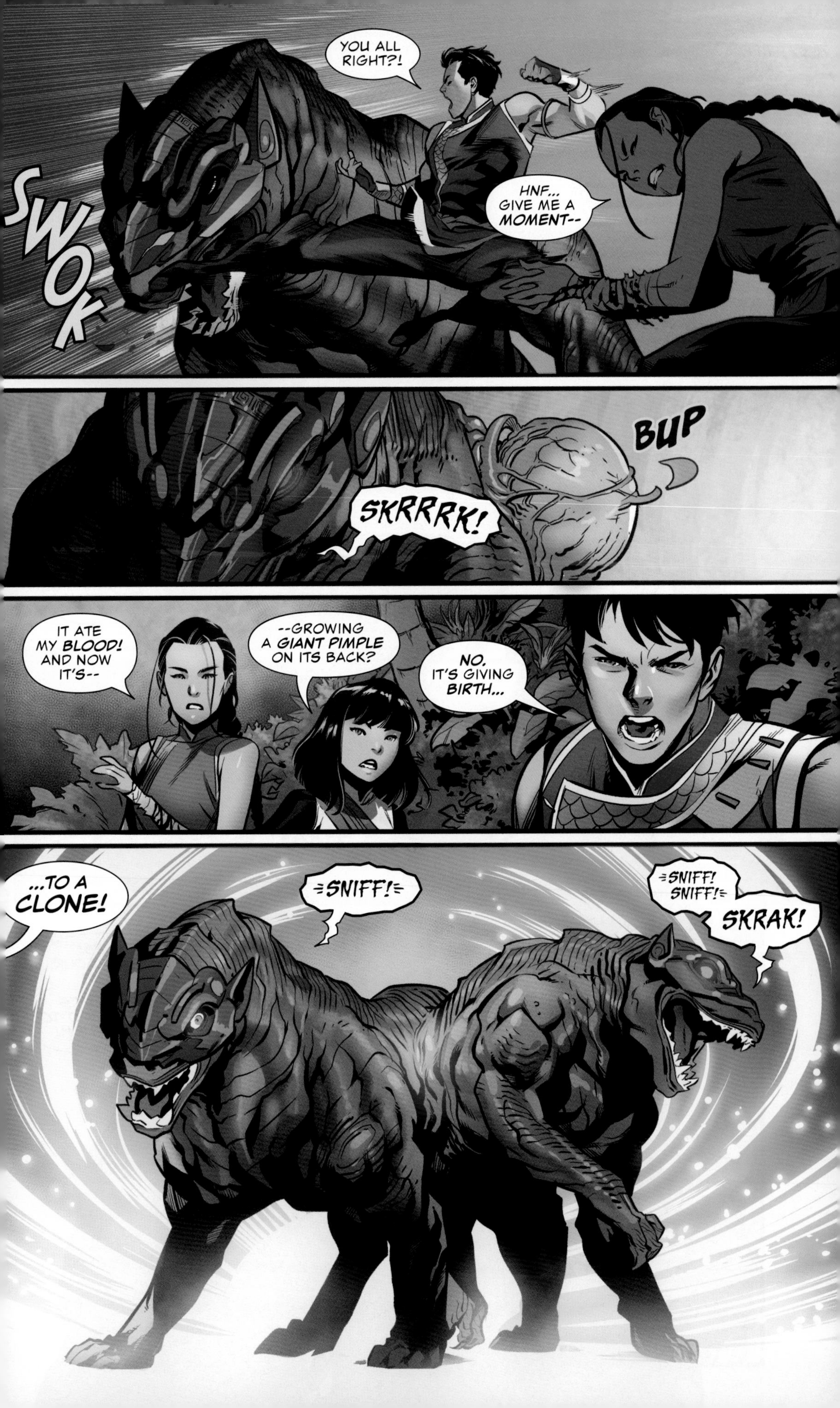
YOU ALL RIGHT?!
SWOK
HNF... GIVE ME A MOMENT--
BUP
SKRRRK!
IT ATE MY BLOOD! AND NOW IT'S--
--GROWING A GIANT PIMPLE ON ITS BACK?
NO. IT'S GIVING BIRTH...
...TO A CLONE!
SNIFF!
SNIFF! SNIFF!
SKRAK!

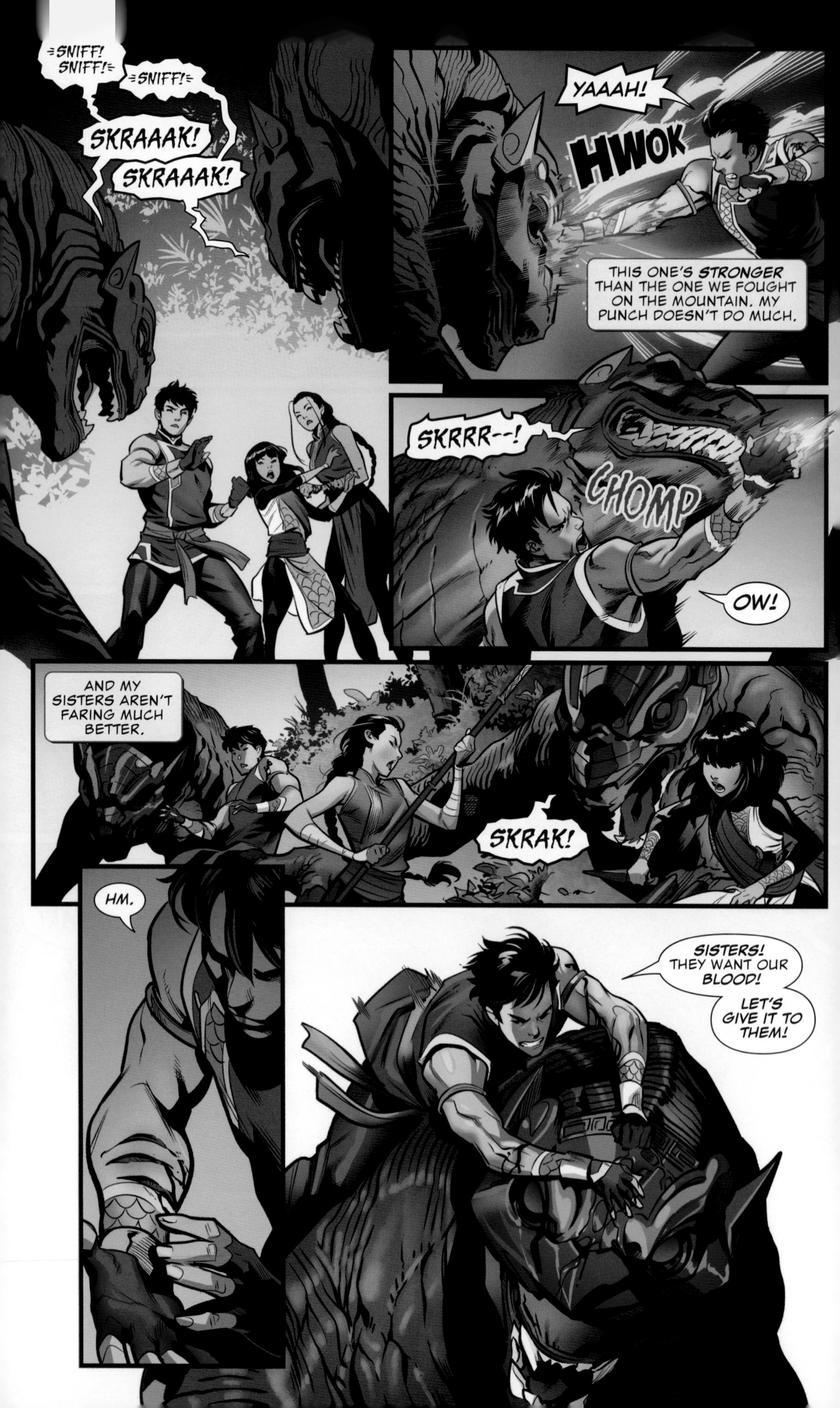

SNIFF! SNIFF!
SNIFF!
SKRAAAK!
SKRAAAK!
YAAAH!
HWOK
THIS ONE'S STRONGER THAN THE ONE WE FOUGHT ON THE MOUNTAIN. MY PUNCH DOESN'T DO MUCH.
SKRRR--!
CHOMP
OW!
AND MY SISTERS AREN'T FARING MUCH BETTER.
SKRAK!
HM.
SISTERS! THEY WANT OUR BLOOD!
LET'S GIVE IT TO THEM!

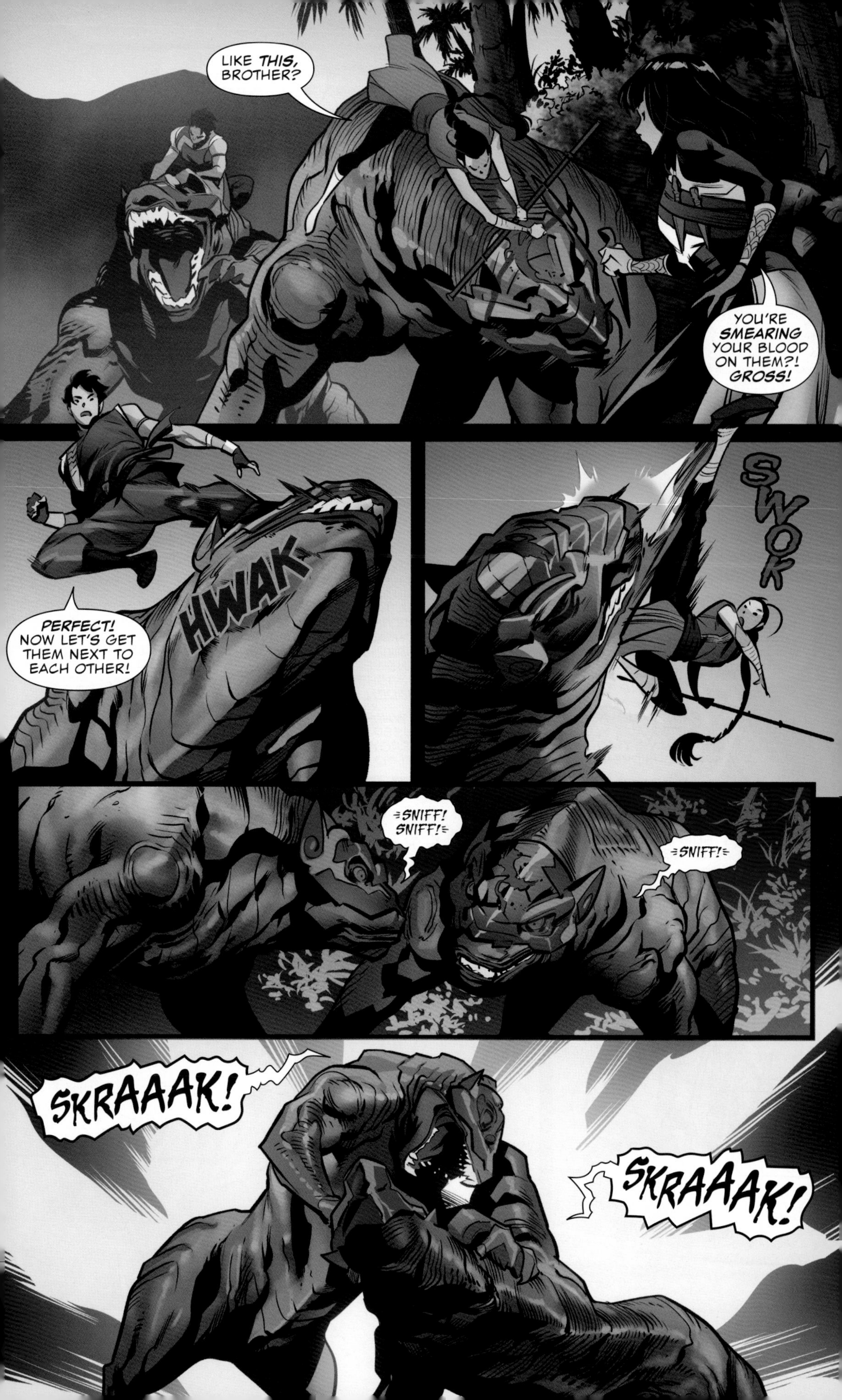
LIKE THIS, BROTHER?
YOU'RE SMEARING YOUR BLOOD ON THEM?! GROSS!
HWAK
PERFECT! NOW LET'S GET THEM NEXT TO EACH OTHER!
SWOK
SNIFF! SNIFF!
SNIFF!
SKRAAAK!
SKRAAAK!

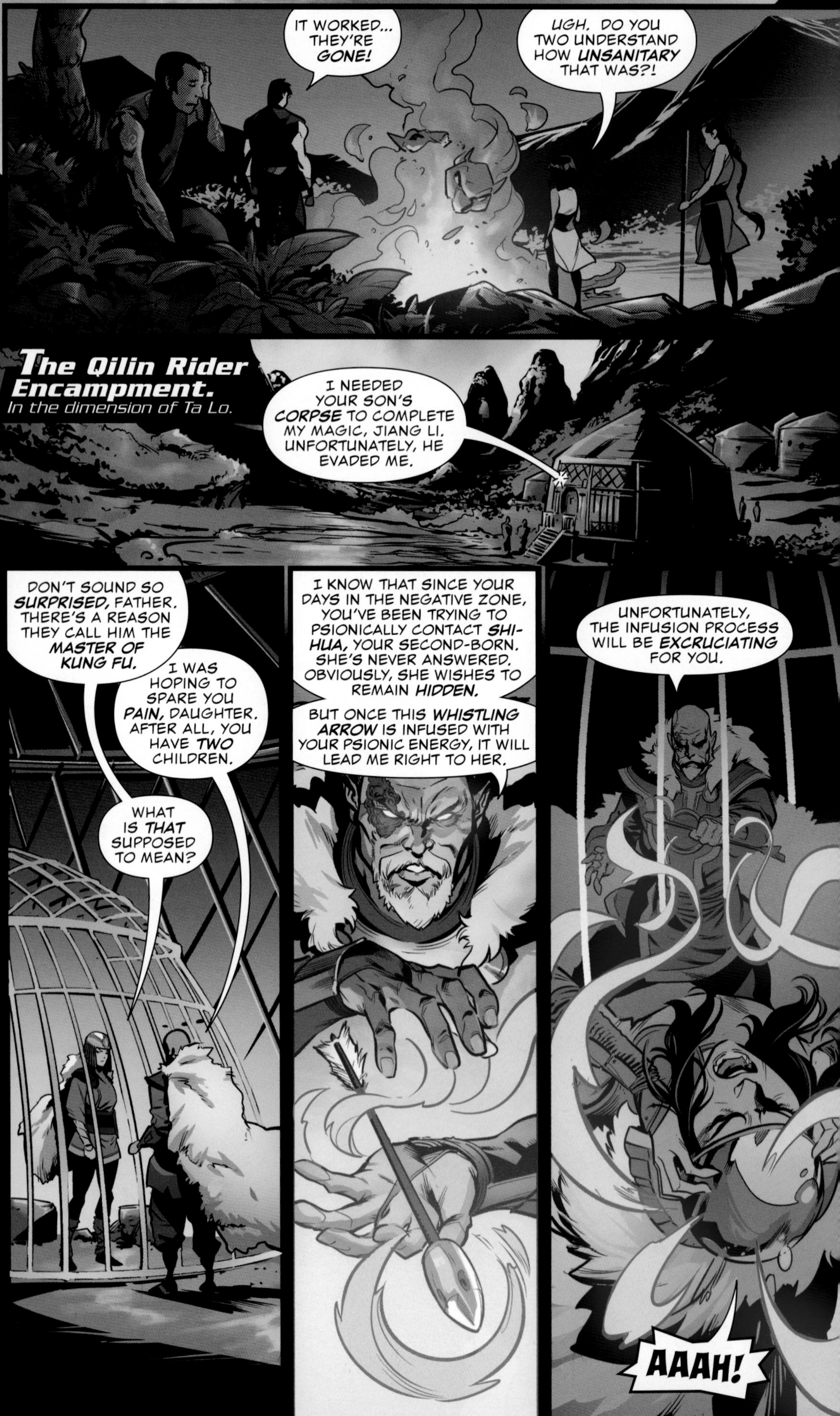
IT WORKED... THEY'RE GONE!
UGH. DO YOU TWO UNDERSTAND HOW UNSANITARY THAT WAS?!
The Qilin Rider Encampment.
In the dimension of Ta Lo.
I NEEDED YOUR SON'S CORPSE TO COMPLETE MY MAGIC, JIANG LI. UNFORTUNATELY, HE EVADED ME.
DON'T SOUND SO SURPRISED, FATHER. THERE'S A REASON THEY CALL HIM THE MASTER OF KUNG FU.
I WAS HOPING TO SPARE YOU PAIN, DAUGHTER. AFTER ALL, YOU HAVE TWO CHILDREN.
WHAT IS THAT SUPPOSED TO MEAN?
I KNOW THAT SINCE YOUR DAYS IN THE NEGATIVE ZONE, YOU'VE BEEN TRYING TO PSIONICALLY CONTACT SHI-HUA, YOUR SECOND-BORN. SHE'S NEVER ANSWERED. OBVIOUSLY, SHE WISHES TO REMAIN HIDDEN.
BUT ONCE THIS WHISTLING ARROW IS INFUSED WITH YOUR PSIONIC ENERGY, IT WILL LEAD ME RIGHT TO HER.
UNFORTUNATELY, THE INFUSION PROCESS WILL BE EXCRUCIATING FOR YOU.
AAAH!

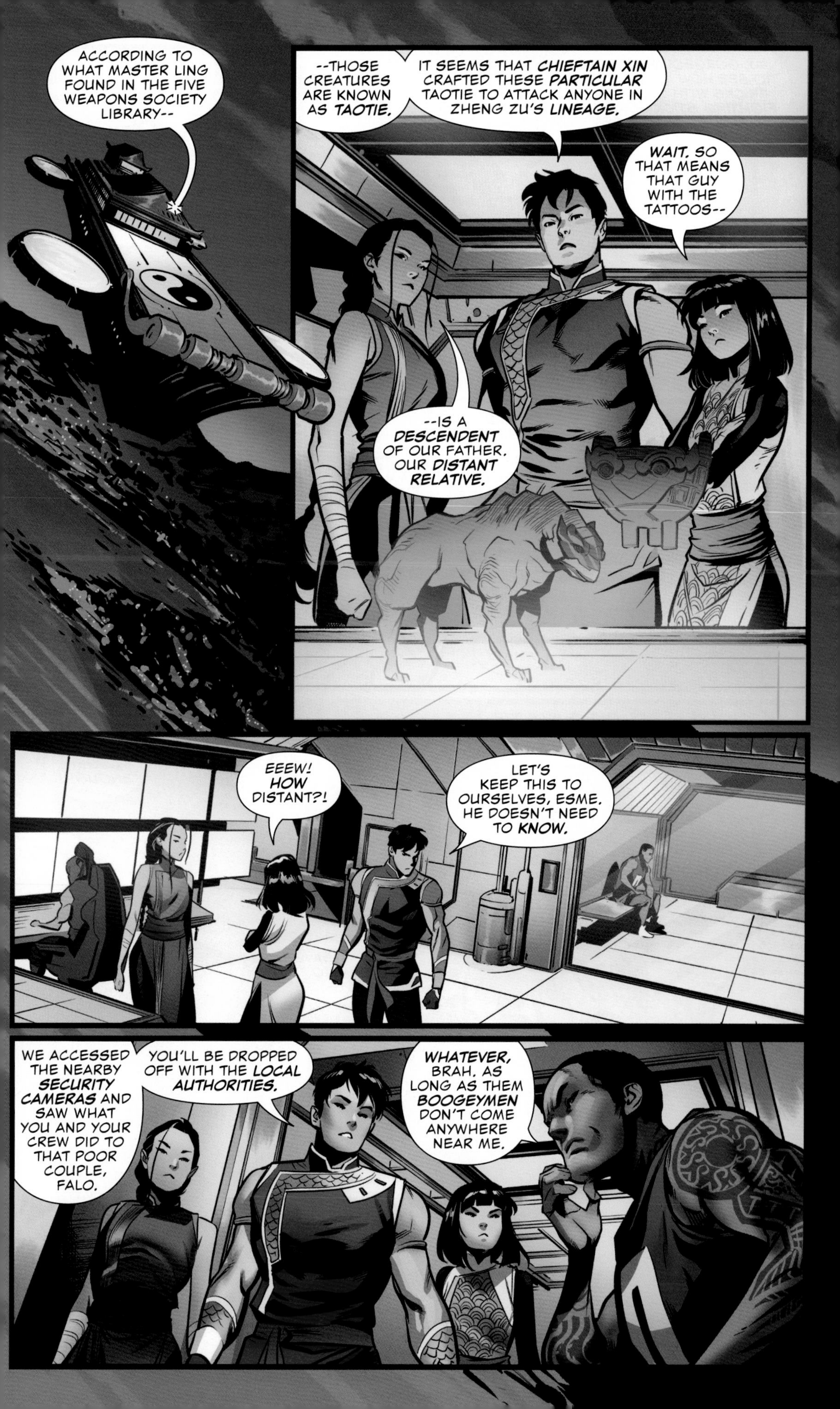
ACCORDING TO WHAT MASTER LING FOUND IN THE FIVE WEAPONS SOCIETY LIBRARY--
--THOSE CREATURES ARE KNOWN AS TAOTIE.
IT SEEMS THAT CHIEFTAIN XIN CRAFTED THESE PARTICULAR TAOTIE TO ATTACK ANYONE IN ZHENG ZU'S LINEAGE.
WAIT. SO THAT MEANS THAT GUY WITH THE TATTOOS--
--IS A DESCENDENT OF OUR FATHER. OUR DISTANT RELATIVE.
EEEW! HOW DISTANT?!
LET'S KEEP THIS TO OURSELVES, ESME. HE DOESN'T NEED TO KNOW.
WE ACCESSED THE NEARBY SECURITY CAMERAS AND SAW WHAT YOU AND YOUR CREW DID TO THAT POOR COUPLE, FALO.
YOU'LL BE DROPPED OFF WITH THE LOCAL AUTHORITIES.
WHATEVER, BRAH. AS LONG AS THEM BOOGEYMEN DON'T COME ANYWHERE NEAR ME.

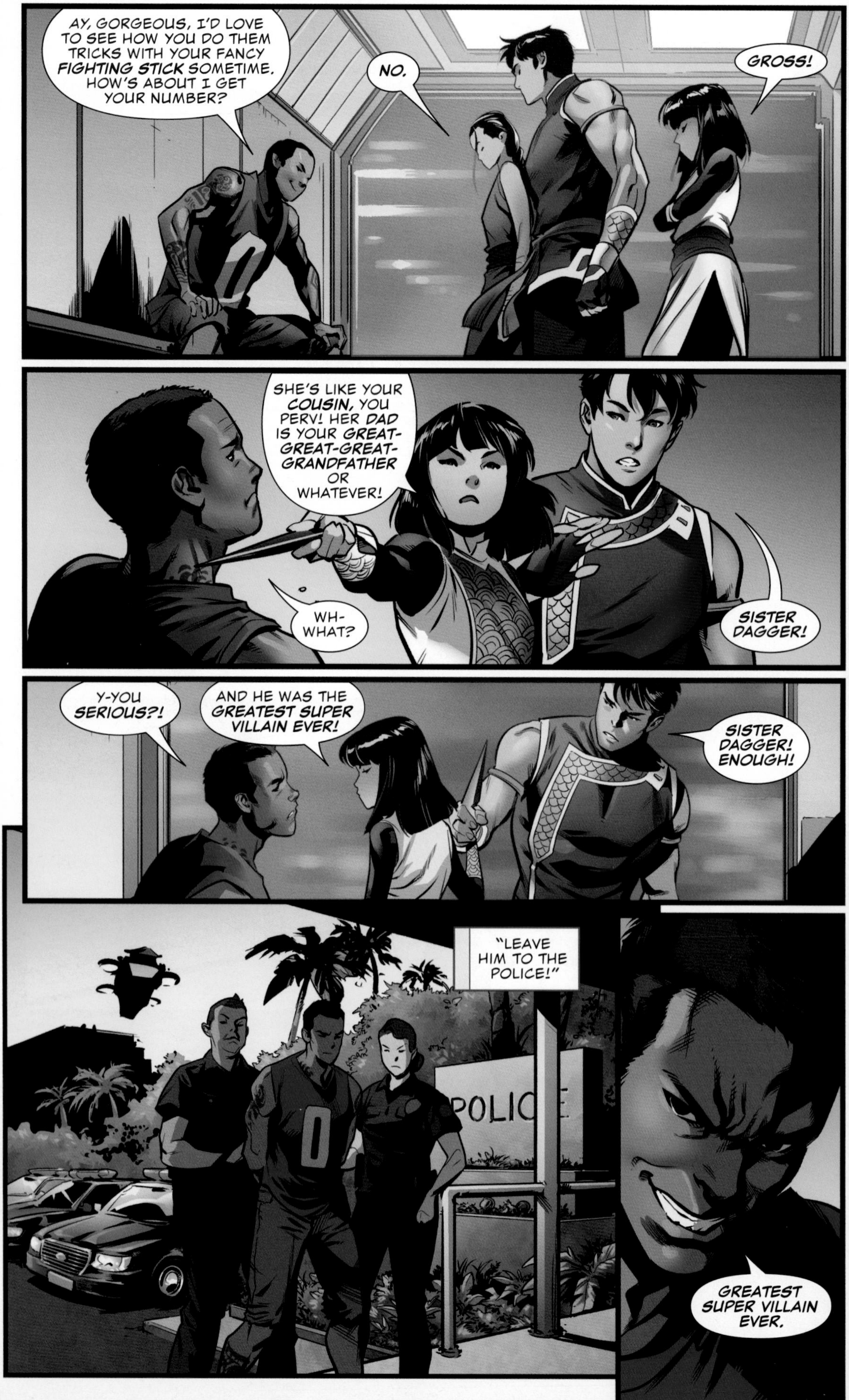
AY, GORGEOUS, I'D LOVE TO SEE HOW YOU DO THEM TRICKS WITH YOUR FANCY FIGHTING STICK SOMETIME. HOW'S ABOUT I GET YOUR NUMBER?
NO.
GROSS!
SHE'S LIKE YOUR COUSIN, YOU PERV! HER DAD IS YOUR GREAT-GREAT-GREAT-GRANDFATHER OR WHATEVER!
WH-WHAT?
SISTER DAGGER!
Y-YOU SERIOUS?!
AND HE WAS THE GREATEST SUPER VILLAIN EVER!
SISTER DAGGER! ENOUGH!
"LEAVE HIM TO THE POLICE!"
POLICE
GREATEST SUPER VILLAIN EVER.

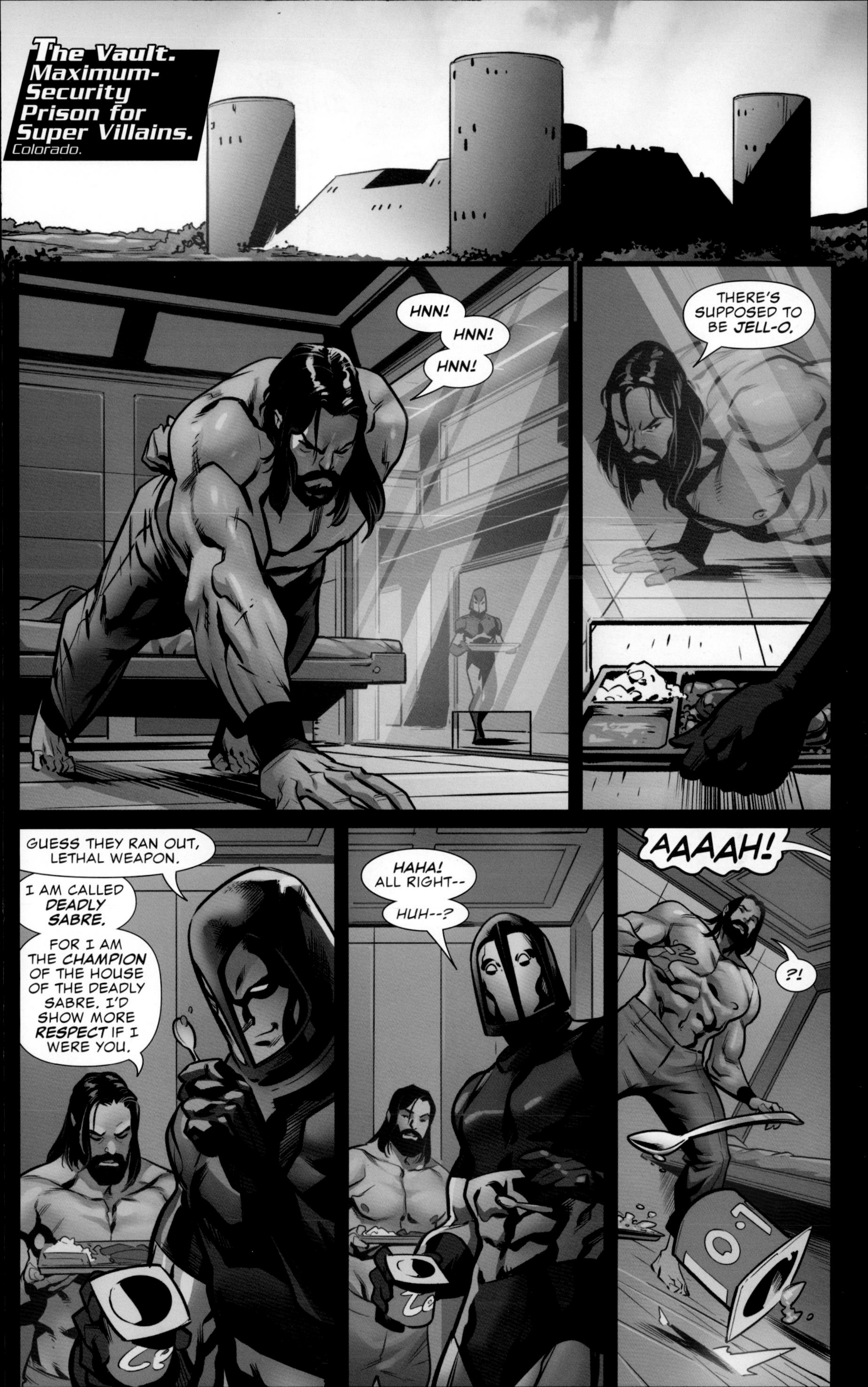
The Vault. Maximum-Security Prison for Super Villains.
Colorado.
HNN!
HNN!
HNN!
THERE'S SUPPOSED TO BE JELL-O.
GUESS THEY RAN OUT, LETHAL WEAPON.
I AM CALLED DEADLY SABRE.
FOR I AM THE CHAMPION OF THE HOUSE OF THE DEADLY SABRE. I'D SHOW MORE RESPECT IF I WERE YOU.
HAHA! ALL RIGHT--
HUH--?
AAAAH!
?!

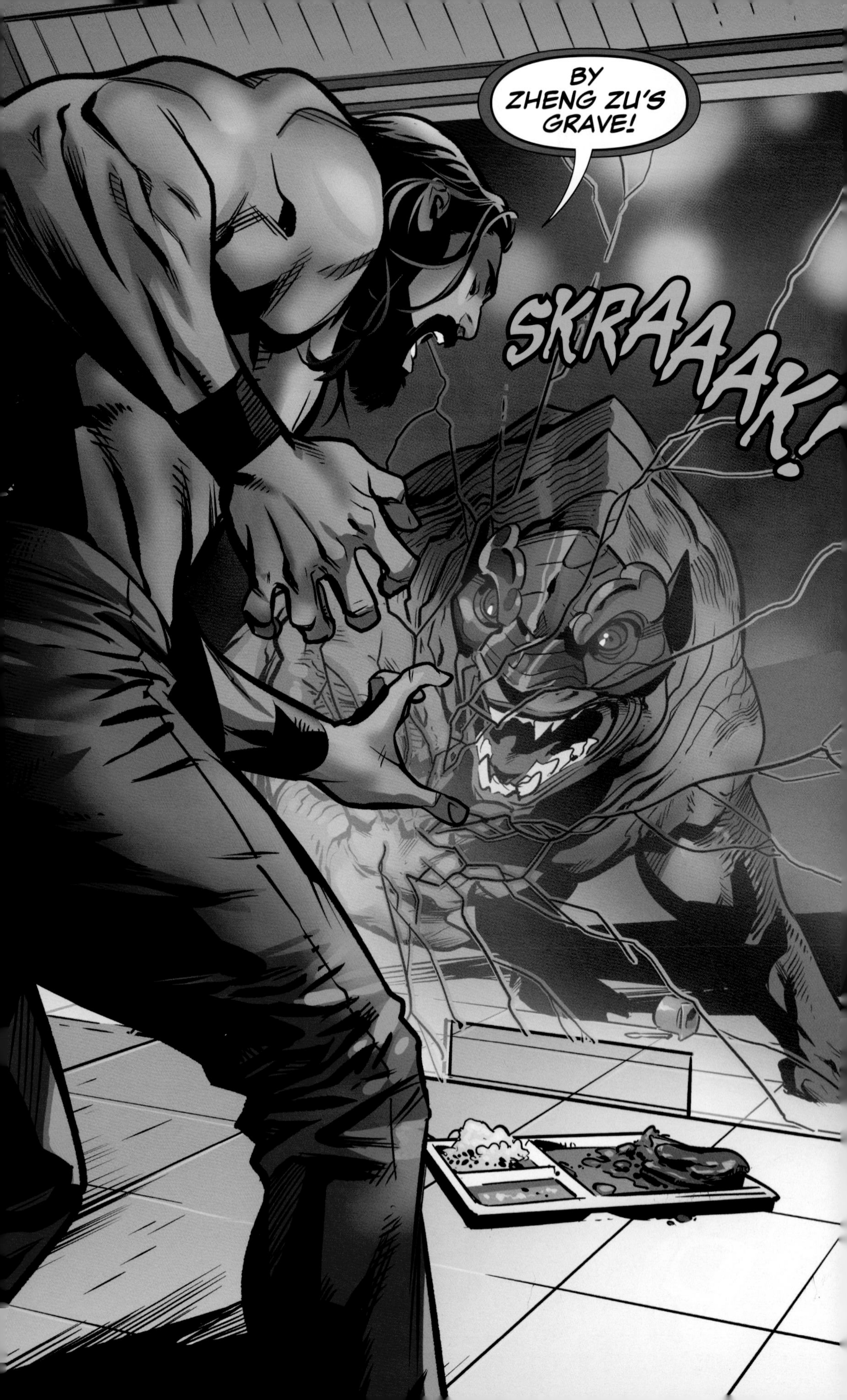
BY ZHENG ZU'S GRAVE!
SKRAAAK!

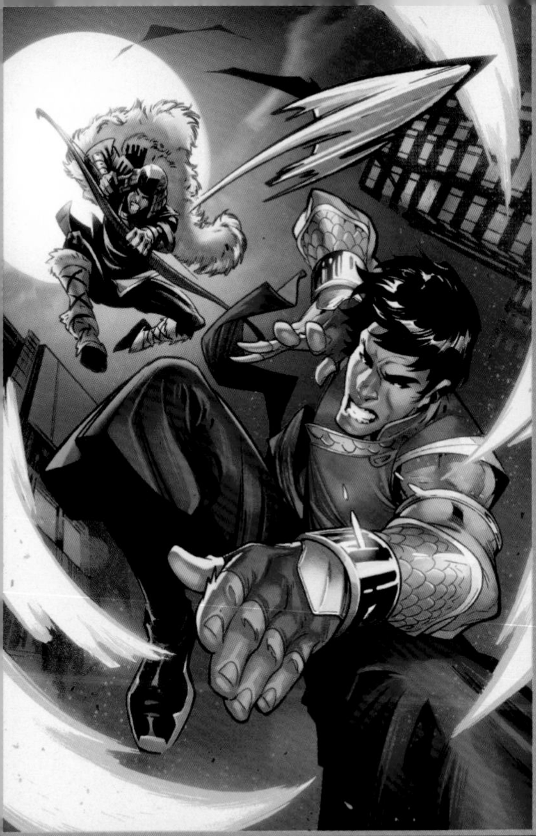

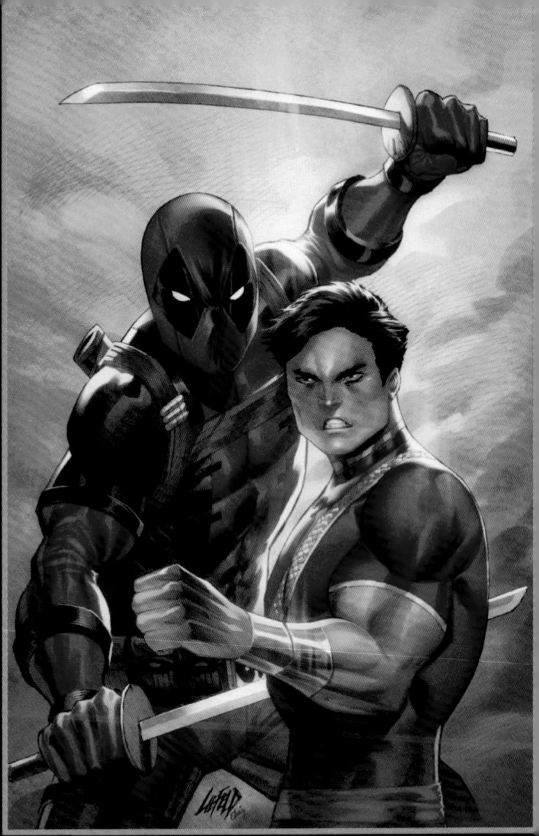

#7 VARIANT BY
RANCESCO MANNA & RACHELLE ROSENBERG

#7 DEADPOOL 30TH ANNIVERSARY VARIANT BY
ROB LIEFELD

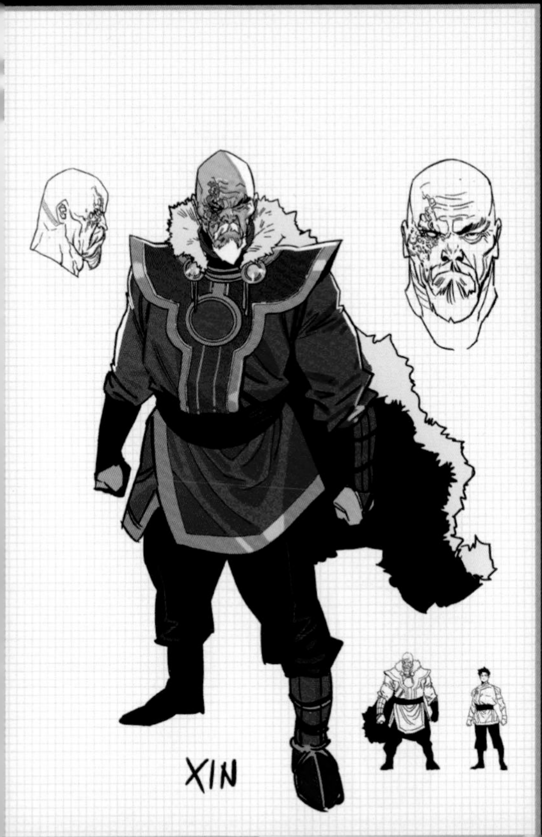
XIN

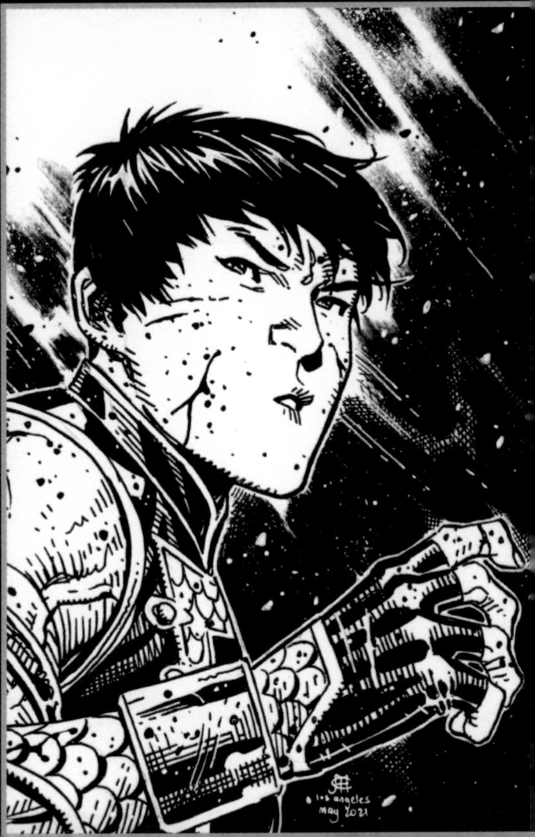
los angeles
may 2021

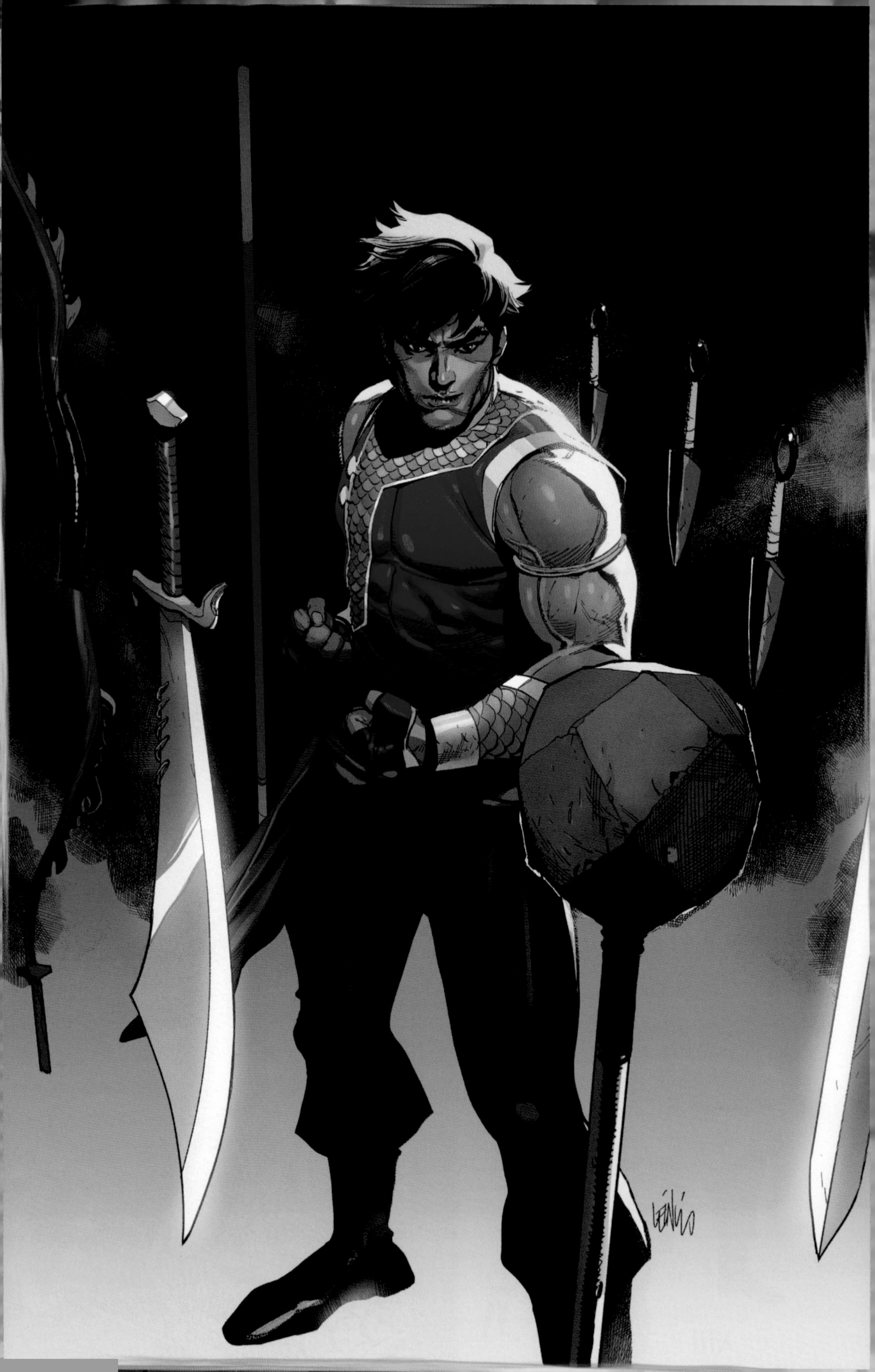

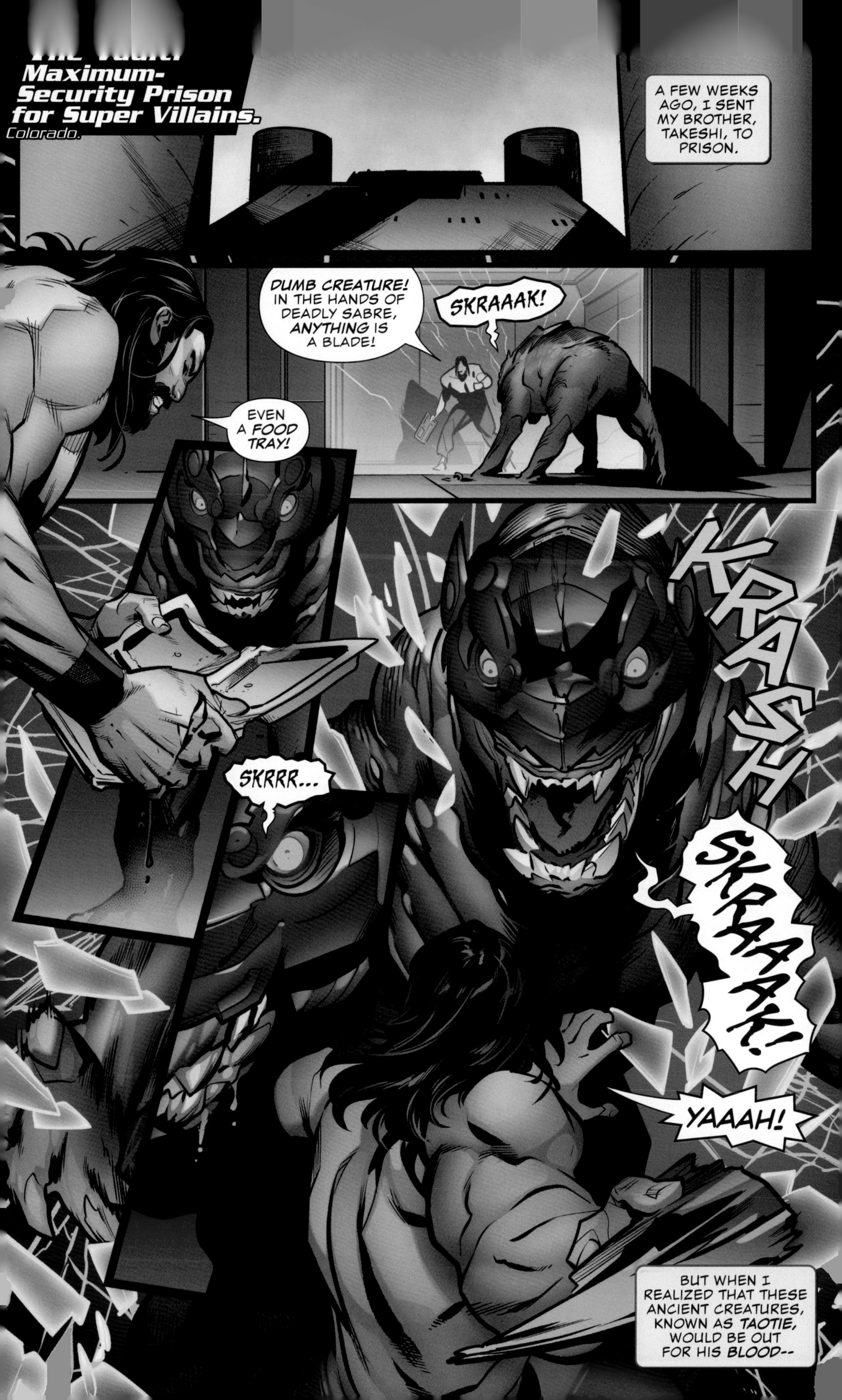

Maximum-Security Prison for Super Villains.
Colorado.
A FEW WEEKS AGO, I SENT MY BROTHER, TAKESHI, TO PRISON.
DUMB CREATURE! IN THE HANDS OF DEADLY SABRE, ANYTHING IS A BLADE!
SKRAAAK!
EVEN A FOOD TRAY!
KRASH
SKRRR...
SKRAAAK!
YAAAH!
BUT WHEN I REALIZED THAT THESE ANCIENT CREATURES, KNOWN AS TAOTIE, WOULD BE OUT FOR HIS BLOOD--

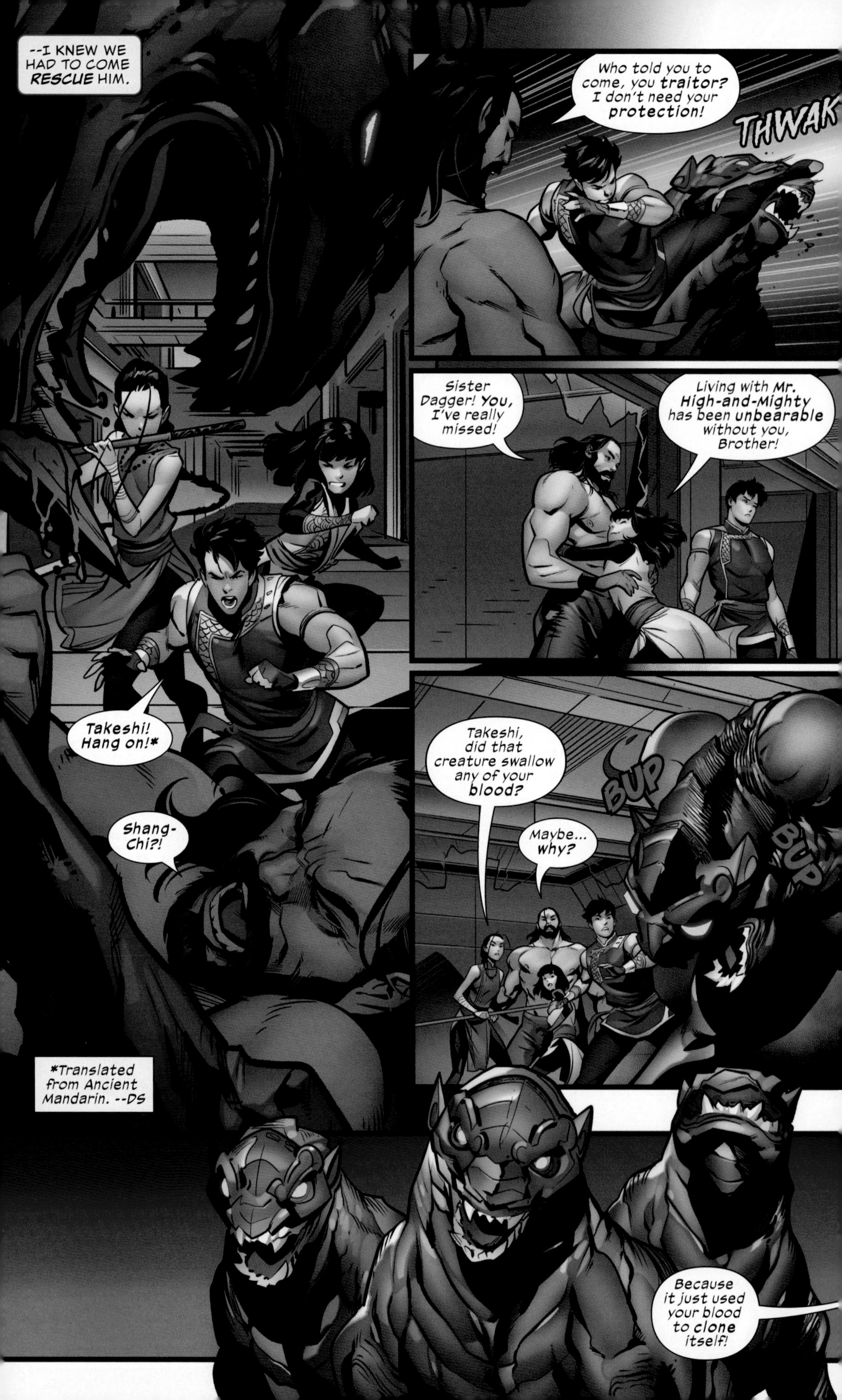
--I KNEW WE HAD TO COME RESCUE HIM.
Who told you to come, you traitor? I don't need your protection!
THWAK
Sister Dagger! You, I've really missed!
Living with Mr. High-and-Mighty has been unbearable without you, Brother!
Takeshi! Hang on!*
Shang-Chi?!
Takeshi, did that creature swallow any of your blood?
Maybe... why?
BUP
BUP
Because it just used your blood to clone itself!
*Translated from Ancient Mandarin. --DS

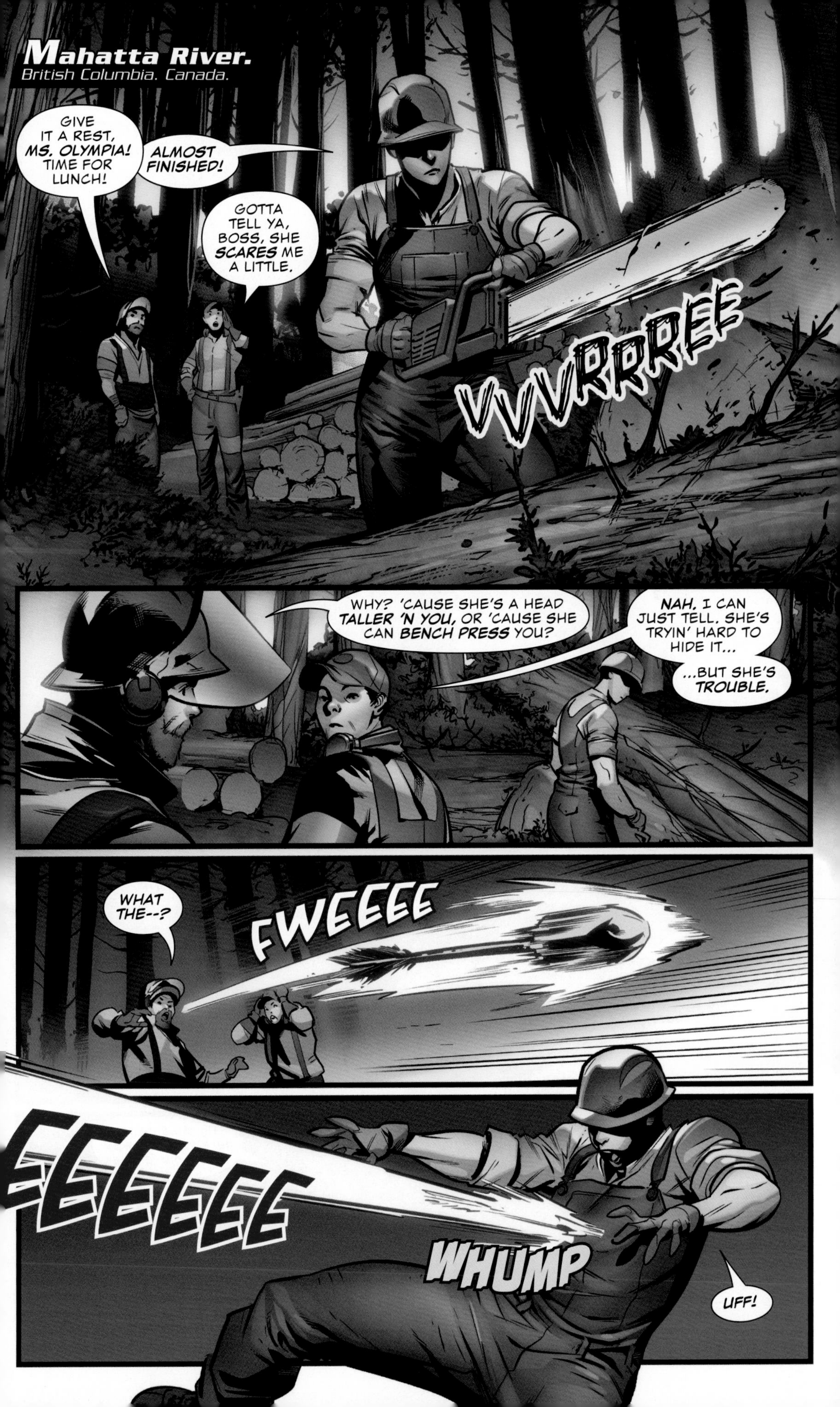
Mahatta River.
British Columbia. Canada.
GIVE IT A REST, MS. OLYMPIA! TIME FOR LUNCH!
ALMOST FINISHED!
GOTTA TELL YA, BOSS, SHE SCARES ME A LITTLE.
VVVRRRREE
WHY? 'CAUSE SHE'S A HEAD TALLER 'N YOU, OR 'CAUSE SHE CAN BENCH PRESS YOU?
NAH. I CAN JUST TELL. SHE'S TRYIN' HARD TO HIDE IT...
...BUT SHE'S TROUBLE.
WHAT THE--?
FWEEEE
EEEEEEE
WHUMP
UFF!

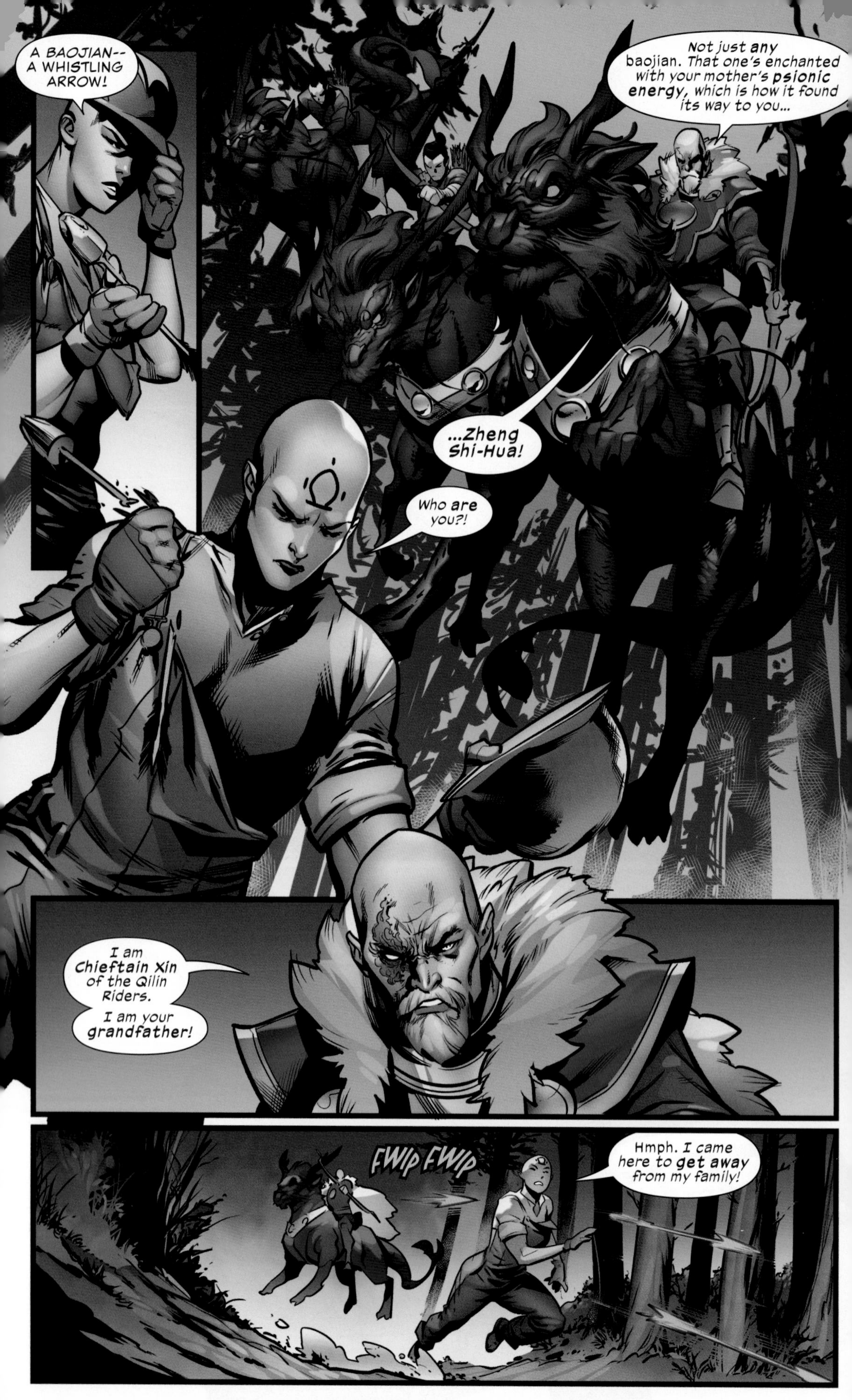

A BAOJIAN-- A WHISTLING ARROW!
Not just any baojian. That one's enchanted with your mother's psionic energy, which is how it found its way to you...
...Zheng Shi-Hua!
Who are you?!
I am Chieftain Xin of the Qilin Riders.
I am your grandfather!
FWIP FWIP
Hmph. I came here to get away from my family!

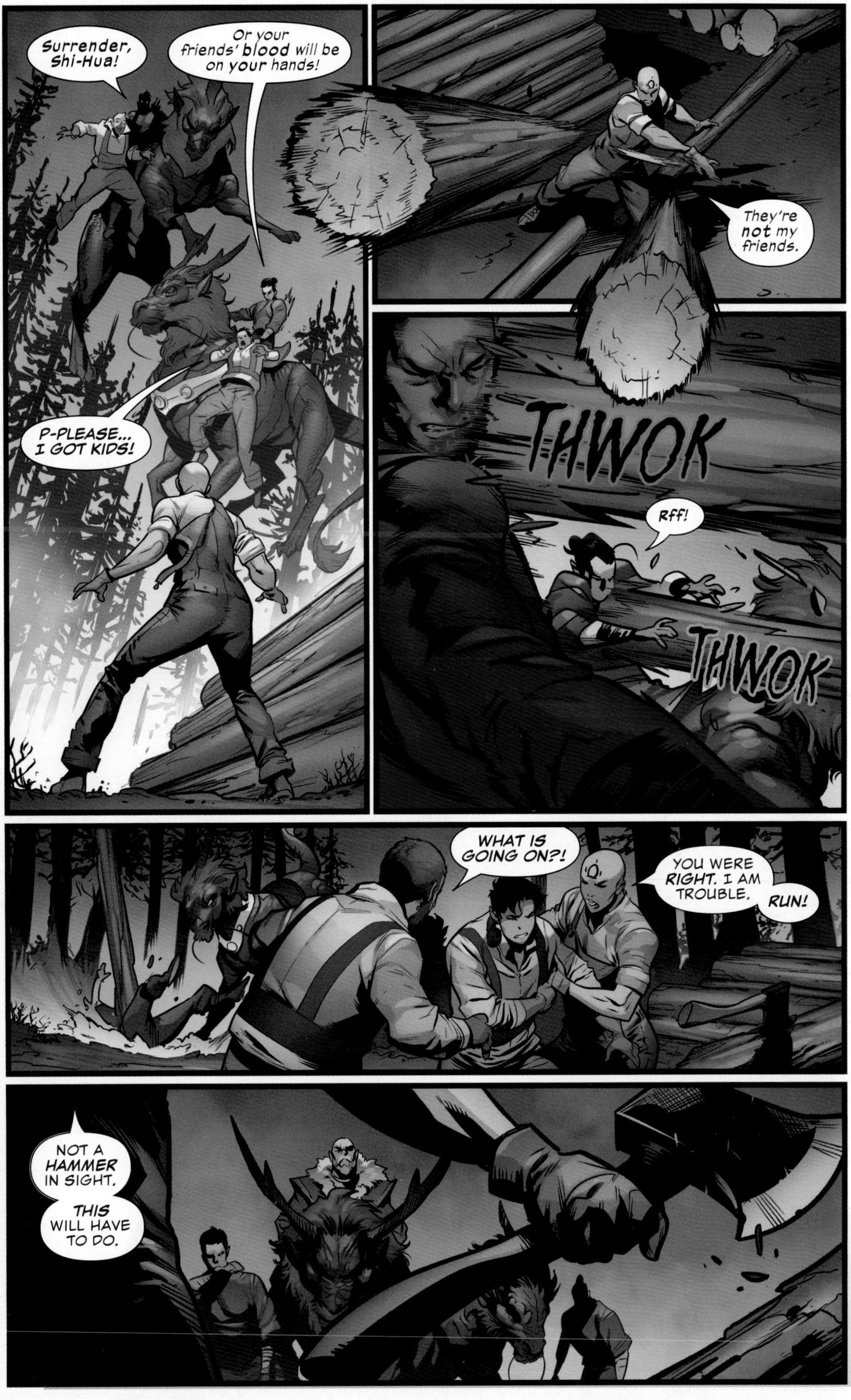
Surrender, Shi-Hua!
Or your friends' blood will be on your hands!
P-PLEASE... I GOT KIDS!
They're not my friends.
THWOK
Rff!
THWOK
WHAT IS GOING ON?!
YOU WERE RIGHT. I AM TROUBLE.
RUN!
NOT A HAMMER IN SIGHT.
THIS WILL HAVE TO DO.

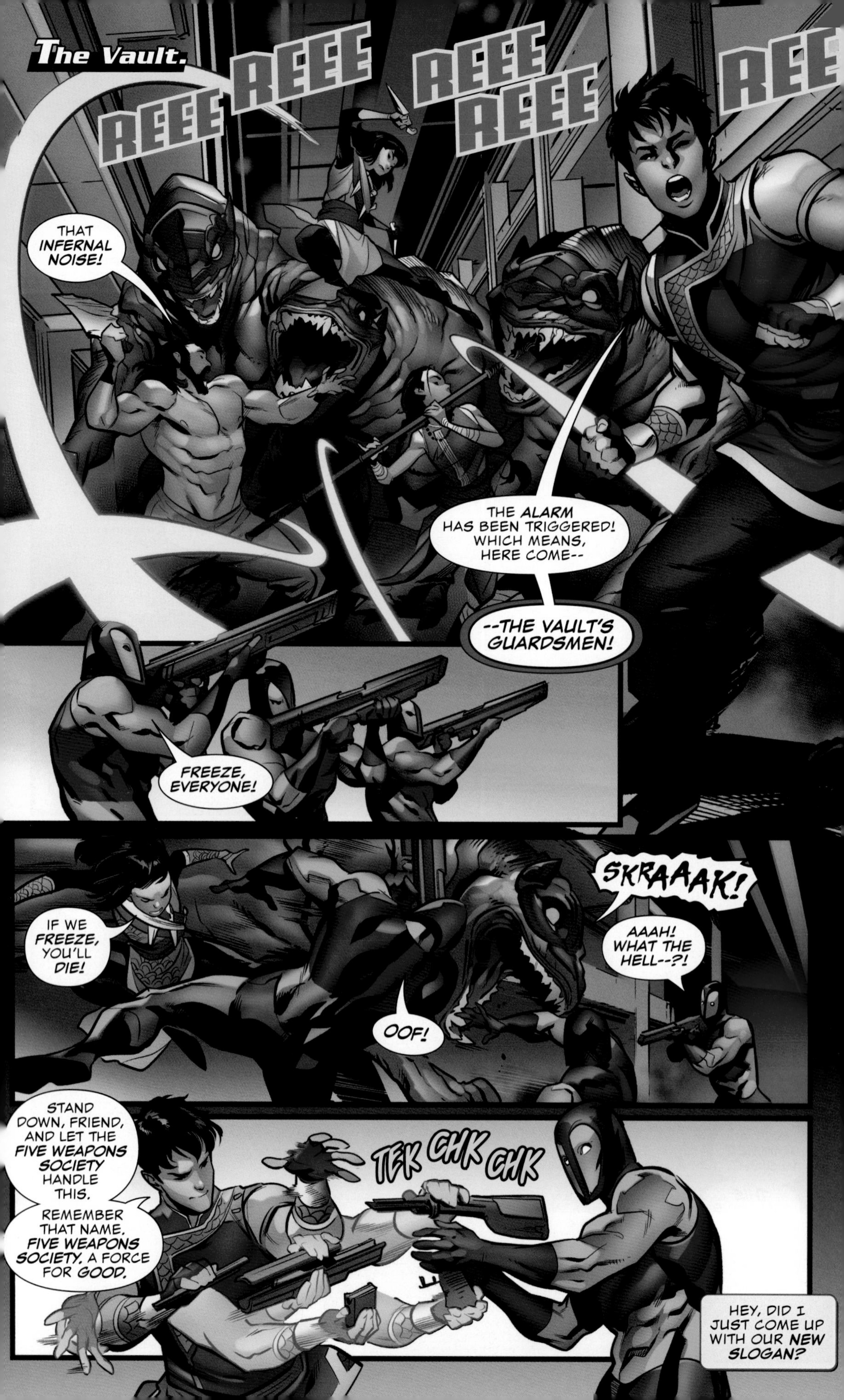
The Vault.
REEE REEE REEE REEE REE
THAT INFERNAL NOISE!
THE ALARM HAS BEEN TRIGGERED! WHICH MEANS, HERE COME--
--THE VAULT'S GUARDSMEN!
FREEZE, EVERYONE!
IF WE FREEZE, YOU'LL DIE!
SKRAAAK!
AAAH! WHAT THE HELL--?!
OOF!
STAND DOWN, FRIEND, AND LET THE FIVE WEAPONS SOCIETY HANDLE THIS.
REMEMBER THAT NAME. FIVE WEAPONS SOCIETY. A FORCE FOR GOOD.
TEK CHK CHK
HEY, DID I JUST COME UP WITH OUR NEW SLOGAN?

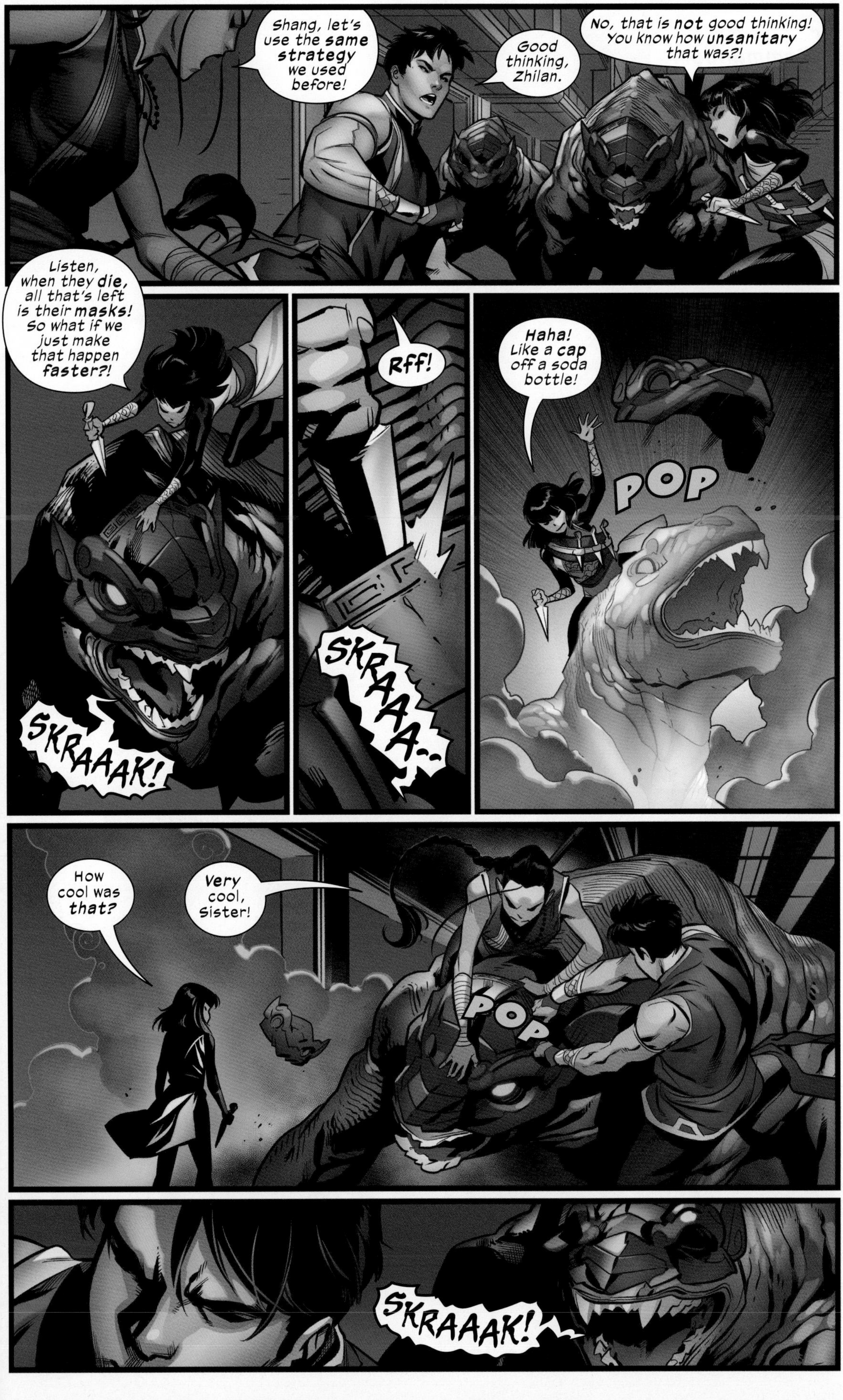

Shang, let's use the same strategy we used before!
Good thinking, Zhilan.
No, that is not good thinking! You know how unsanitary that was?!
Listen, when they die, all that's left is their masks! So what if we just make that happen faster?!
SKRAAAK!
Rff!
SKRAAAA--
Haha! Like a cap off a soda bottle!
POP
How cool was that?
Very cool, Sister!
POP
SKRAAAK!

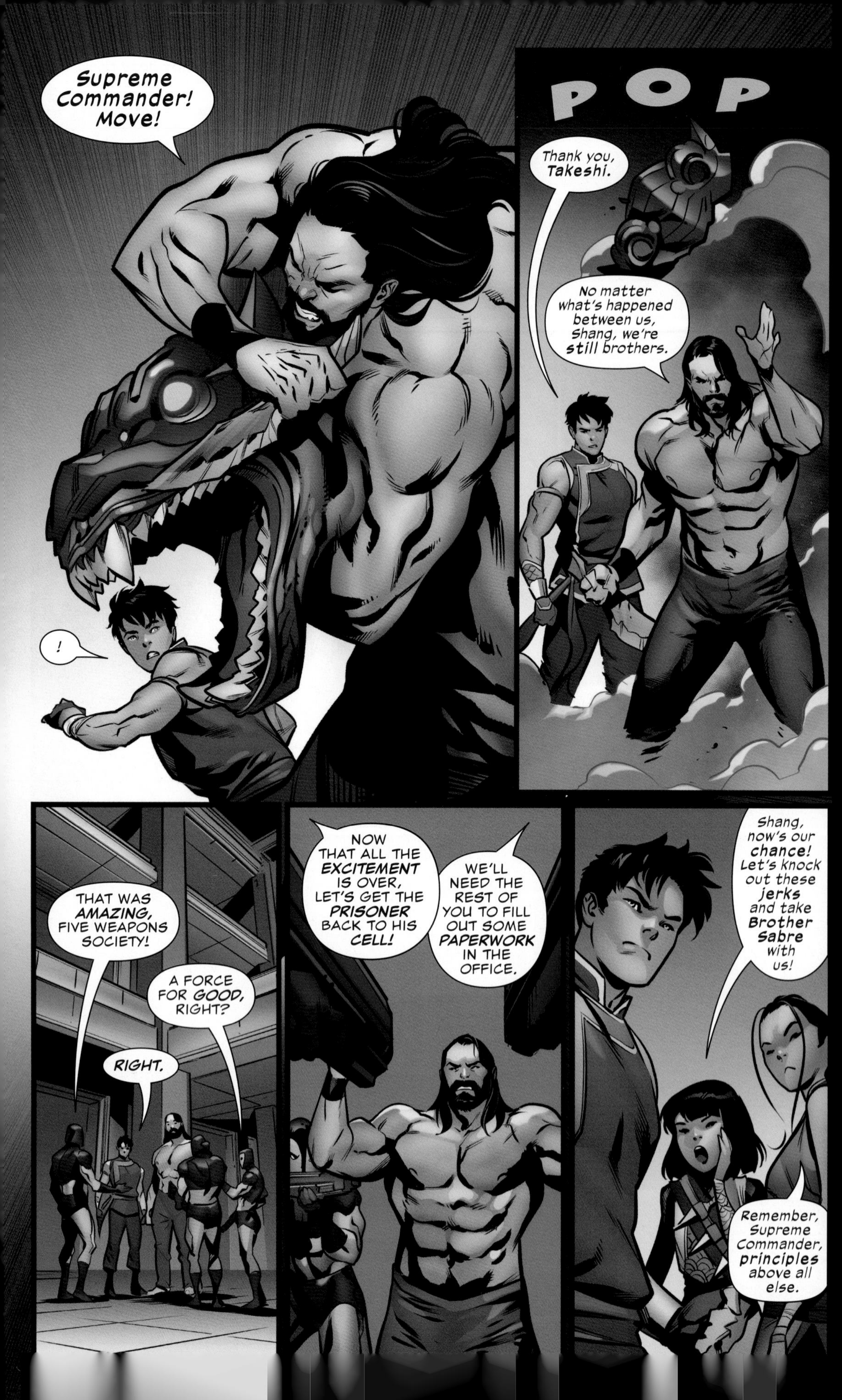

Supreme Commander! Move!
!
POP
Thank you, Takeshi.
No matter what's happened between us, Shang, we're still brothers.
THAT WAS AMAZING, FIVE WEAPONS SOCIETY!
A FORCE FOR GOOD, RIGHT?
RIGHT.
NOW THAT ALL THE EXCITEMENT IS OVER, LET'S GET THE PRISONER BACK TO HIS CELL!
WE'LL NEED THE REST OF YOU TO FILL OUT SOME PAPERWORK IN THE OFFICE.
Shang, now's our chance! Let's knock out these jerks and take Brother Sabre with us!
Remember, Supreme Commander, principles above all else.

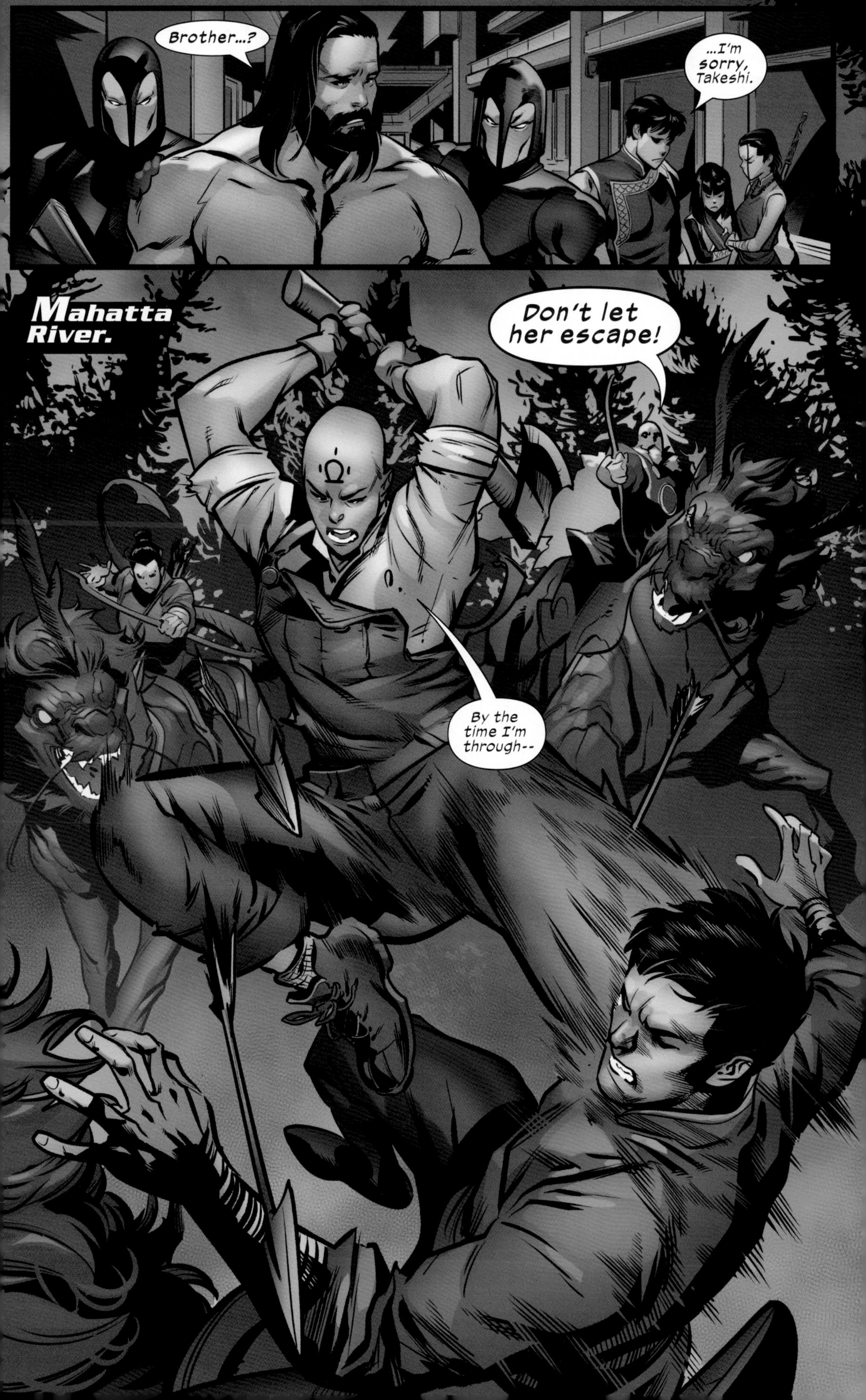
Brother...?
...I'm sorry, Takeshi.
Mahatta River.
Don't let her escape!
By the time I'm through--

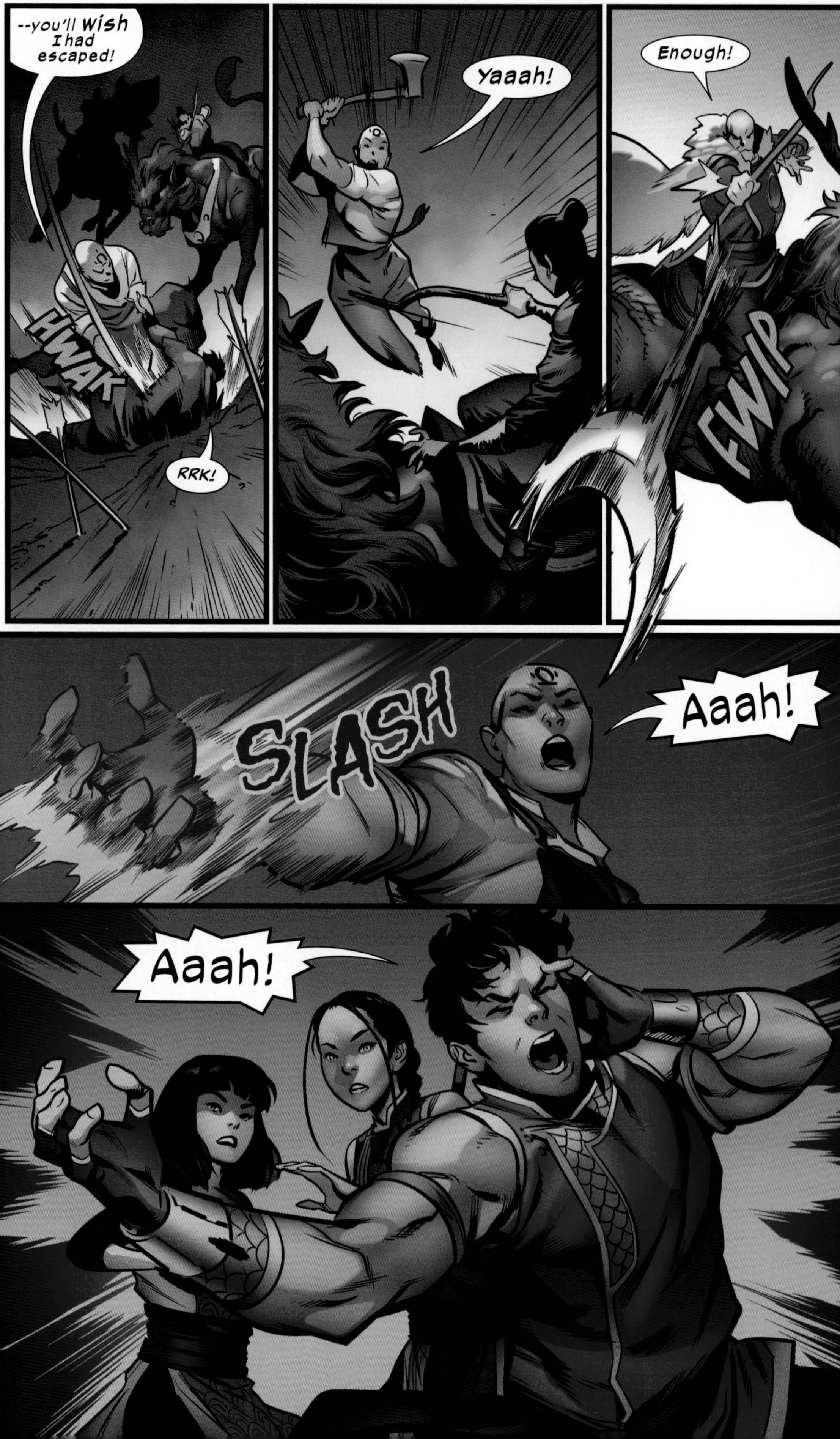
--you'll wish I had escaped!
HWAK
RRK!
Yaaah!
Enough!
FWIP
SLASH
Aaah!
Aaah!

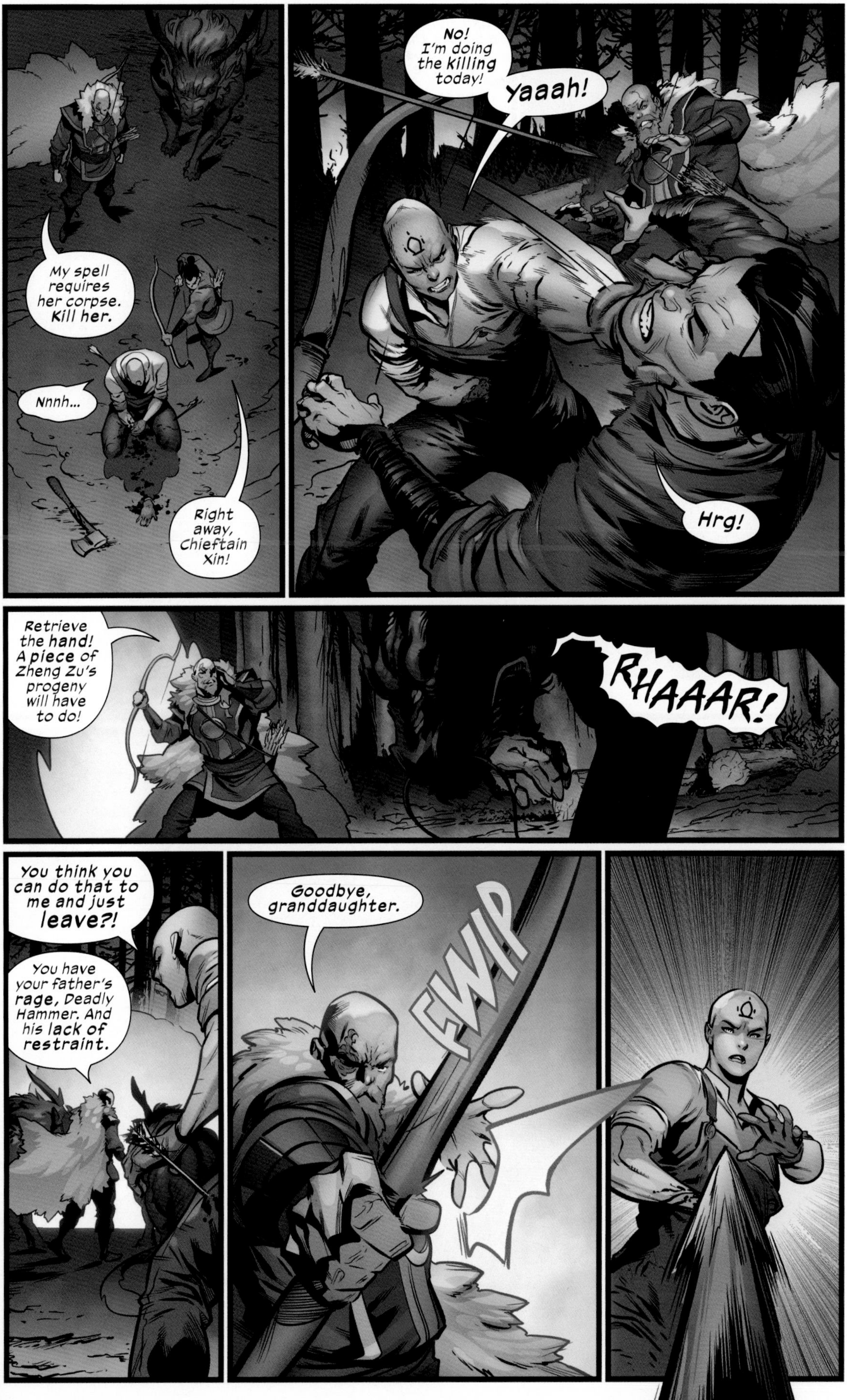
My spell requires her corpse. Kill her.
Nnnh...
Right away, Chieftain Xin!
No! I'm doing the killing today!
Yaaah!
Hrg!
Retrieve the hand! A piece of Zheng Zu's progeny will have to do!
RHAAAR!
You think you can do that to me and just leave?!
You have your father's rage, Deadly Hammer. And his lack of restraint.
Goodbye, granddaughter.
FWIP

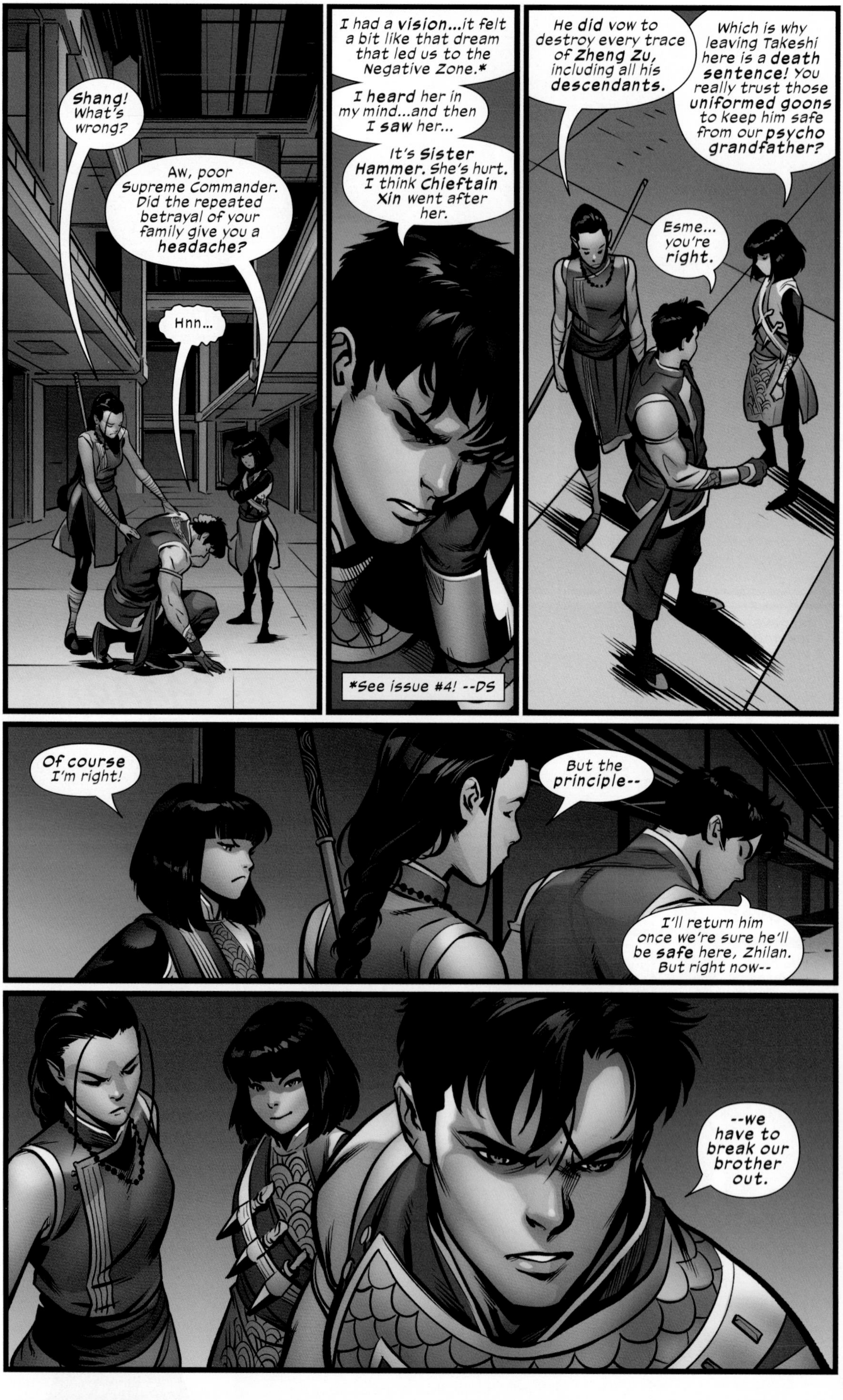
Shang! What's wrong?
Aw, poor Supreme Commander. Did the repeated betrayal of your family give you a headache?
Hnn...
I had a vision...it felt a bit like that dream that led us to the Negative Zone.*
I heard her in my mind...and then I saw her...
It's Sister Hammer. She's hurt. I think Chieftain Xin went after her.
*See issue #4! --DS
He did vow to destroy every trace of Zheng Zu, including all his descendants.
Which is why leaving Takeshi here is a death sentence! You really trust those uniformed goons to keep him safe from our psycho grandfather?
Esme... you're right.
Of course I'm right!
But the principle--
I'll return him once we're sure he'll be safe here, Zhilan. But right now--
--we have to break our brother out.

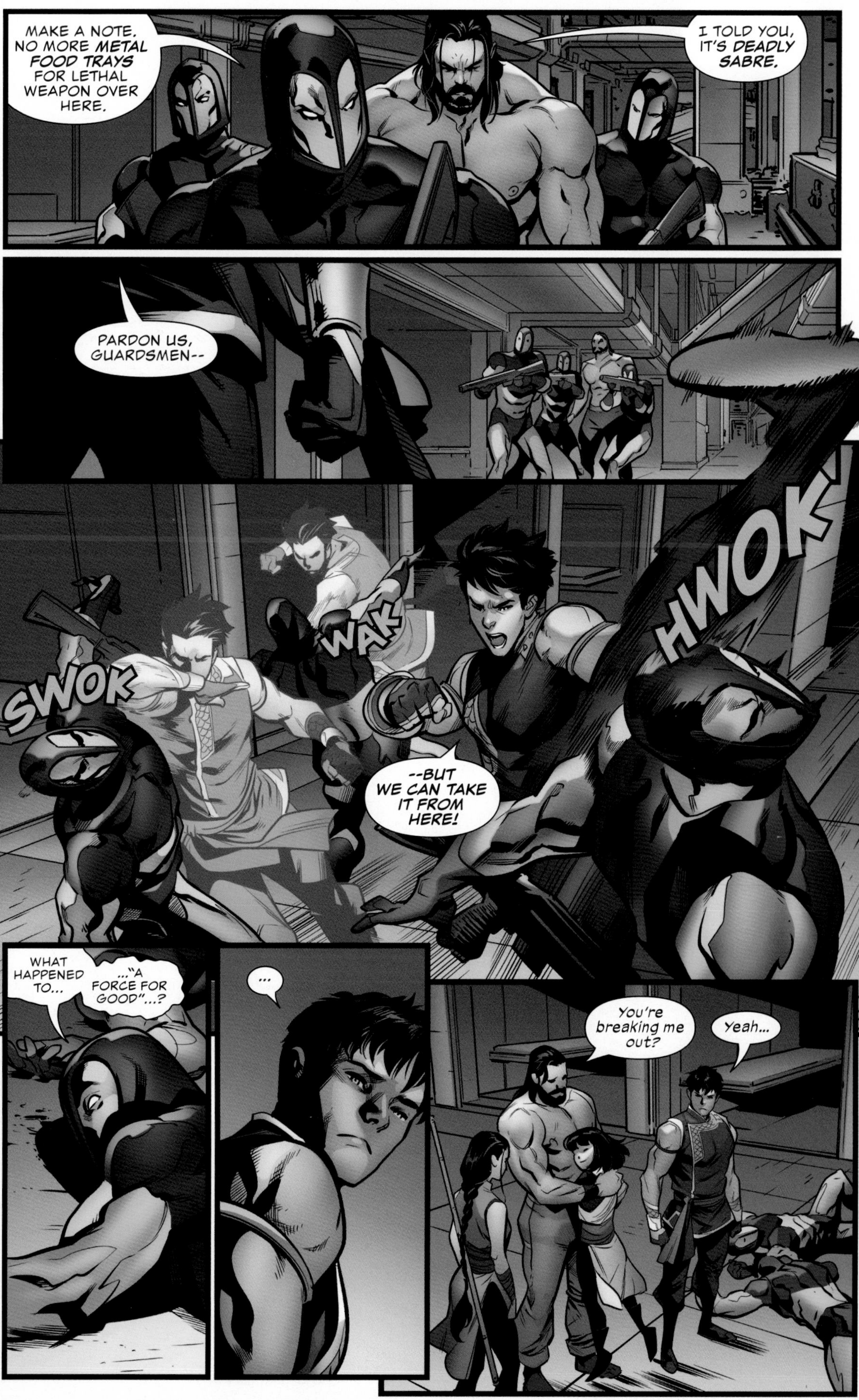

MAKE A NOTE. NO MORE METAL FOOD TRAYS FOR LETHAL WEAPON OVER HERE.
I TOLD YOU, IT'S DEADLY SABRE.
PARDON US, GUARDSMEN--
HWOK
WAK
SWOK
--BUT WE CAN TAKE IT FROM HERE!
WHAT HAPPENED TO...
..."A FORCE FOR GOOD"...?
...
You're breaking me out?
Yeah...

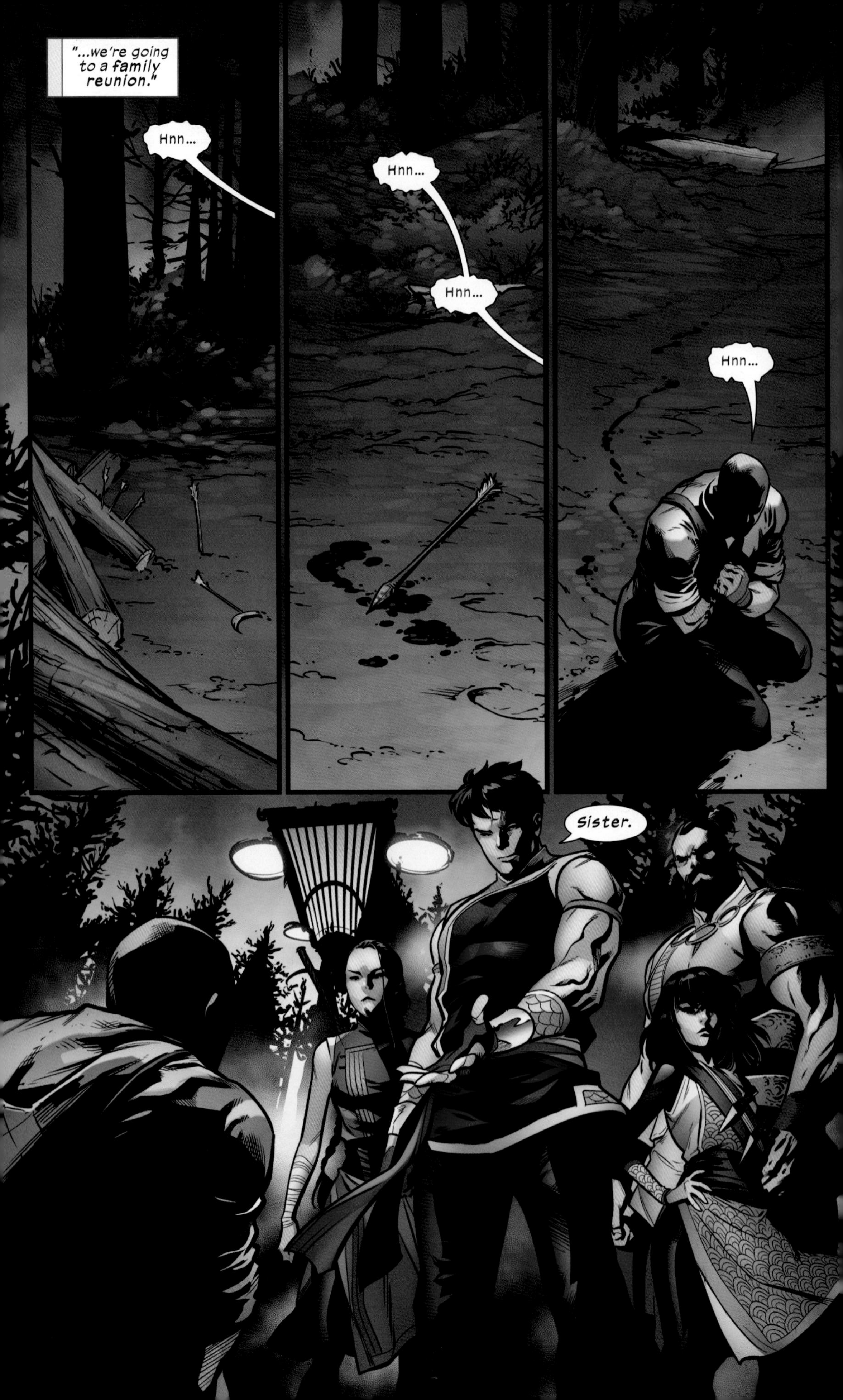
"...we're going to a family reunion."
Hnn...
Hnn...
Hnn...
Hnn...
Sister.

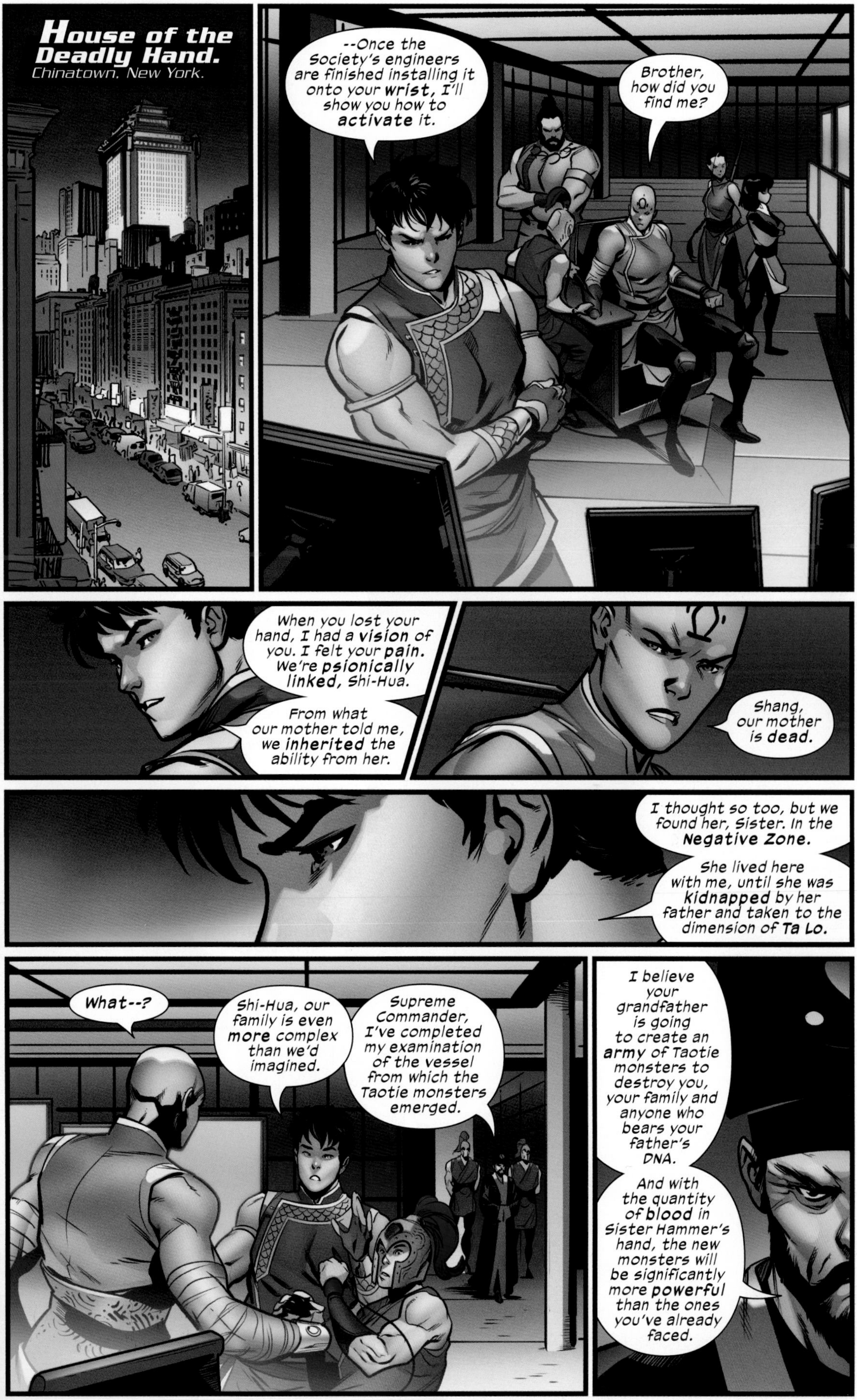
House of the Deadly Hand.
Chinatown, New York.
--Once the Society's engineers are finished installing it onto your wrist, I'll show you how to activate it.
Brother, how did you find me?
When you lost your hand, I had a vision of you. I felt your pain. We're psionically linked, Shi-Hua.
From what our mother told me, we inherited the ability from her.
Shang, our mother is dead.
I thought so too, but we found her, Sister. In the Negative Zone.
She lived here with me, until she was kidnapped by her father and taken to the dimension of Ta Lo.
What--?
Shi-Hua, our family is even more complex than we'd imagined.
Supreme Commander, I've completed my examination of the vessel from which the Taotie monsters emerged.
I believe your grandfather is going to create an army of Taotie monsters to destroy you, your family and anyone who bears your father's DNA.
And with the quantity of blood in Sister Hammer's hand, the new monsters will be significantly more powerful than the ones you've already faced.

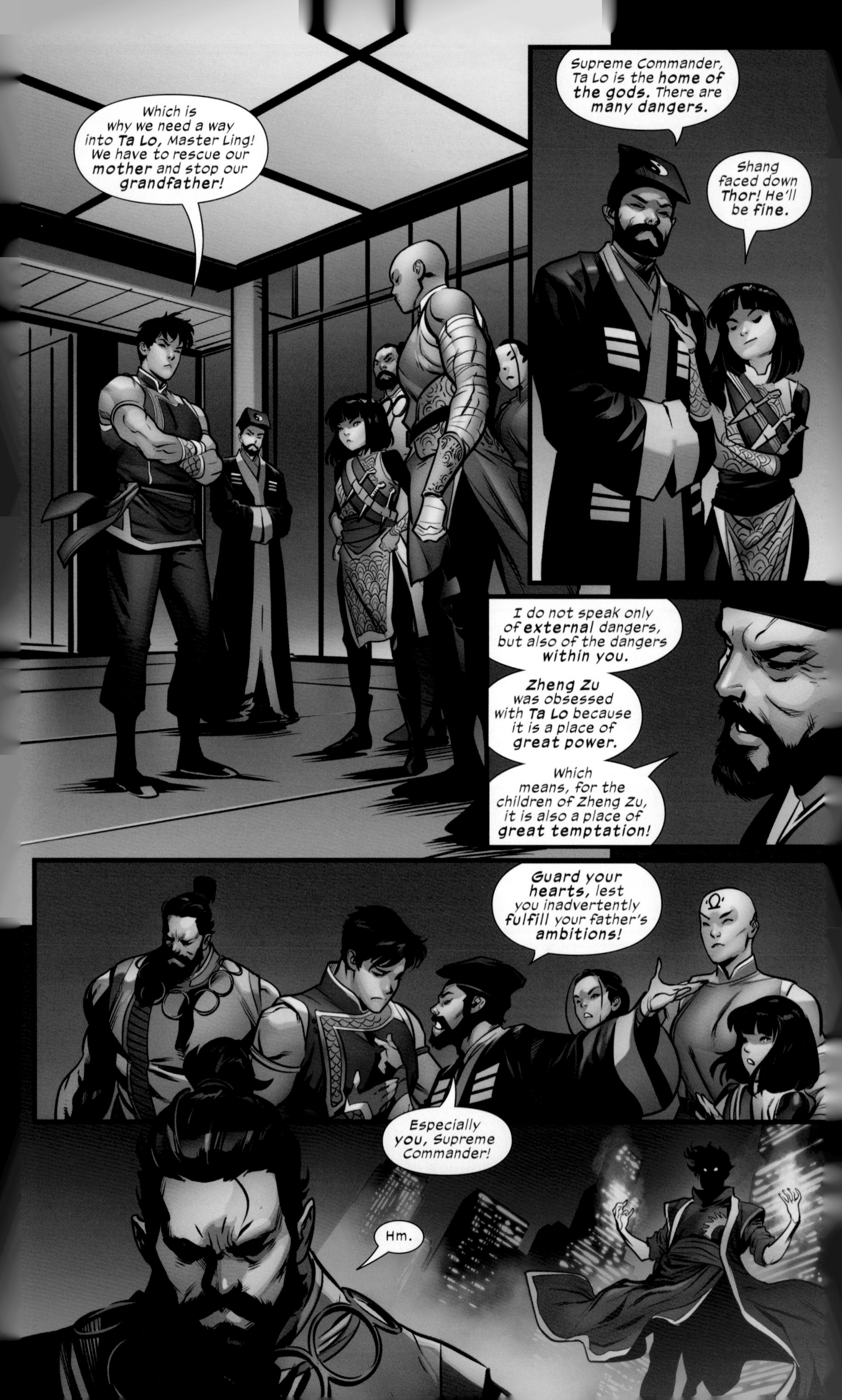

Which is why we need a way into Ta Lo, Master Ling! We have to rescue our mother and stop our grandfather!
Supreme Commander, Ta Lo is the home of the gods. There are many dangers.
Shang faced down Thor! He'll be fine.
I do not speak only of external dangers, but also of the dangers within you.
Zheng Zu was obsessed with Ta Lo because it is a place of great power.
Which means, for the children of Zheng Zu, it is also a place of great temptation!
Guard your hearts, lest you inadvertently fulfill your father's ambitions!
Especially you, Supreme Commander!
Hm.

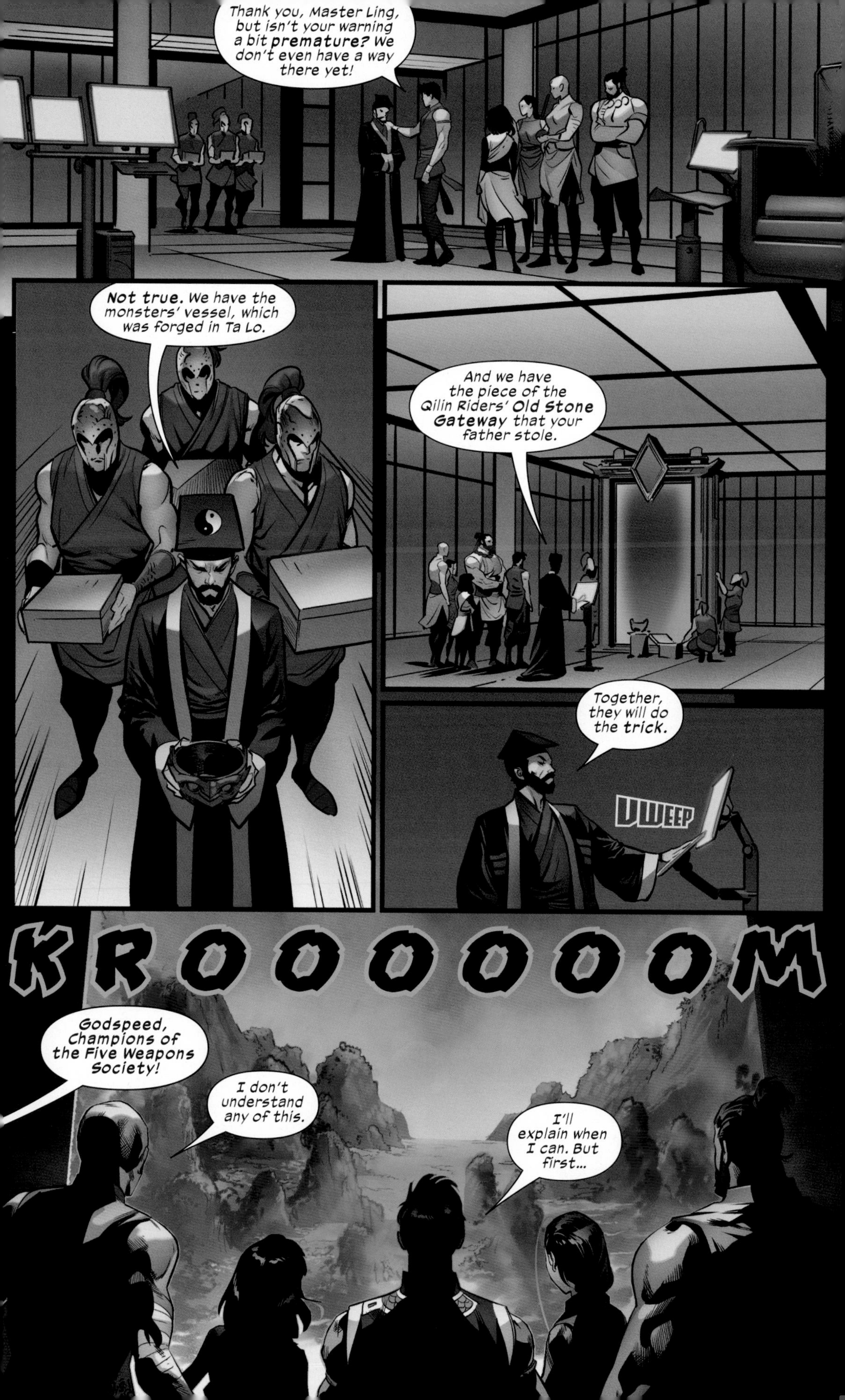
Thank you, Master Ling, but isn't your warning a bit **premature?** We don't even have a way there yet!
Not true. We have the monsters' vessel, which was forged in Ta Lo.
And we have the piece of the Qilin Riders' **Old Stone Gateway** that your father stole.
Together, they will do the **trick.**
VWEEP
KROOOOOOM
Godspeed, Champions of the Five Weapons Society!
I don't understand any of this.
I'll explain when I can. But first...

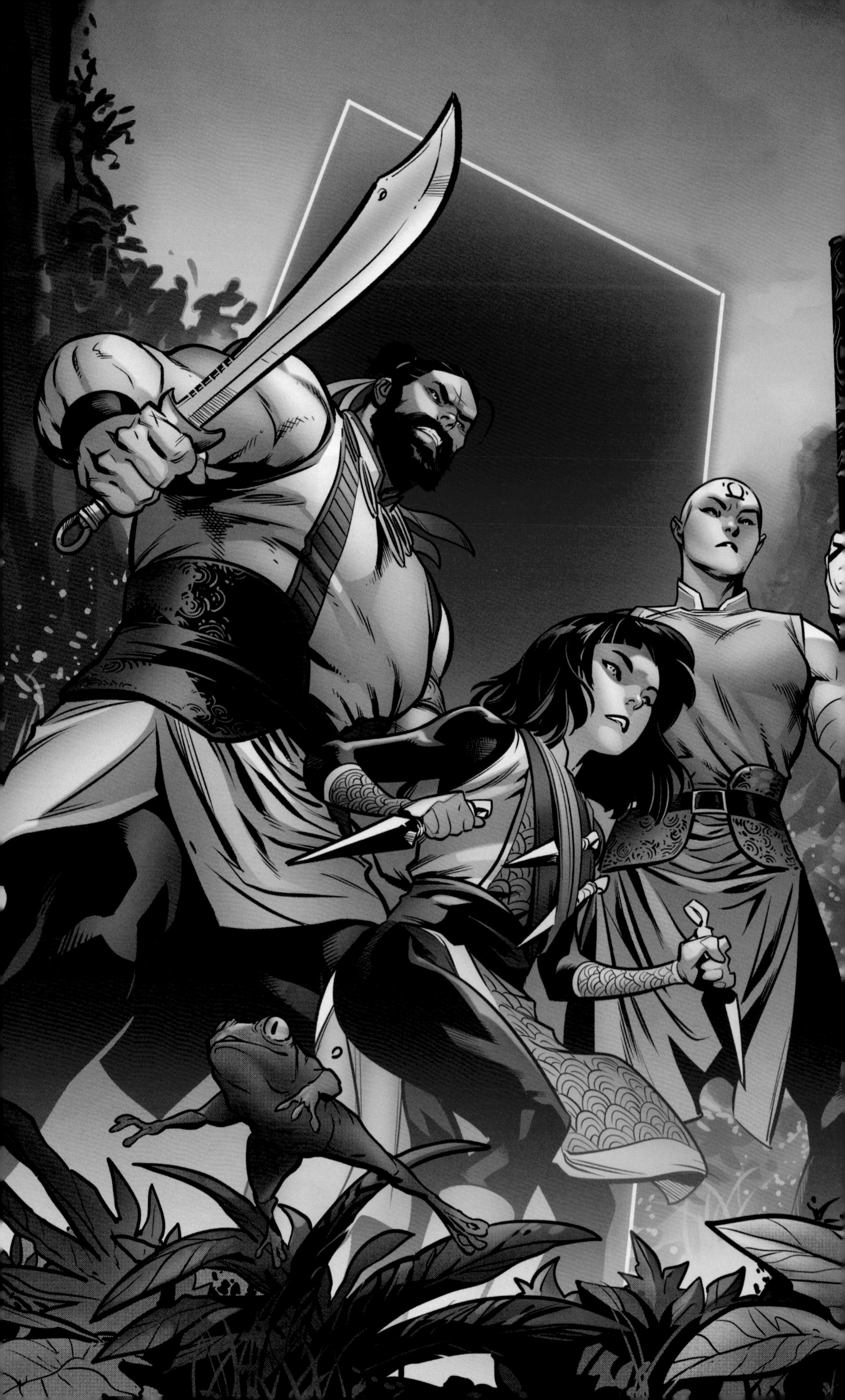

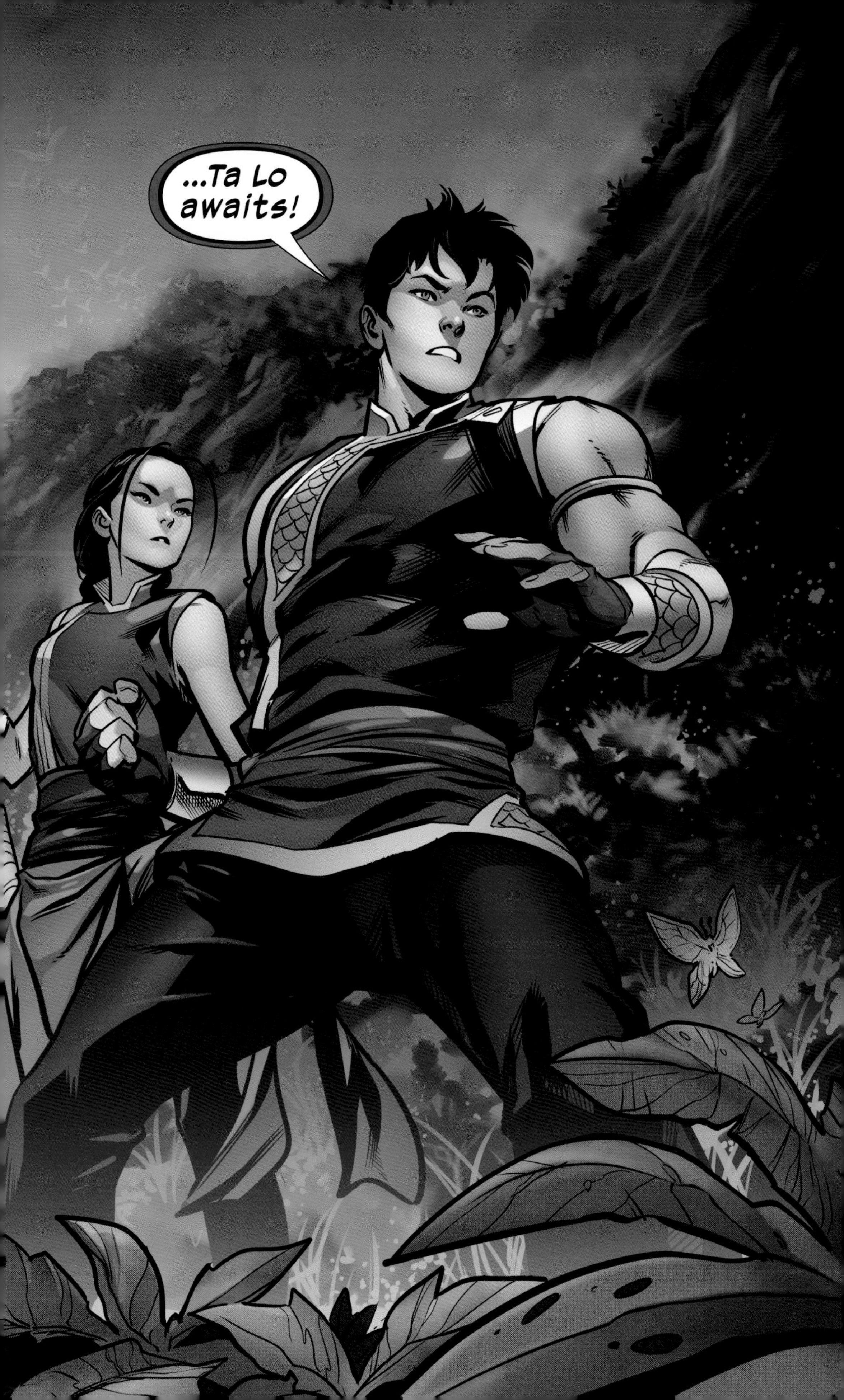
...Ta Lo awaits!

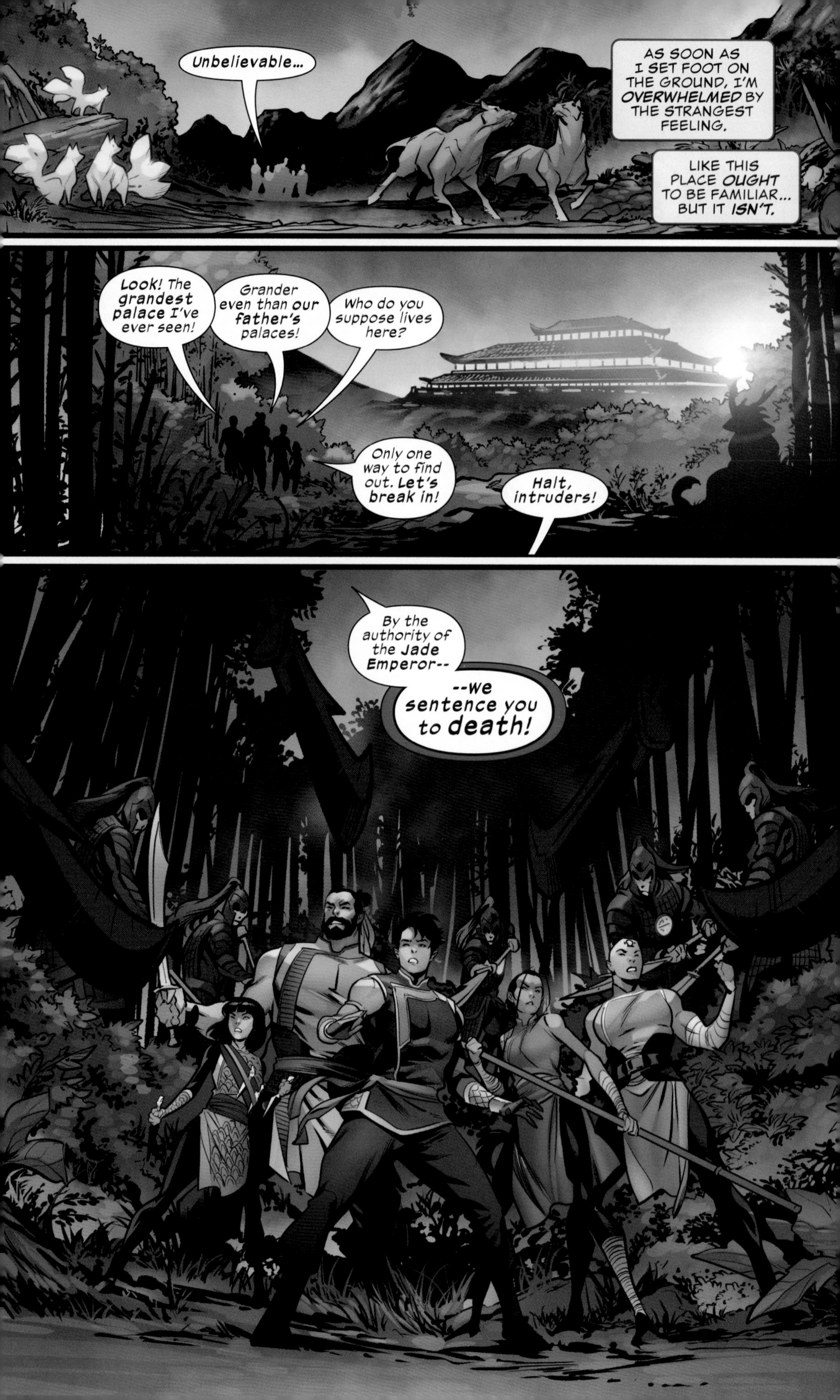

Unbelievable...
AS SOON AS I SET FOOT ON THE GROUND, I'M OVERWHELMED BY THE STRANGEST FEELING.
LIKE THIS PLACE OUGHT TO BE FAMILIAR... BUT IT ISN'T.
Look! The grandest palace I've ever seen!
Grander even than our father's palaces!
Who do you suppose lives here?
Only one way to find out. Let's break in!
Halt, intruders!
By the authority of the Jade Emperor--
--we sentence you to death!

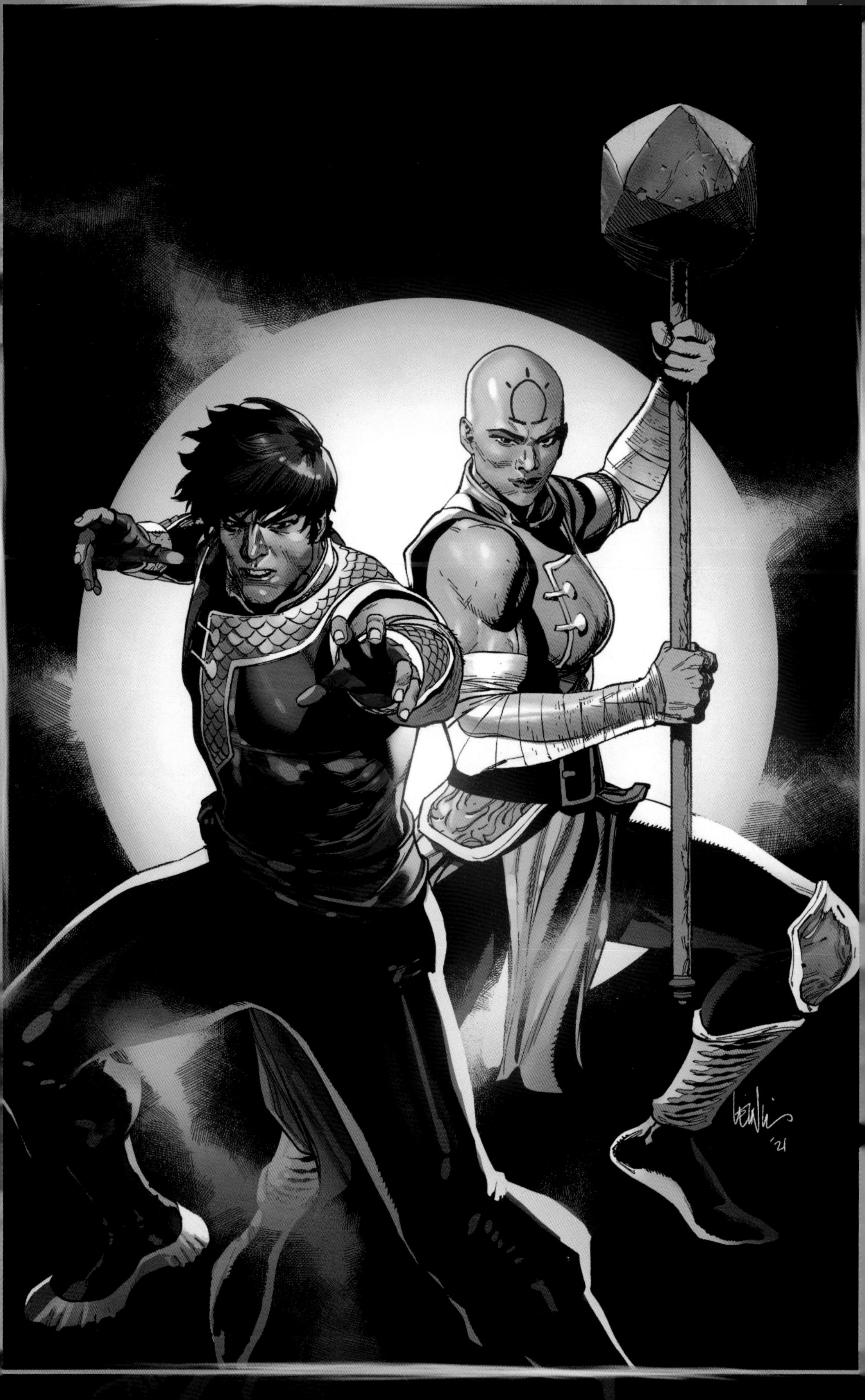

ELEVEN

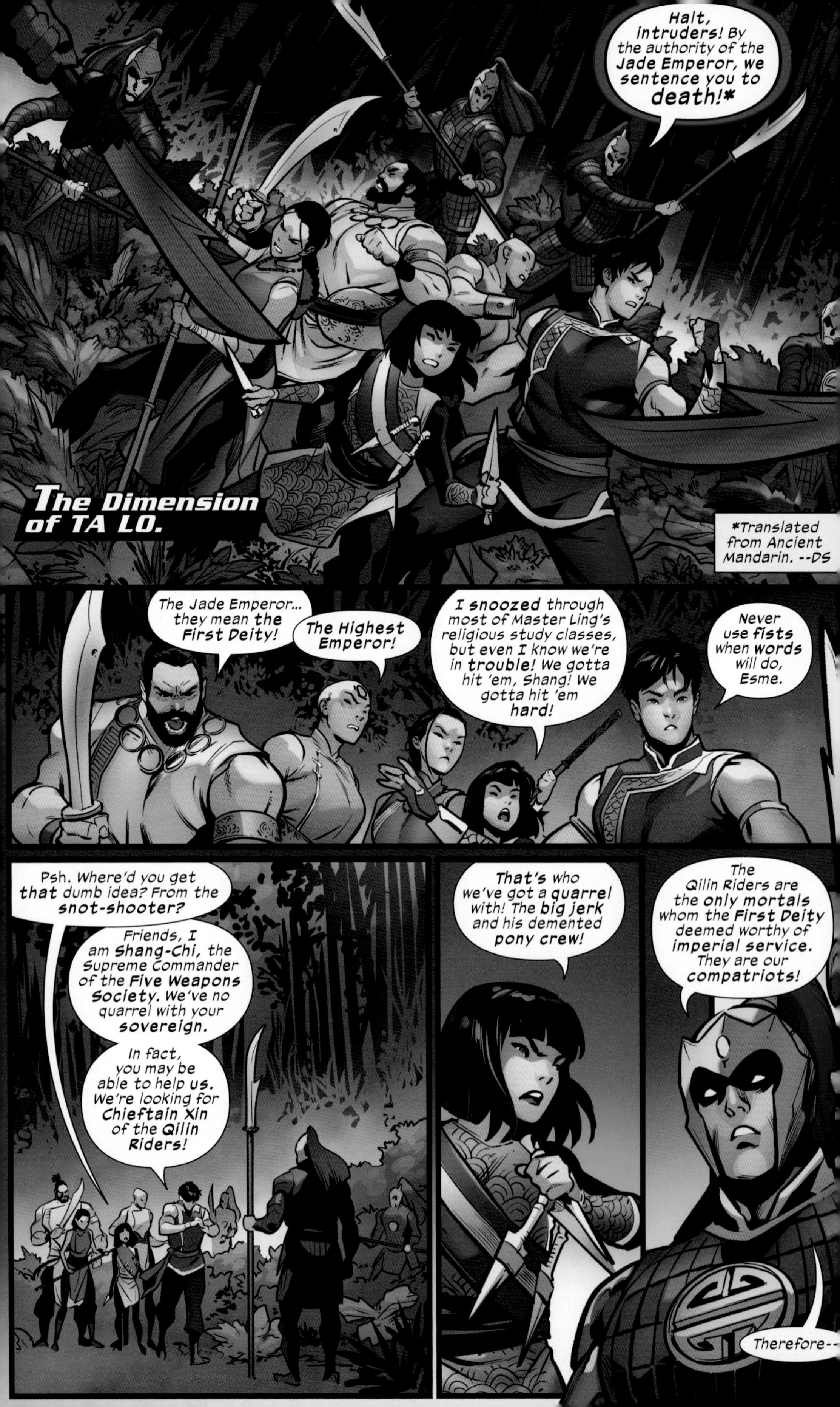

Halt, intruders! By the authority of the Jade Emperor, we sentence you to death!*
The Dimension of TA LO.
*Translated from Ancient Mandarin. --DS
The Jade Emperor... they mean the First Deity!
The Highest Emperor!
I snoozed through most of Master Ling's religious study classes, but even I know we're in trouble! We gotta hit 'em, Shang! We gotta hit 'em hard!
Never use fists when words will do, Esme.
Psh. Where'd you get that dumb idea? From the snot-shooter?
Friends, I am Shang-Chi, the Supreme Commander of the Five Weapons Society. We've no quarrel with your sovereign.
In fact, you may be able to help us. We're looking for Chieftain Xin of the Qilin Riders!
That's who we've got a quarrel with! The big jerk and his demented pony crew!
The Qilin Riders are the only mortals whom the First Deity deemed worthy of imperial service. They are our compatriots!
Therefore--

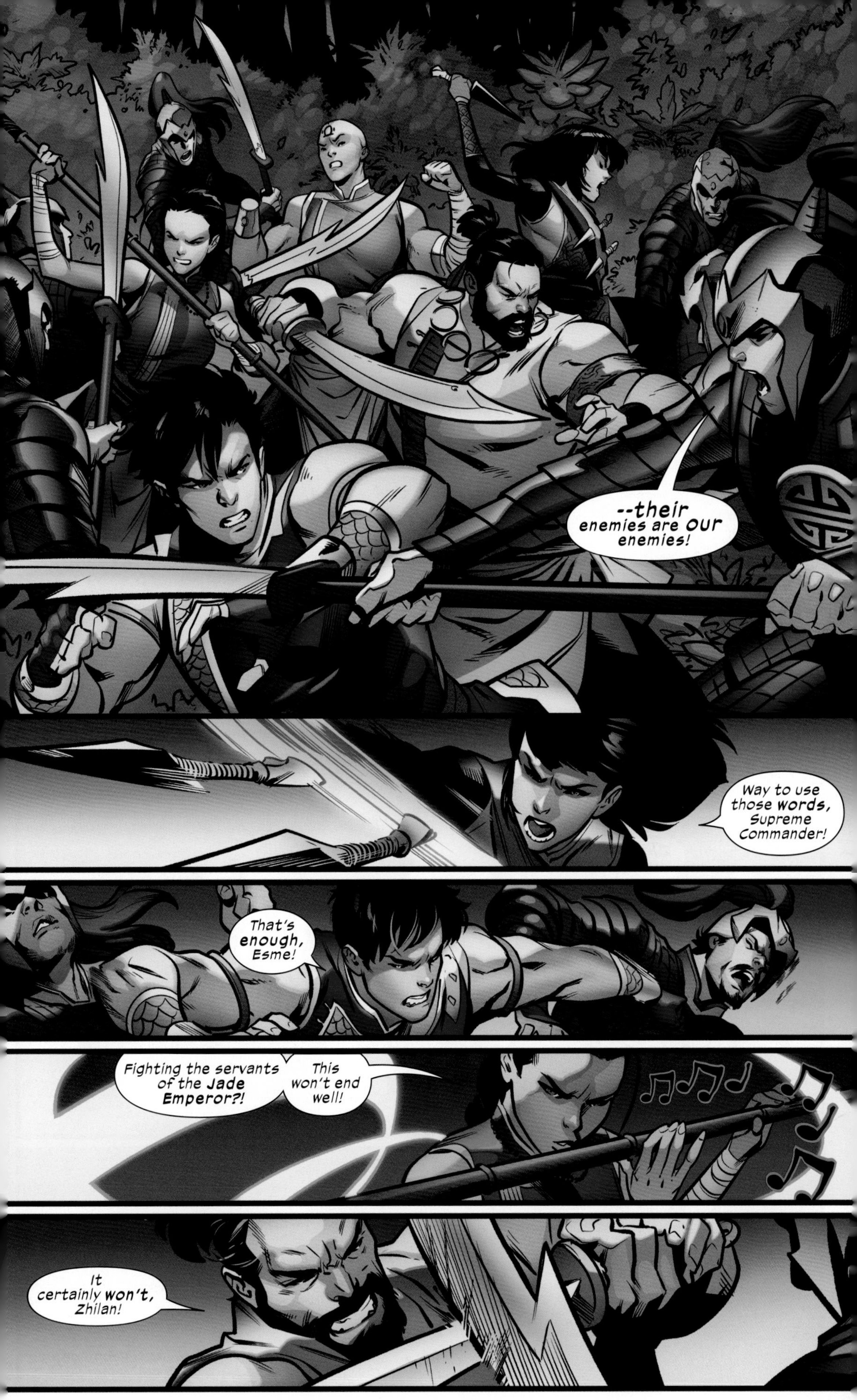
--their enemies are OUR enemies!
Way to use those words, Supreme Commander!
That's enough, Esme!
Fighting the servants of the Jade Emperor?!
This won't end well!
It certainly won't, Zhilan!

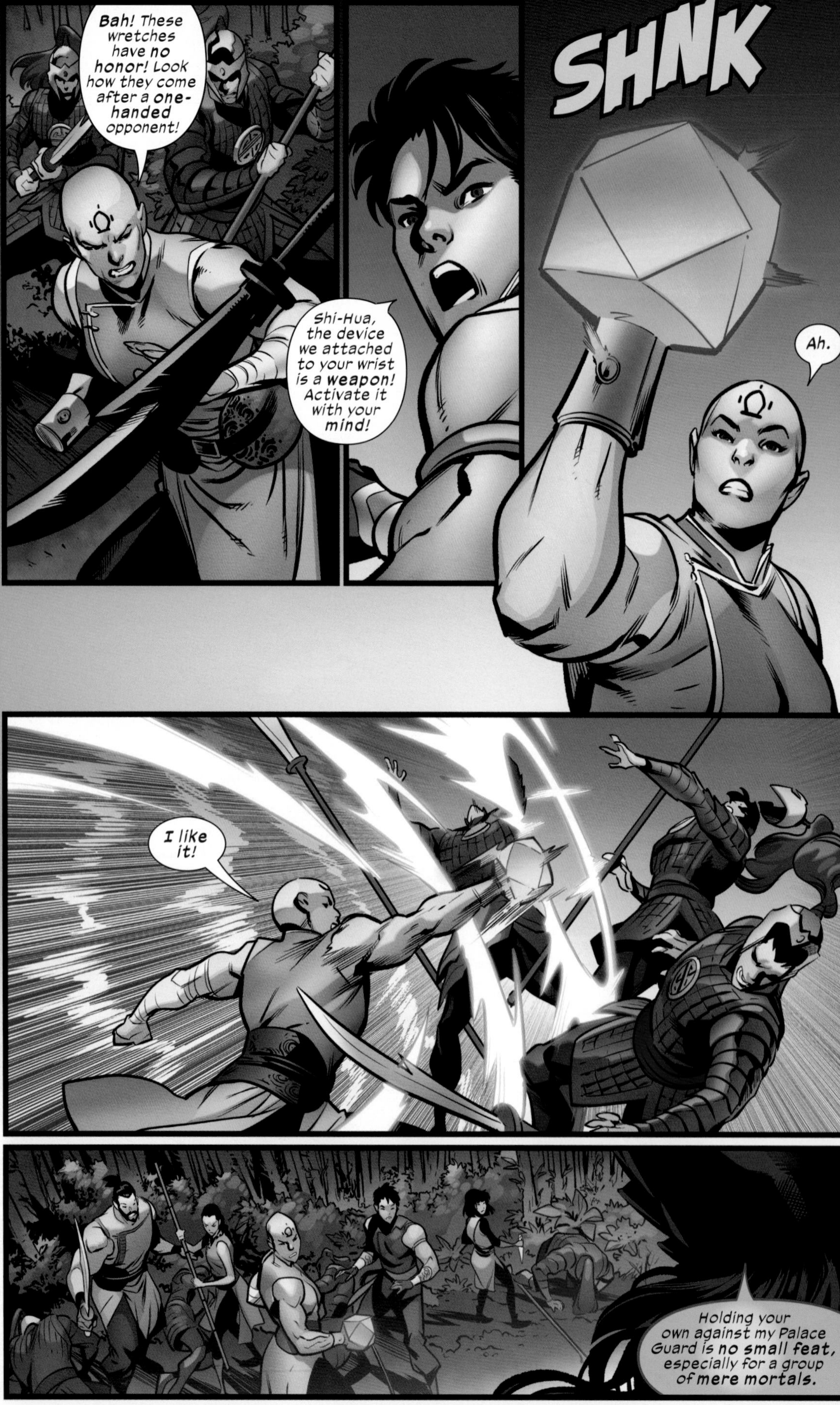

Bah! These wretches have no honor! Look how they come after a one-handed opponent!
Shi-Hua, the device we attached to your wrist is a weapon! Activate it with your mind!
SHNK
Ah.
I like it!
Holding your own against my Palace Guard is no small feat, especially for a group of mere mortals.

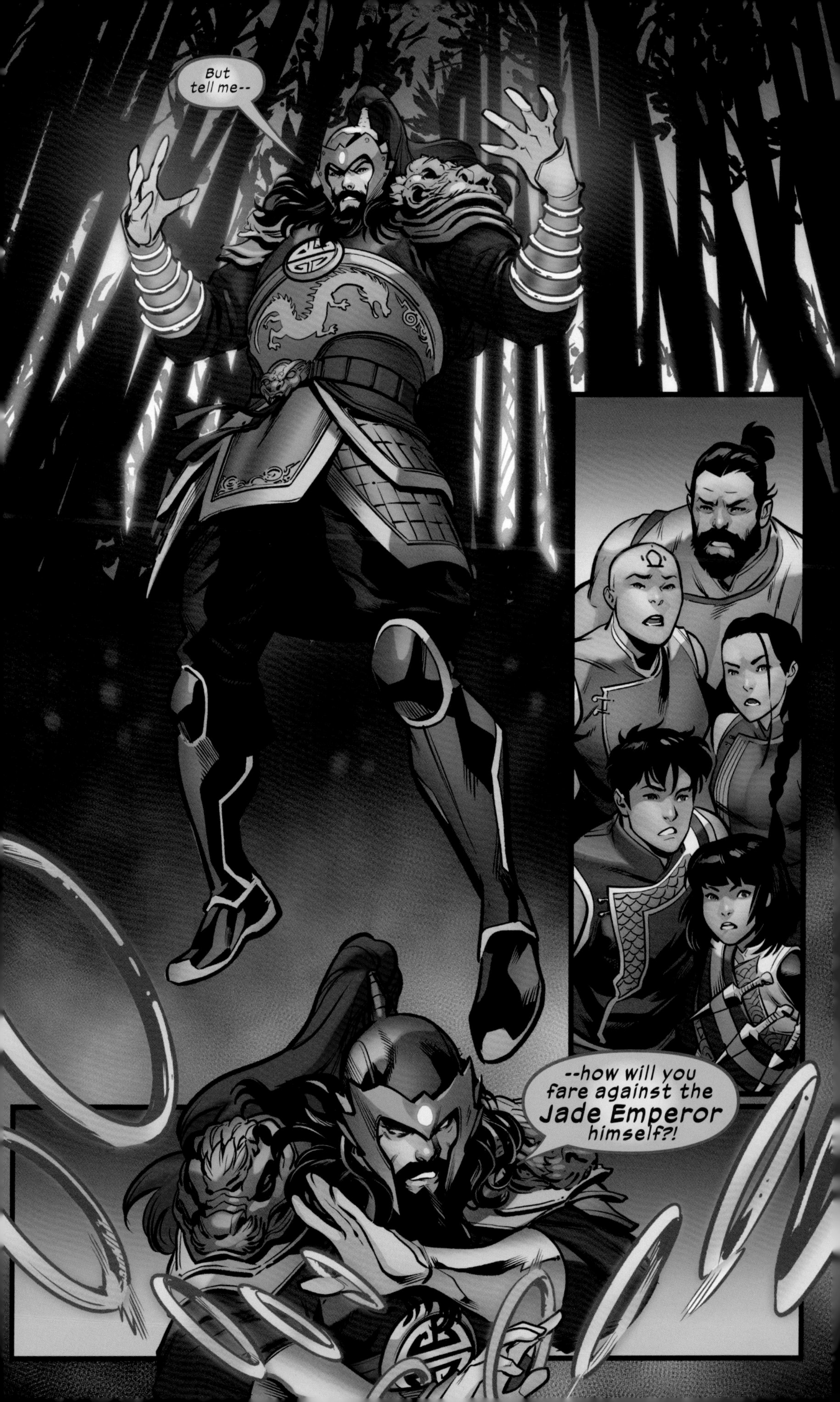
But tell me--
--how will you fare against the Jade Emperor himself?!

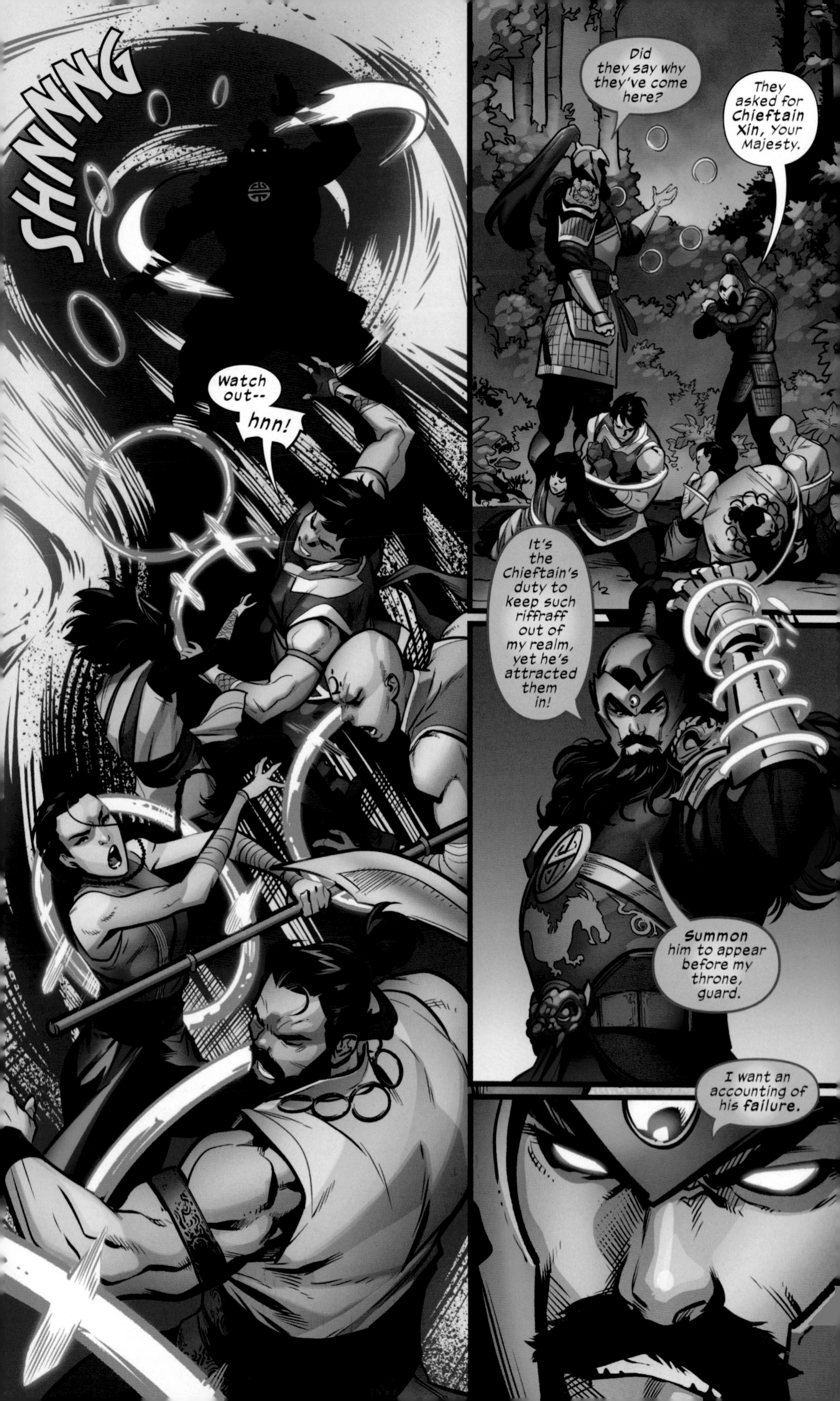
SHNNNG
Watch out--
hnn!
Did they say why they've come here?
They asked for Chieftain Xin, Your Majesty.
It's the Chieftain's duty to keep such riffraff out of my realm, yet he's attracted them in!
Summon him to appear before my throne, guard.
I want an accounting of his failure.

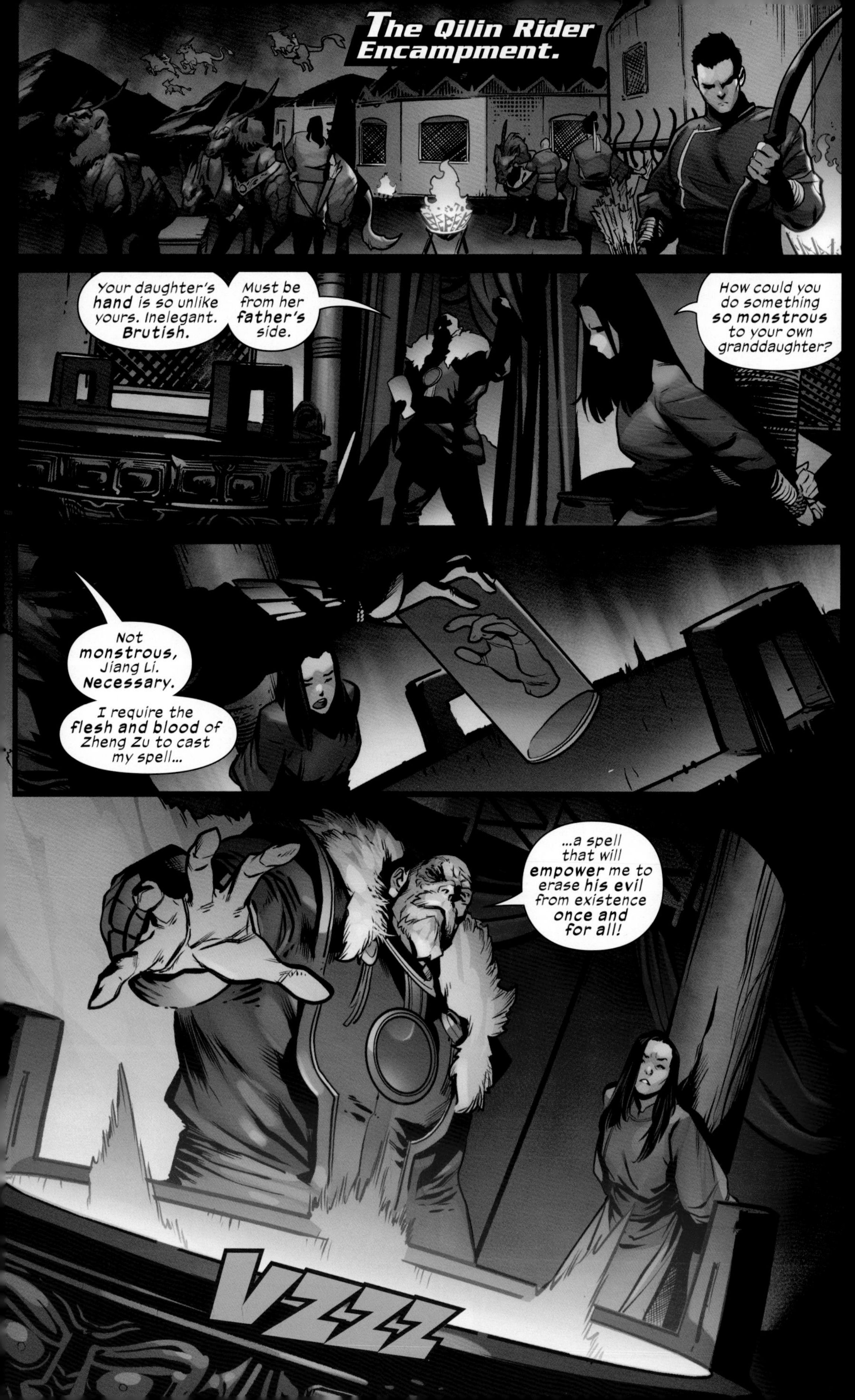
The Qilin Rider Encampment.
Your daughter's hand is so unlike yours. Inelegant. Brutish.
Must be from her father's side.
How could you do something so monstrous to your own granddaughter?
Not monstrous, Jiang Li. Necessary.
I require the flesh and blood of Zheng Zu to cast my spell...
...a spell that will empower me to erase his evil from existence once and for all!
VZZZ

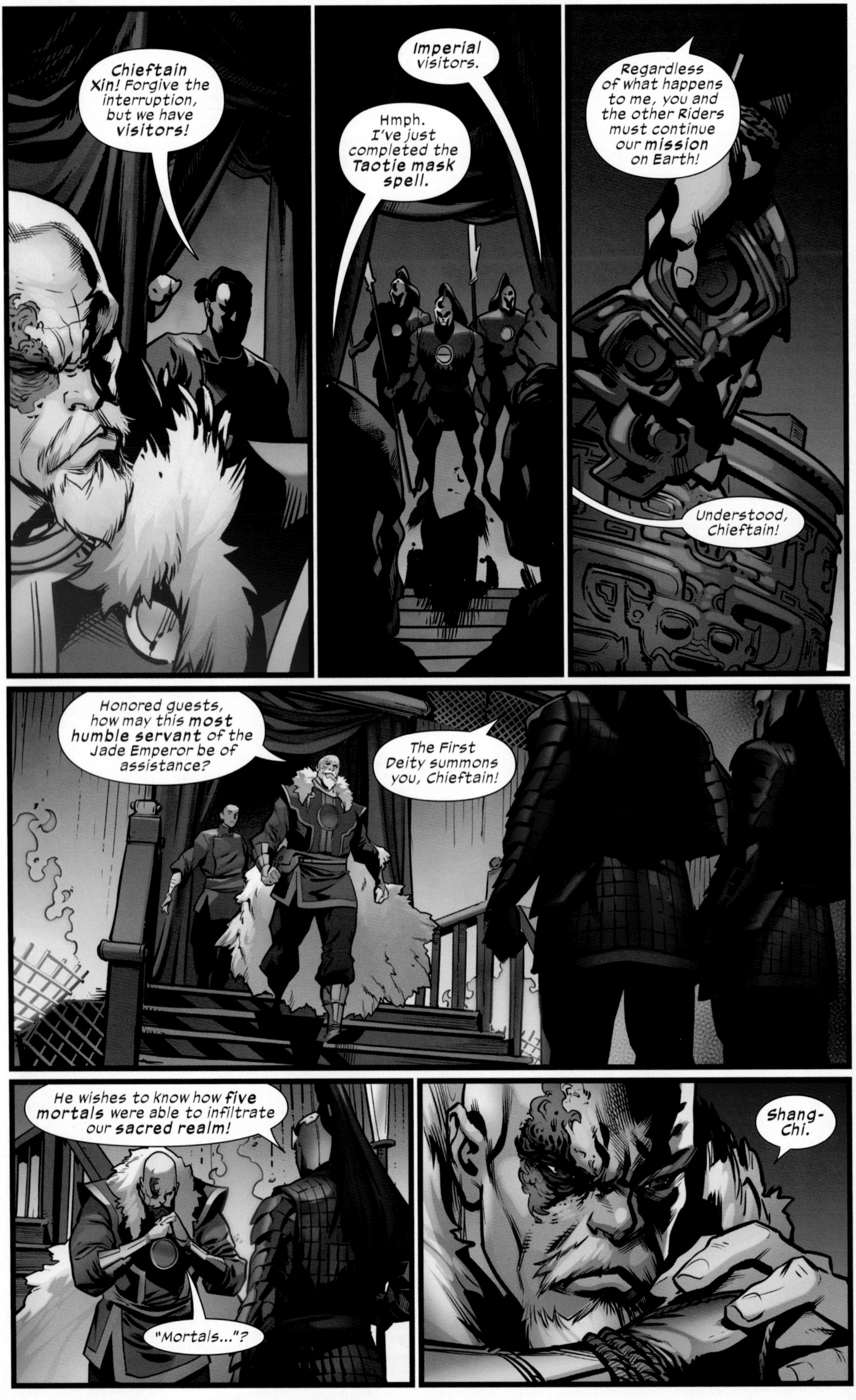

Chieftain Xin! Forgive the interruption, but we have visitors!
Imperial visitors.
Hmph. I've just completed the Taotie mask spell.
Regardless of what happens to me, you and the other Riders must continue our mission on Earth!
Understood, Chieftain!
Honored guests, how may this most humble servant of the Jade Emperor be of assistance?
The First Deity summons you, Chieftain!
He wishes to know how five mortals were able to infiltrate our sacred realm!
"Mortals..."?
Shang-Chi.

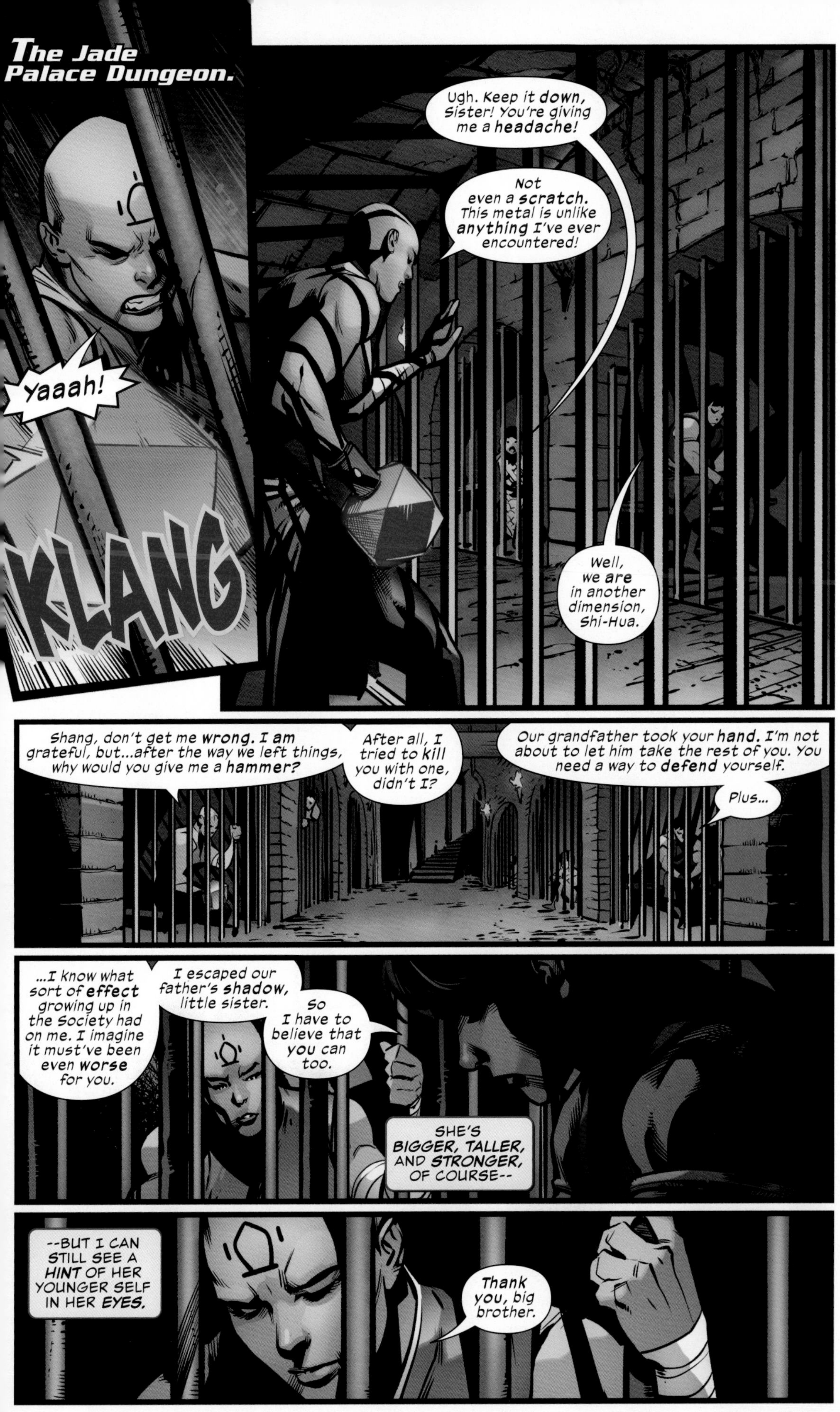

The Jade Palace Dungeon.
Yaaah!
KLANG
Ugh. Keep it down, Sister! You're giving me a headache!
Not even a scratch. This metal is unlike anything I've ever encountered!
Well, we are in another dimension, Shi-Hua.
Shang, don't get me wrong. I am grateful, but...after the way we left things, why would you give me a hammer?
After all, I tried to kill you with one, didn't I?
Our grandfather took your hand. I'm not about to let him take the rest of you. You need a way to defend yourself.
Plus...
...I know what sort of effect growing up in the Society had on me. I imagine it must've been even worse for you.
I escaped our father's shadow, little sister.
So I have to believe that you can too.
SHE'S BIGGER, TALLER, AND STRONGER, OF COURSE--
--BUT I CAN STILL SEE A HINT OF HER YOUNGER SELF IN HER EYES.
Thank you, big brother.

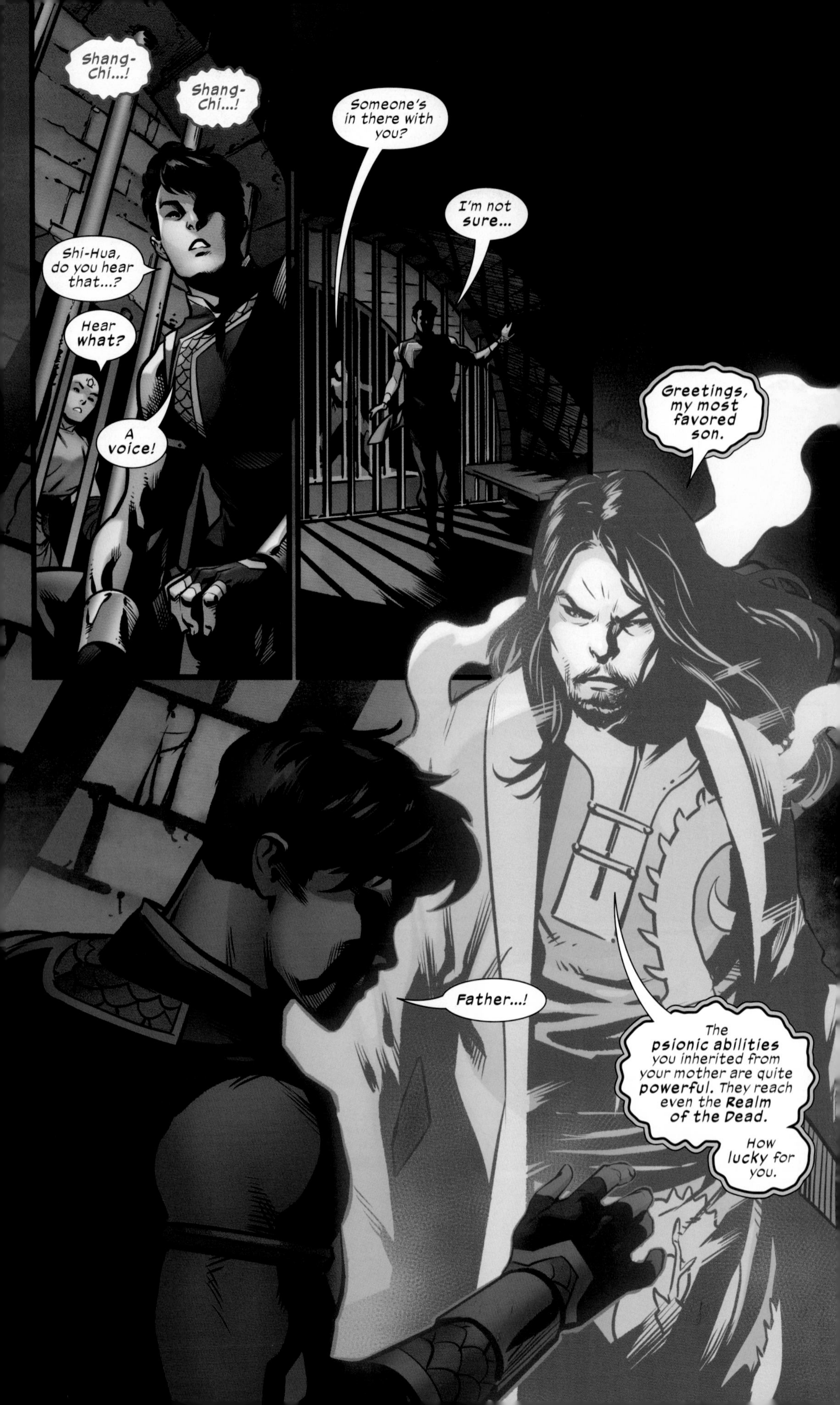
Shang-Chi...!
Shang-Chi...!
Shi-Hua, do you hear that...?
Hear what?
A voice!
Someone's in there with you?
I'm not sure...
Greetings, my most favored son.
Father...!
The psionic abilities you inherited from your mother are quite powerful. They reach even the Realm of the Dead.
How lucky for you.

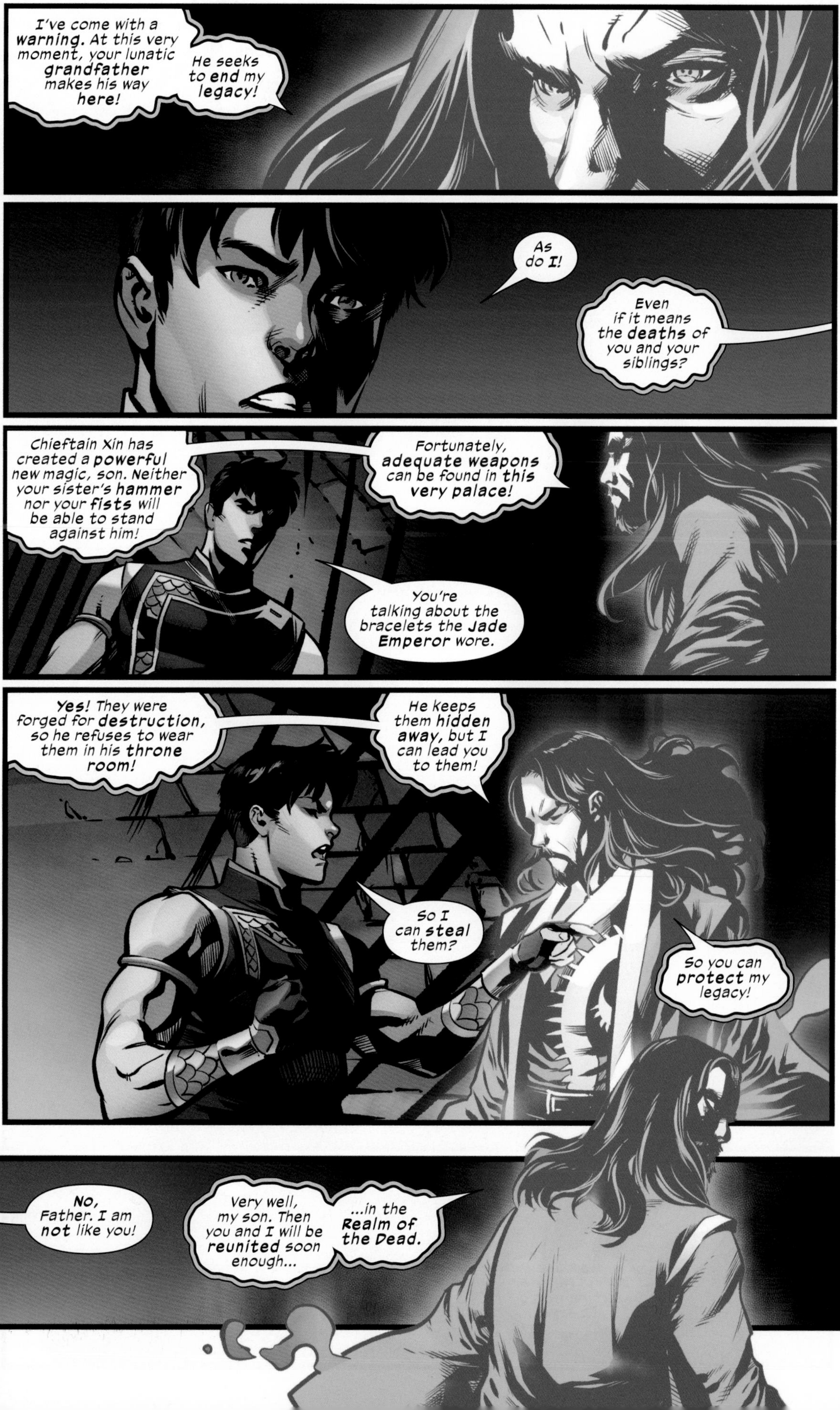
I've come with a warning. At this very moment, your lunatic grandfather makes his way here!
He seeks to end my legacy!
As do I!
Even if it means the deaths of you and your siblings?
Chieftain Xin has created a powerful new magic, son. Neither your sister's hammer nor your fists will be able to stand against him!
Fortunately, adequate weapons can be found in this very palace!
You're talking about the bracelets the Jade Emperor wore.
Yes! They were forged for destruction, so he refuses to wear them in his throne room!
He keeps them hidden away, but I can lead you to them!
So I can steal them?
So you can protect my legacy!
No, Father. I am not like you!
Very well, my son. Then you and I will be reunited soon enough...
...in the Realm of the Dead.

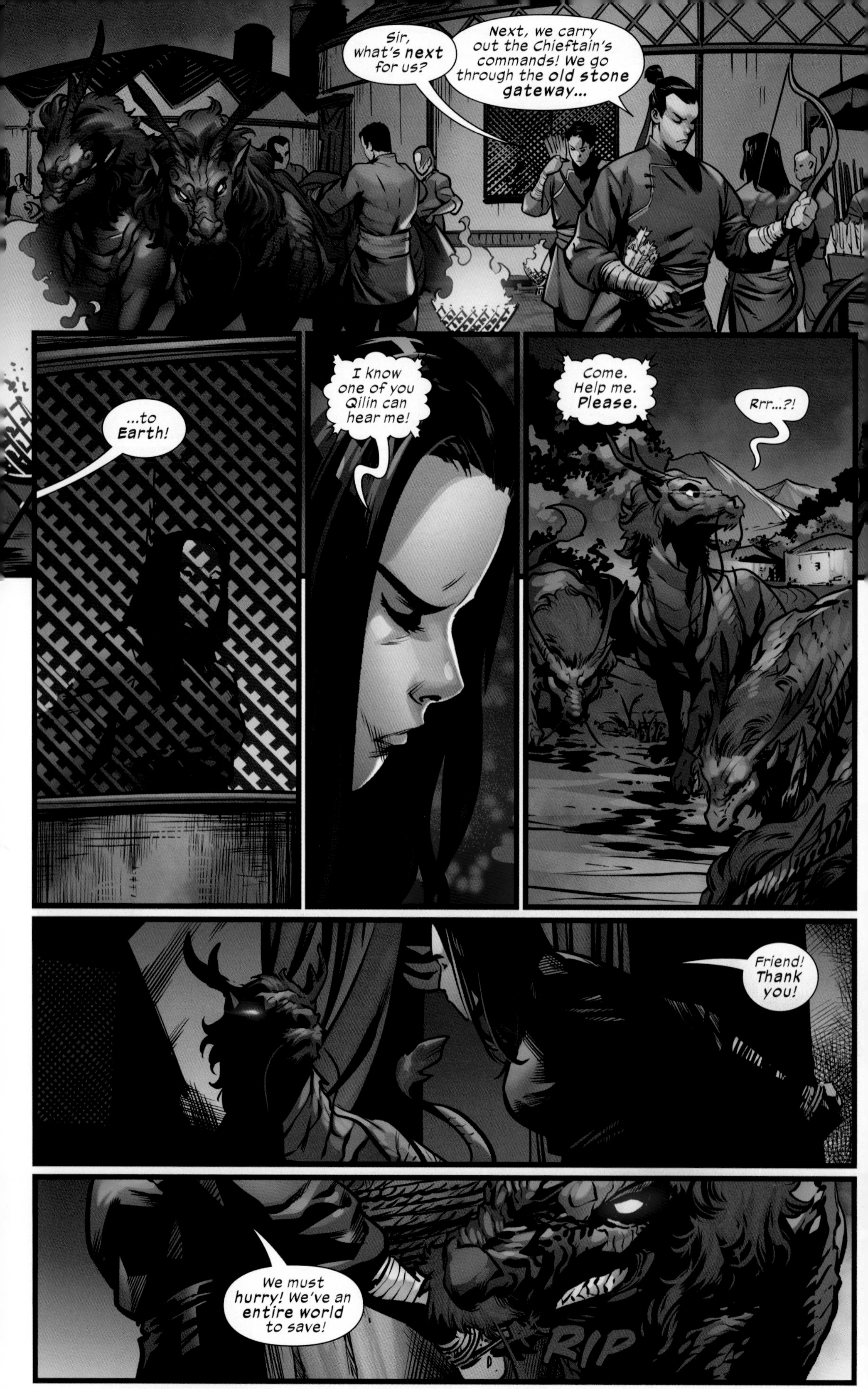
Sir, what's next for us?
Next, we carry out the Chieftain's commands! We go through the old stone gateway...
...to Earth!
I know one of you Qilin can hear me!
Come. Help me. Please.
Rrr...?!
Friend! Thank you!
We must hurry! We've an entire world to save!
RIP

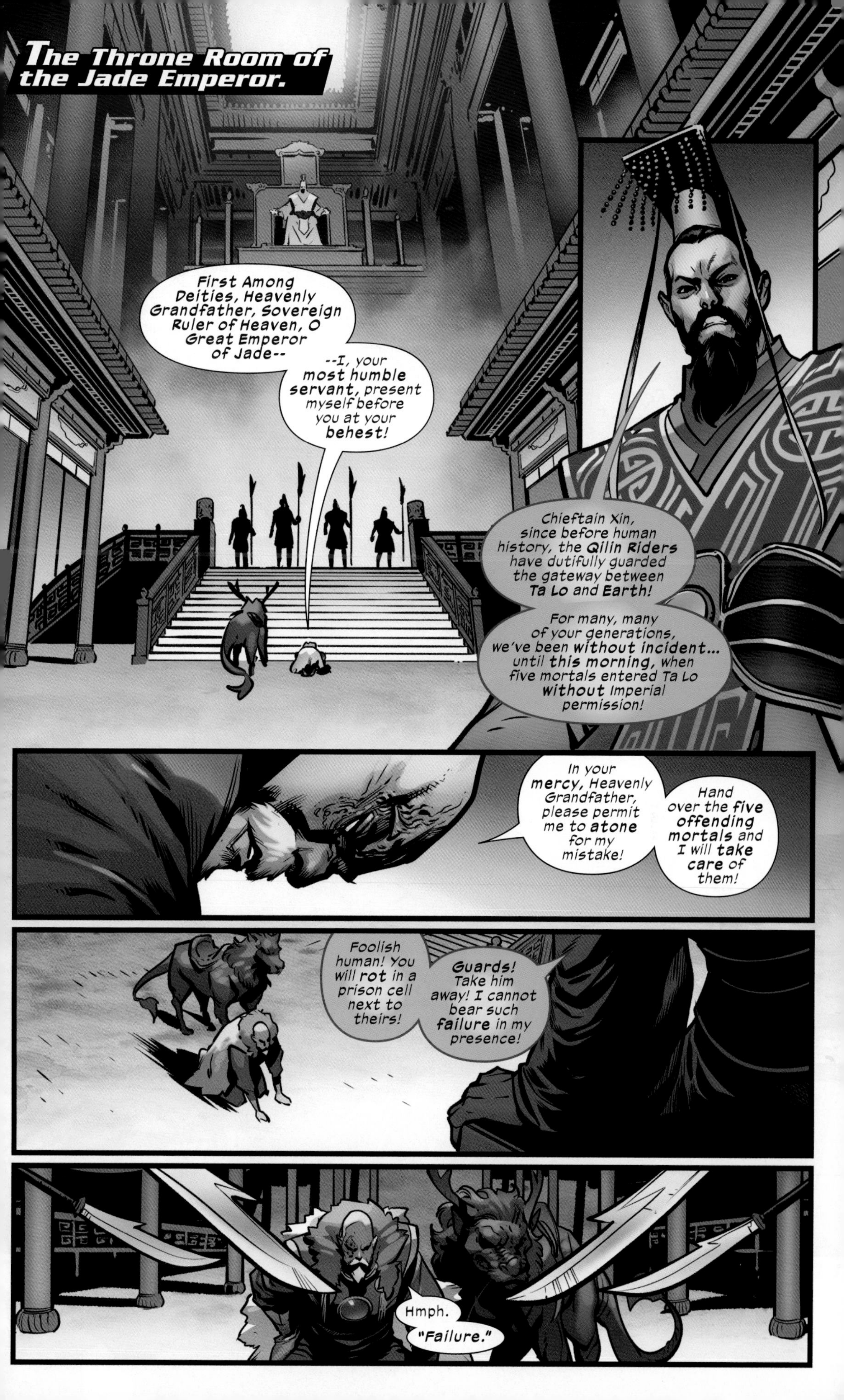
The Throne Room of the Jade Emperor.
First Among Deities, Heavenly Grandfather, Sovereign Ruler of Heaven, O Great Emperor of Jade--
--I, your most humble servant, present myself before you at your behest!
Chieftain Xin, since before human history, the Qilin Riders have dutifully guarded the gateway between Ta Lo and Earth!
For many, many of your generations, we've been without incident... until this morning, when five mortals entered Ta Lo without Imperial permission!
In your mercy, Heavenly Grandfather, please permit me to atone for my mistake!
Hand over the five offending mortals and I will take care of them!
Foolish human! You will rot in a prison cell next to theirs!
Guards! Take him away! I cannot bear such failure in my presence!
Hmph.
"Failure."

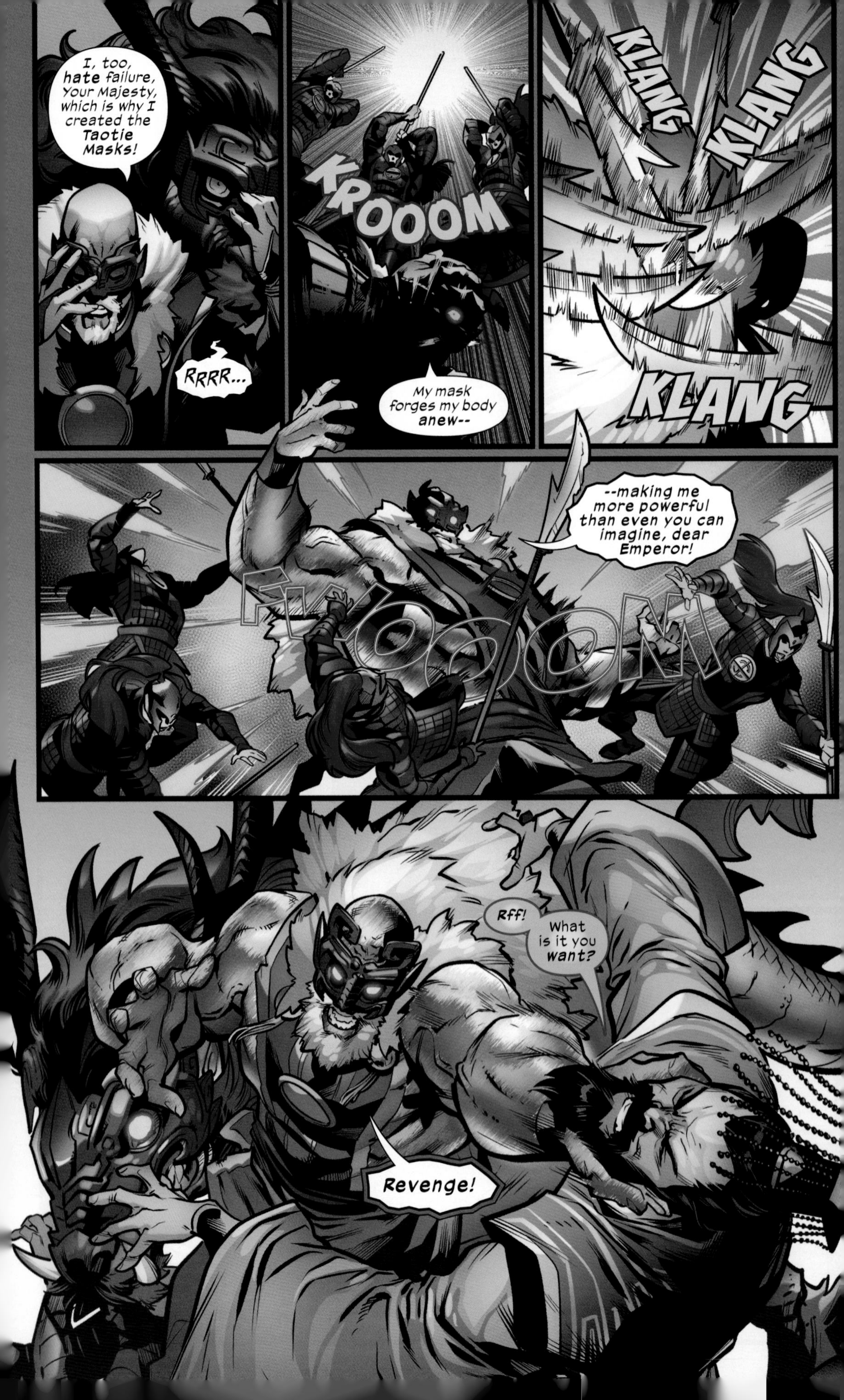
I, too, hate failure, Your Majesty, which is why I created the Taotie Masks!
RRRR...
KROOOM
My mask forges my body anew--
KLANG
KLANG
KLANG
--making me more powerful than even you can imagine, dear Emperor!
FWOOOOM
Rff!
What is it you want?
Revenge!

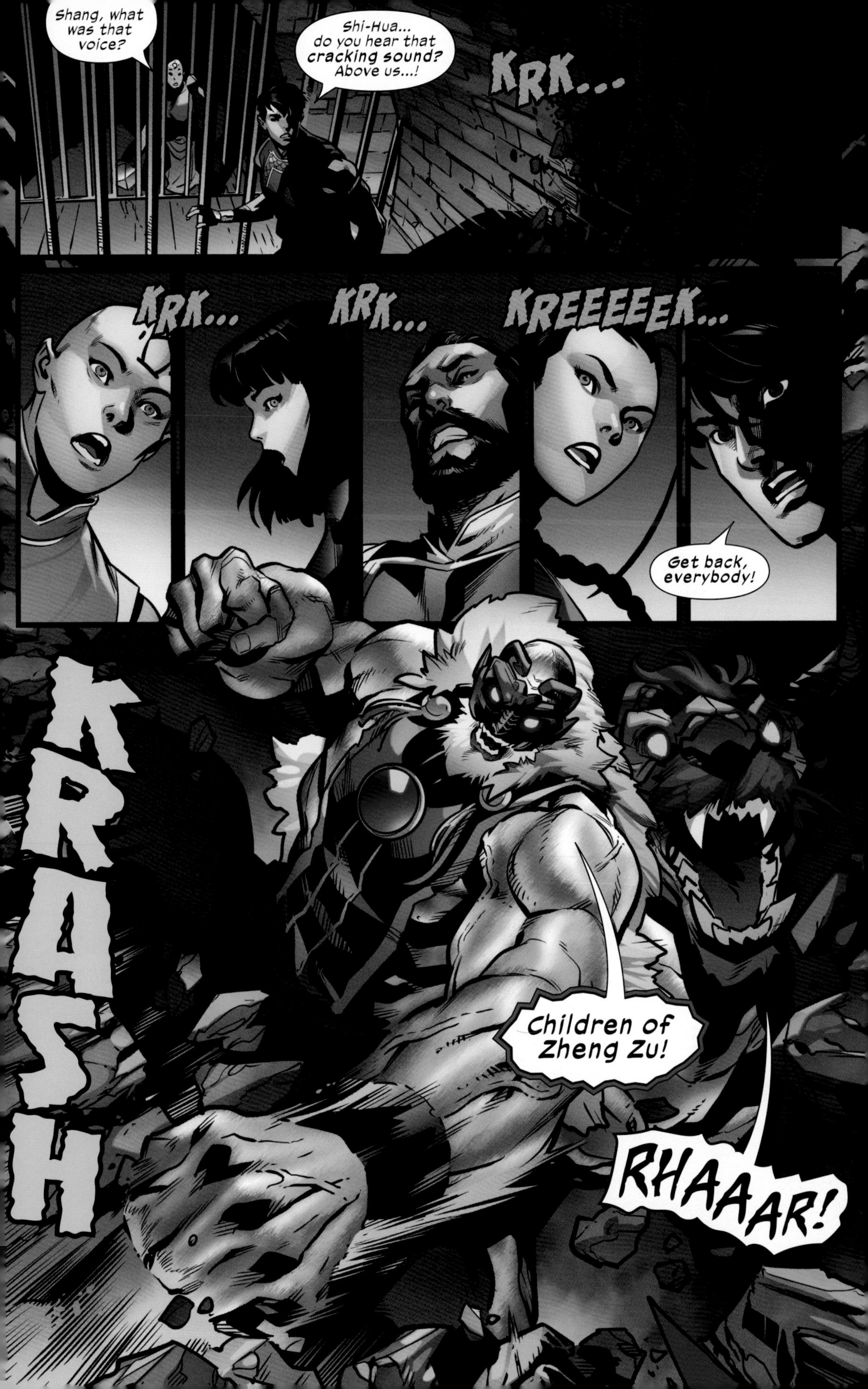
Shang, what was that voice?
Shi-Hua... do you hear that cracking sound? Above us...!
KRK...
KRK...
KRK...
KREEEEEK...
Get back, everybody!
KRASH
Children of Zheng Zu!
RHAAAR!

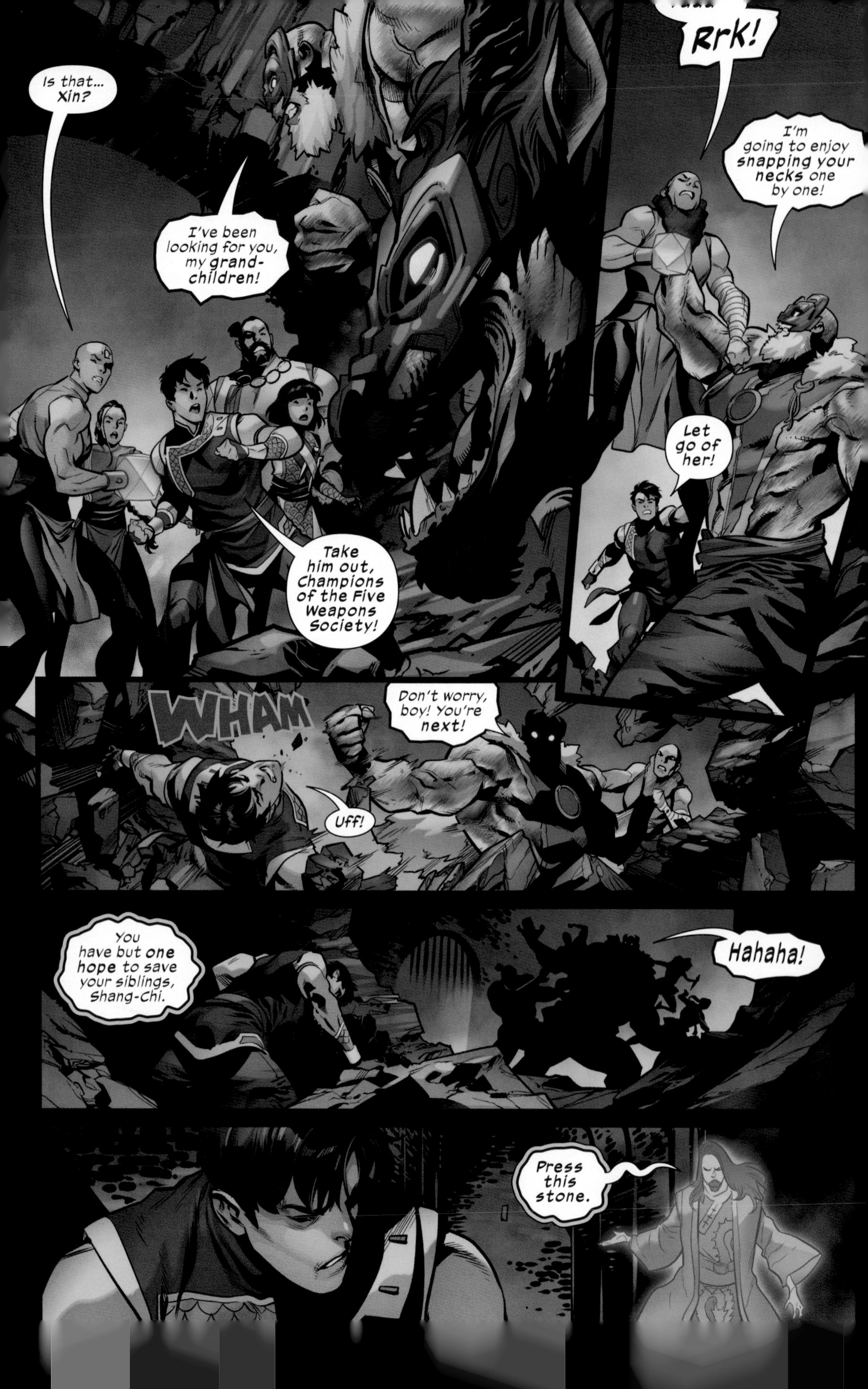
Is that... Xin?
I've been looking for you, my grand-children!
Take him out, Champions of the Five Weapons Society!
Rrk!
I'm going to enjoy snapping your necks one by one!
Let go of her!
WHAM
Don't worry, boy! You're next!
Uff!
You have but one hope to save your siblings, Shang-Chi.
Hahaha!
Press this stone.

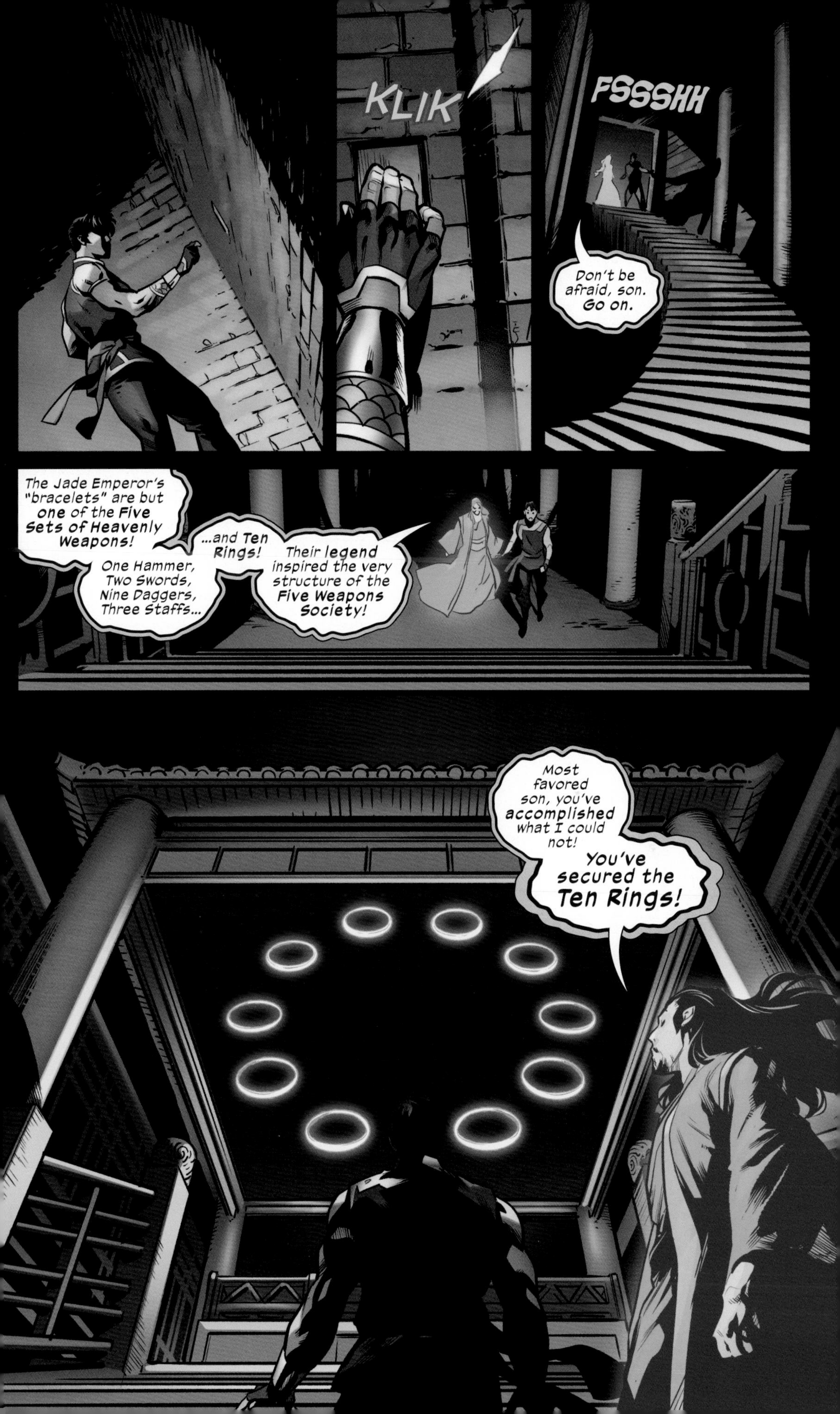
KLIK
FSSSHH
Don't be afraid, son. Go on.
The Jade Emperor's "bracelets" are but one of the Five Sets of Heavenly Weapons!
One Hammer, Two Swords, Nine Daggers, Three Staffs...
...and Ten Rings!
Their legend inspired the very structure of the Five Weapons Society!
Most favored son, you've accomplished what I could not!
You've secured the Ten Rings!

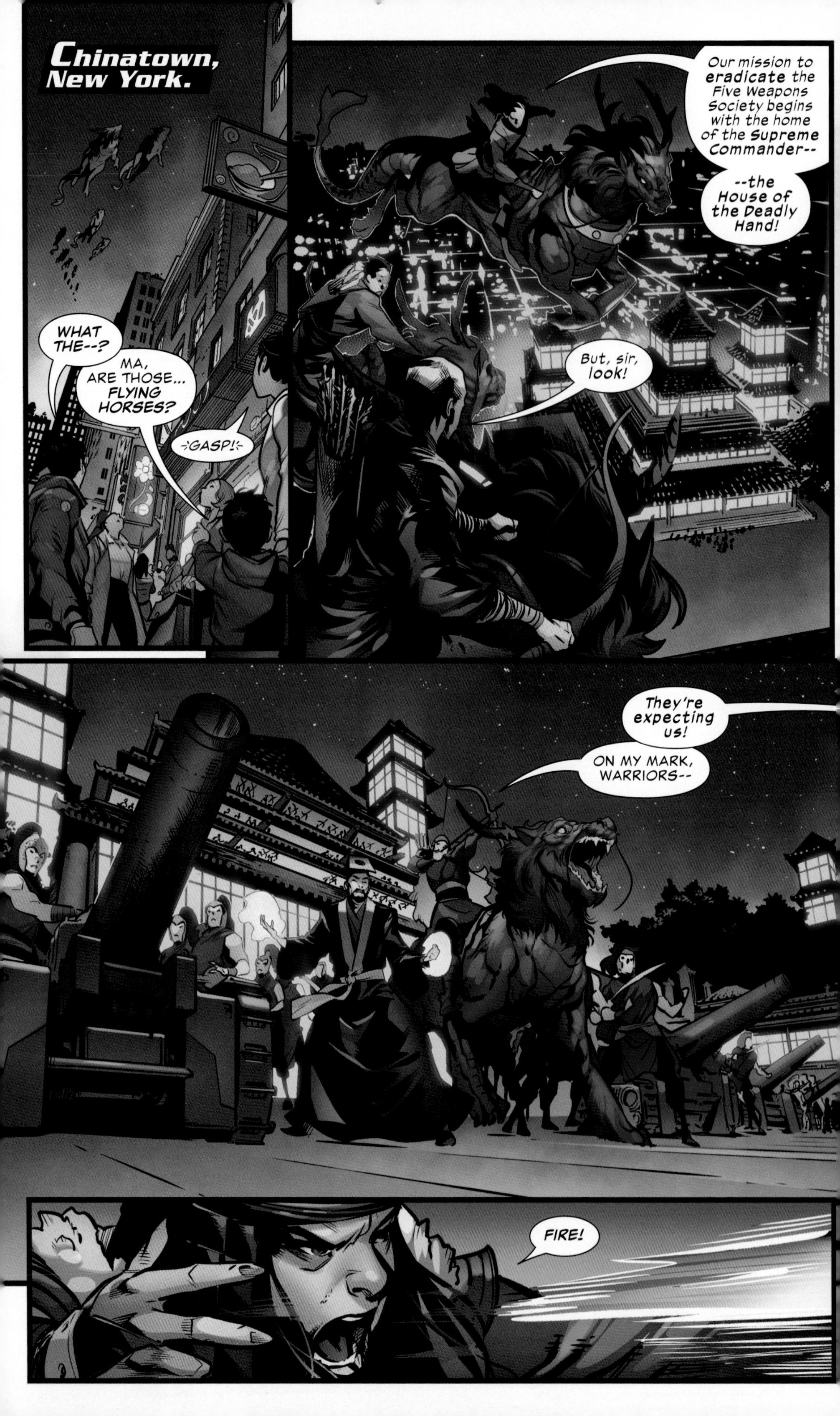
Chinatown, New York.
WHAT THE--?
MA, ARE THOSE... FLYING HORSES?
-GASP!-
Our mission to eradicate the Five Weapons Society begins with the home of the Supreme Commander--
--the House of the Deadly Hand!
But, sir, look!
They're expecting us!
ON MY MARK, WARRIORS--
FIRE!

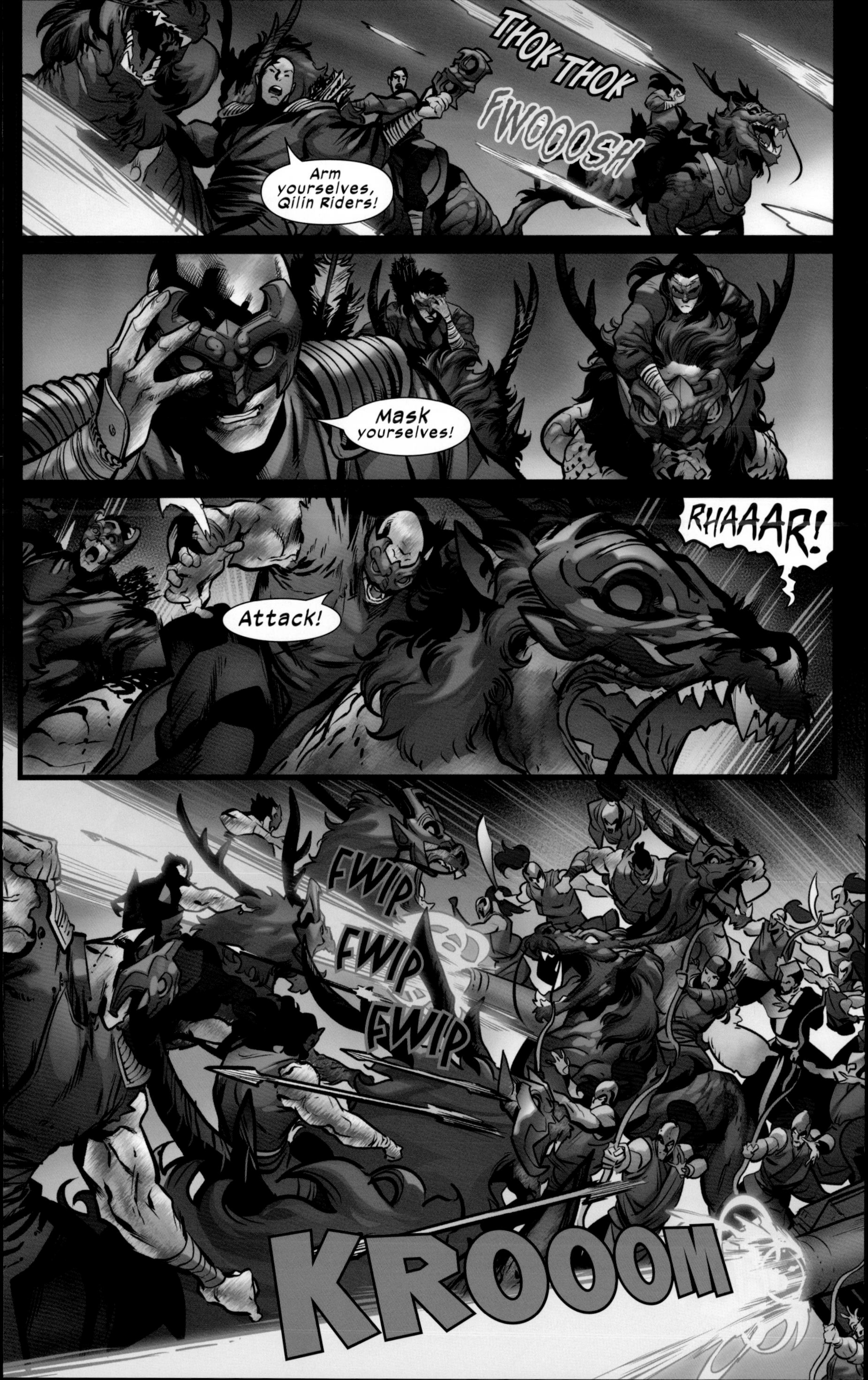
THOK THOK
FWOOOSH
Arm yourselves, Qilin Riders!
Mask yourselves!
RHAAAR!
Attack!
FWIP
FWIP
FWIP
KROOOM

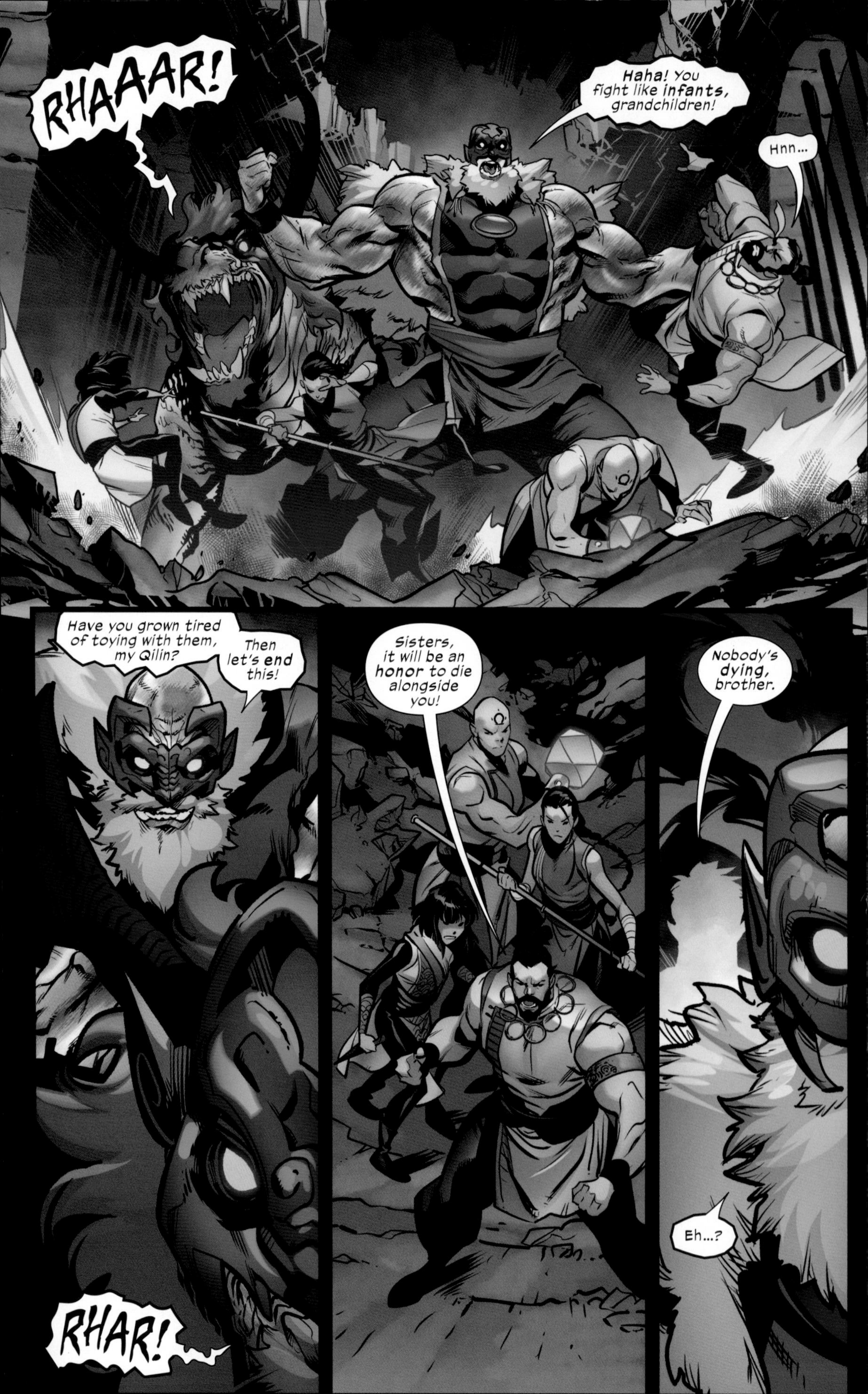

RHAAAR!
Haha! You fight like infants, grandchildren!
Hnn...
Have you grown tired of toying with them, my Qilin?
Then let's end this!
RHAR!
Sisters, it will be an honor to die alongside you!
Nobody's dying, brother.
Eh...?

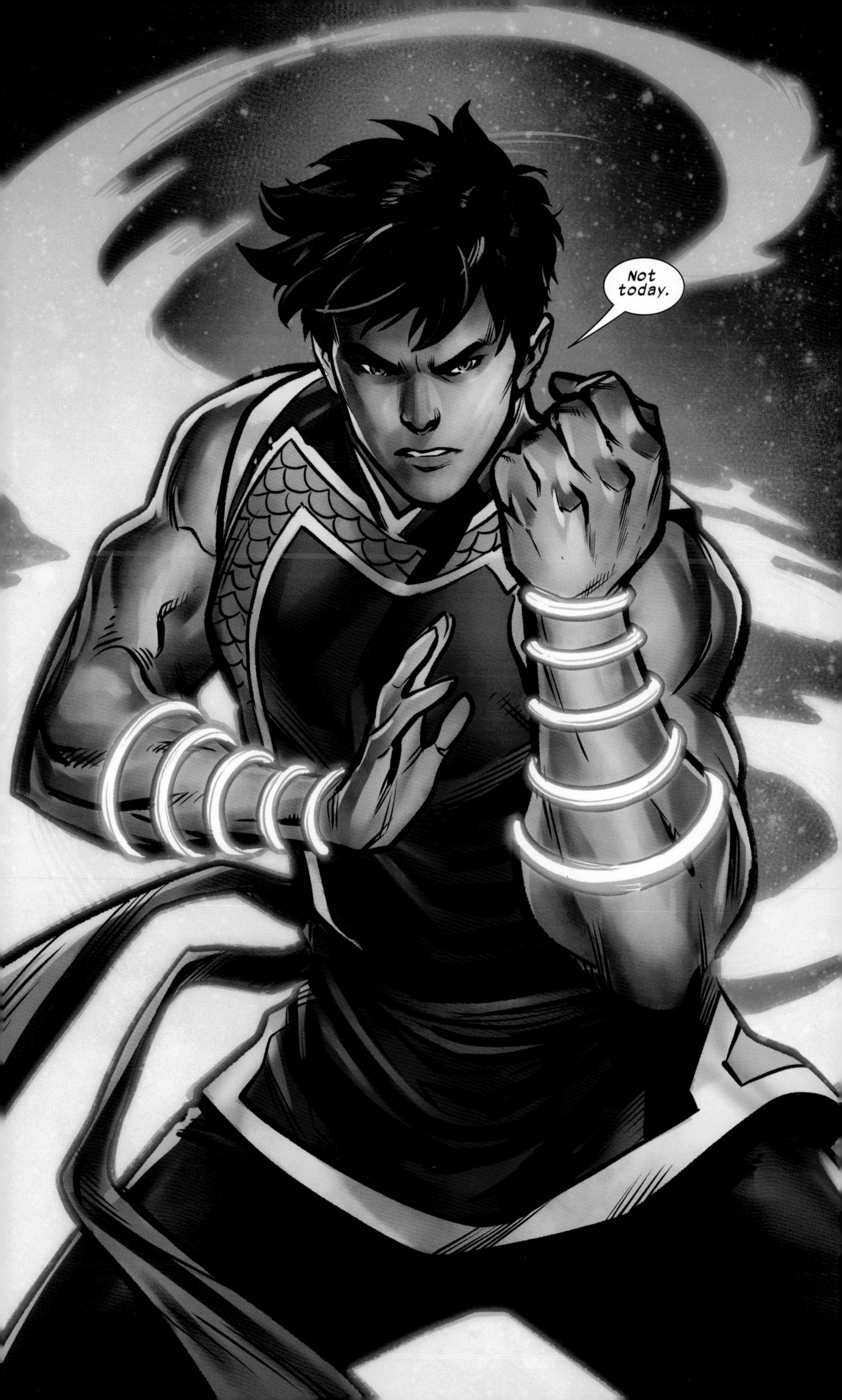
Not today.

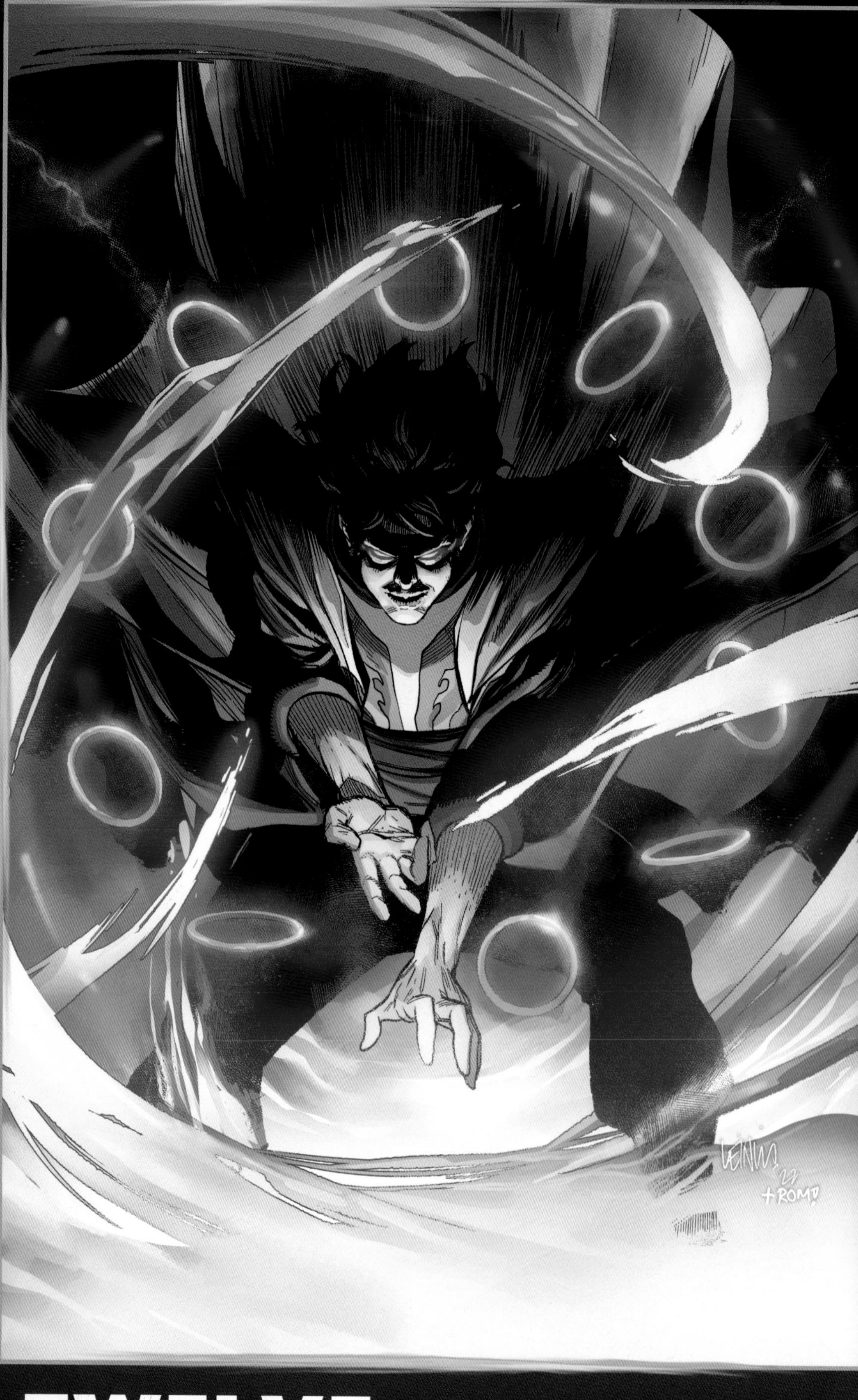

TWELVE

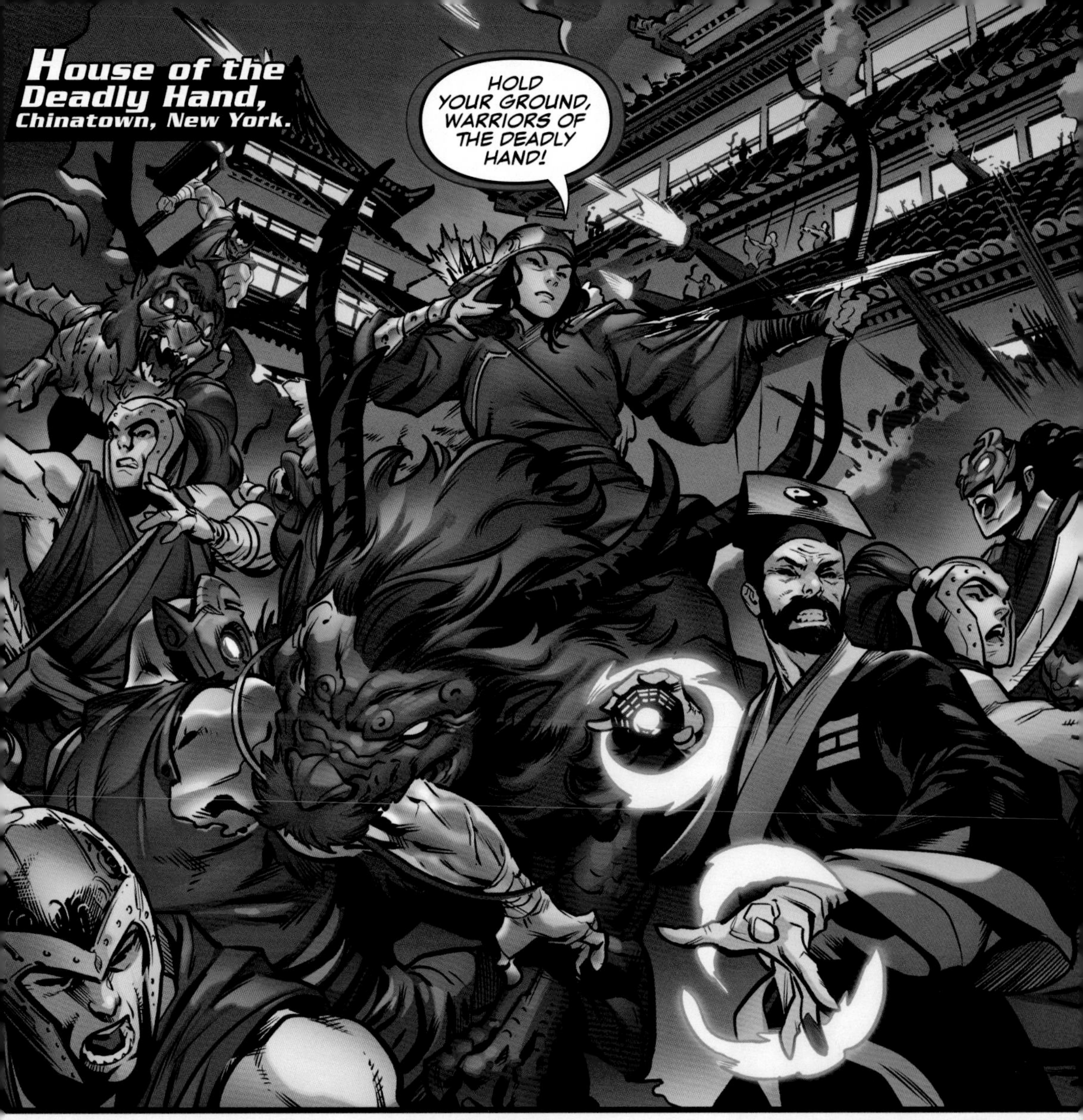
House of the Deadly Hand, Chinatown, New York.
HOLD YOUR GROUND, WARRIORS OF THE DEADLY HAND!
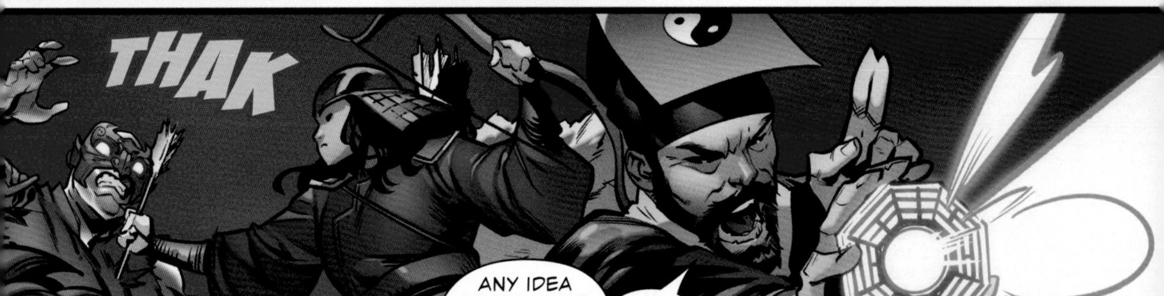
THAK
ANY IDEA WHEN YOUR SON WILL BE BACK, MADAM JIANG LI?!
OR IF...?!
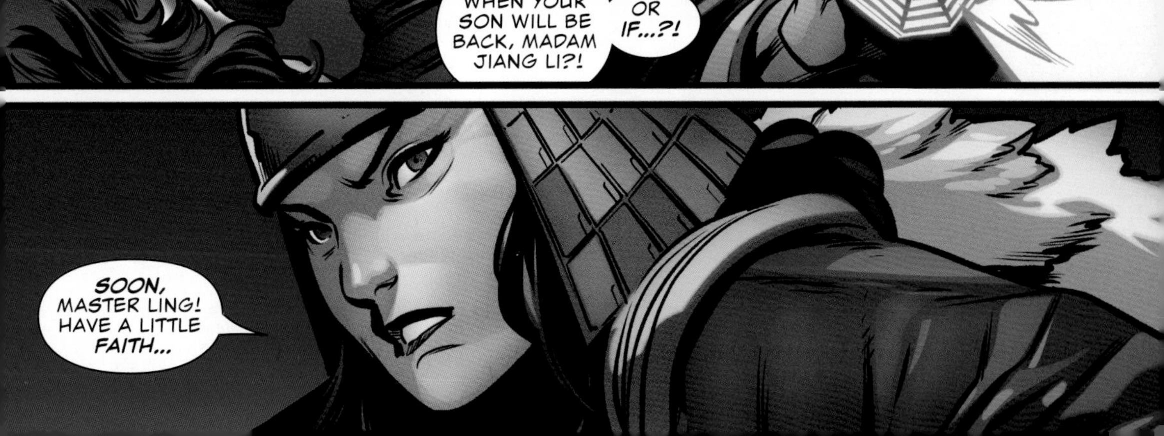
SOON, MASTER LING! HAVE A LITTLE FAITH...

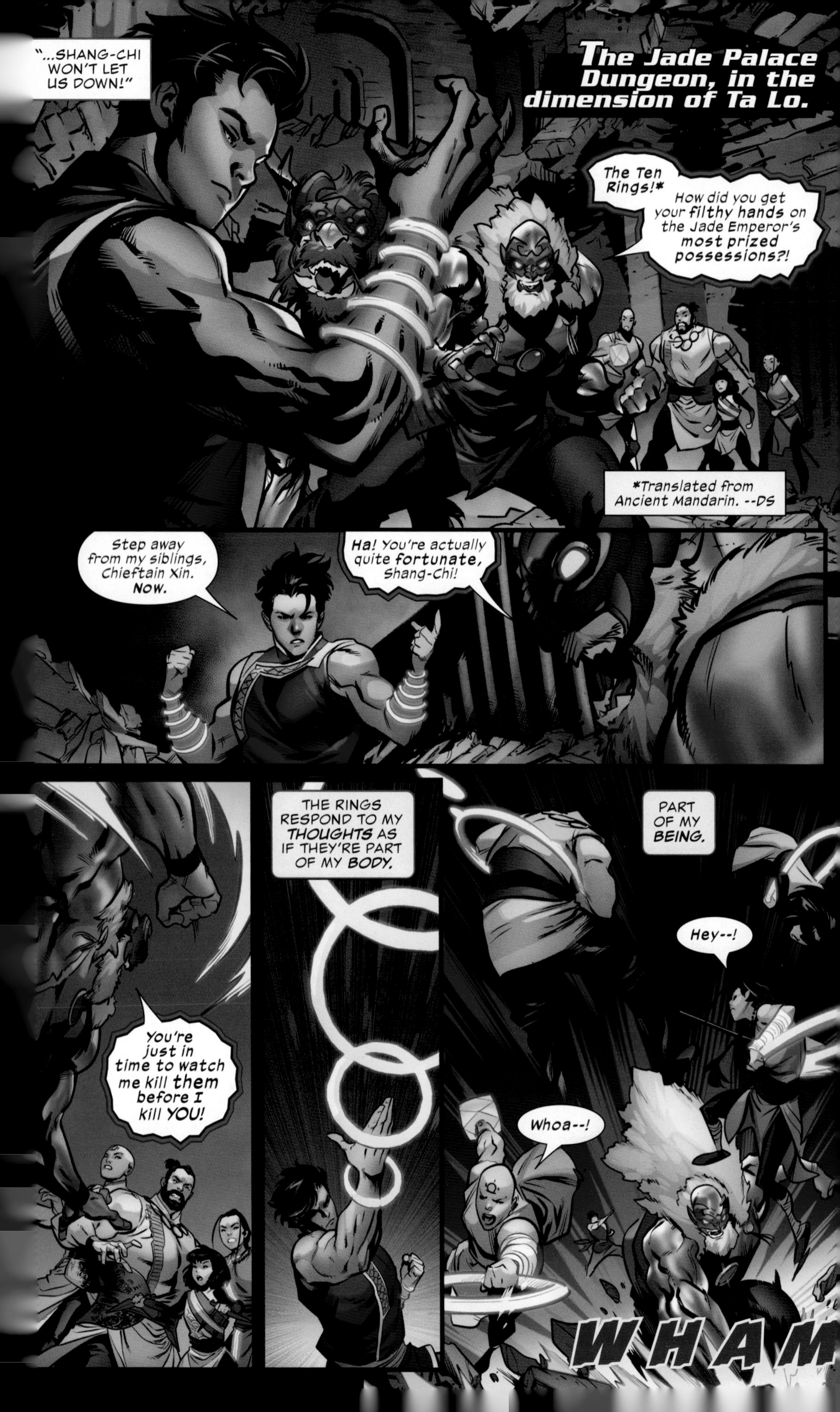
"...SHANG-CHI WON'T LET US DOWN!"
The Jade Palace Dungeon, in the dimension of Ta Lo.
The Ten Rings!*
How did you get your filthy hands on the Jade Emperor's most prized possessions?!
*Translated from Ancient Mandarin. --DS
Step away from my siblings, Chieftain Xin. Now.
Ha! You're actually quite fortunate, Shang-Chi!
You're just in time to watch me kill them before I kill YOU!
THE RINGS RESPOND TO MY THOUGHTS AS IF THEY'RE PART OF MY BODY.
PART OF MY BEING.
Hey--!
Whoa--!
WHAM

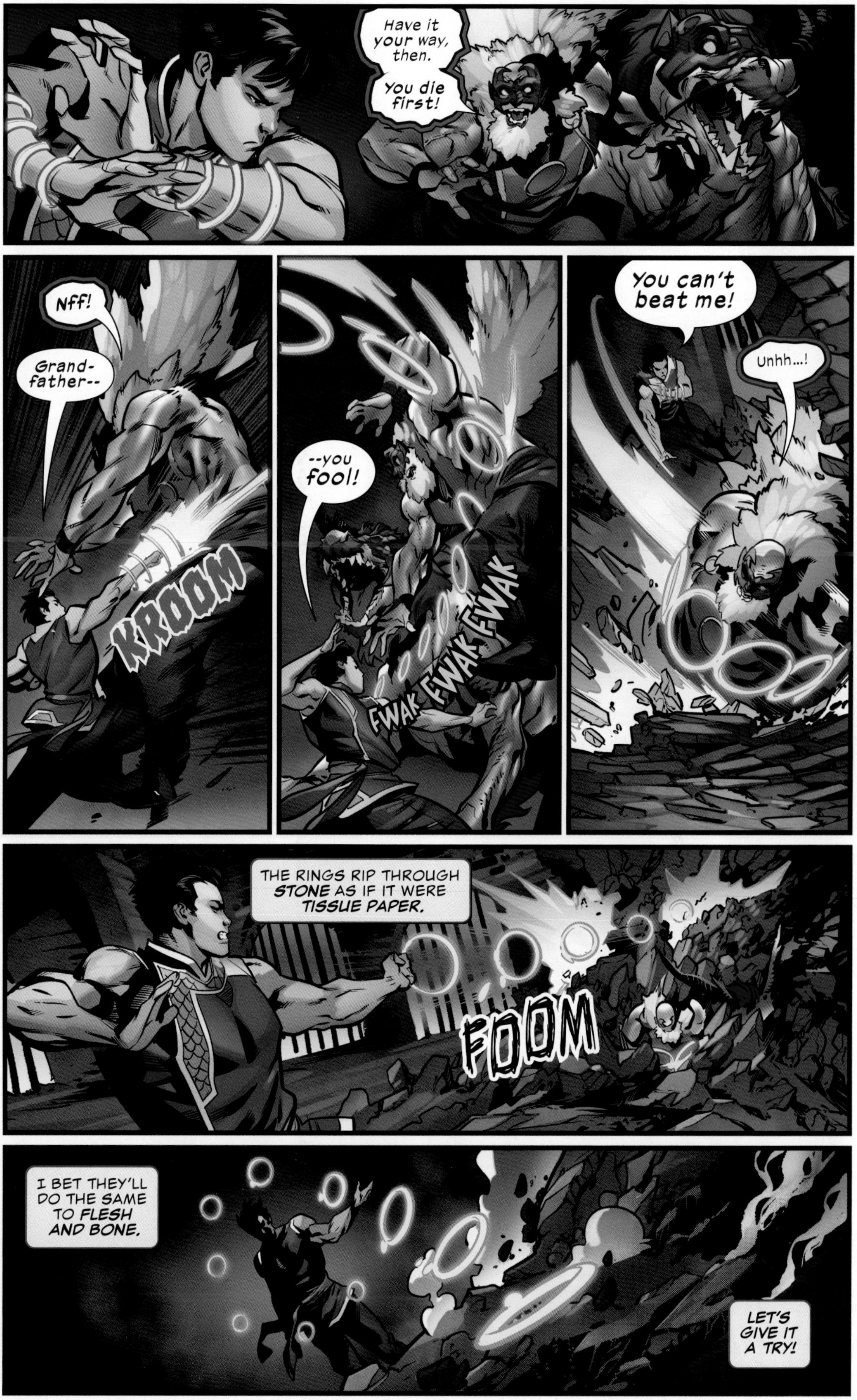

Have it your way, then.
You die first!
Nff!
Grand-father--
KROOM
--you fool!
FWAK FWAK FWAK
You can't beat me!
Unhh...!
THE RINGS RIP THROUGH STONE AS IF IT WERE TISSUE PAPER.
FOOM
I BET THEY'LL DO THE SAME TO FLESH AND BONE.
LET'S GIVE IT A TRY!

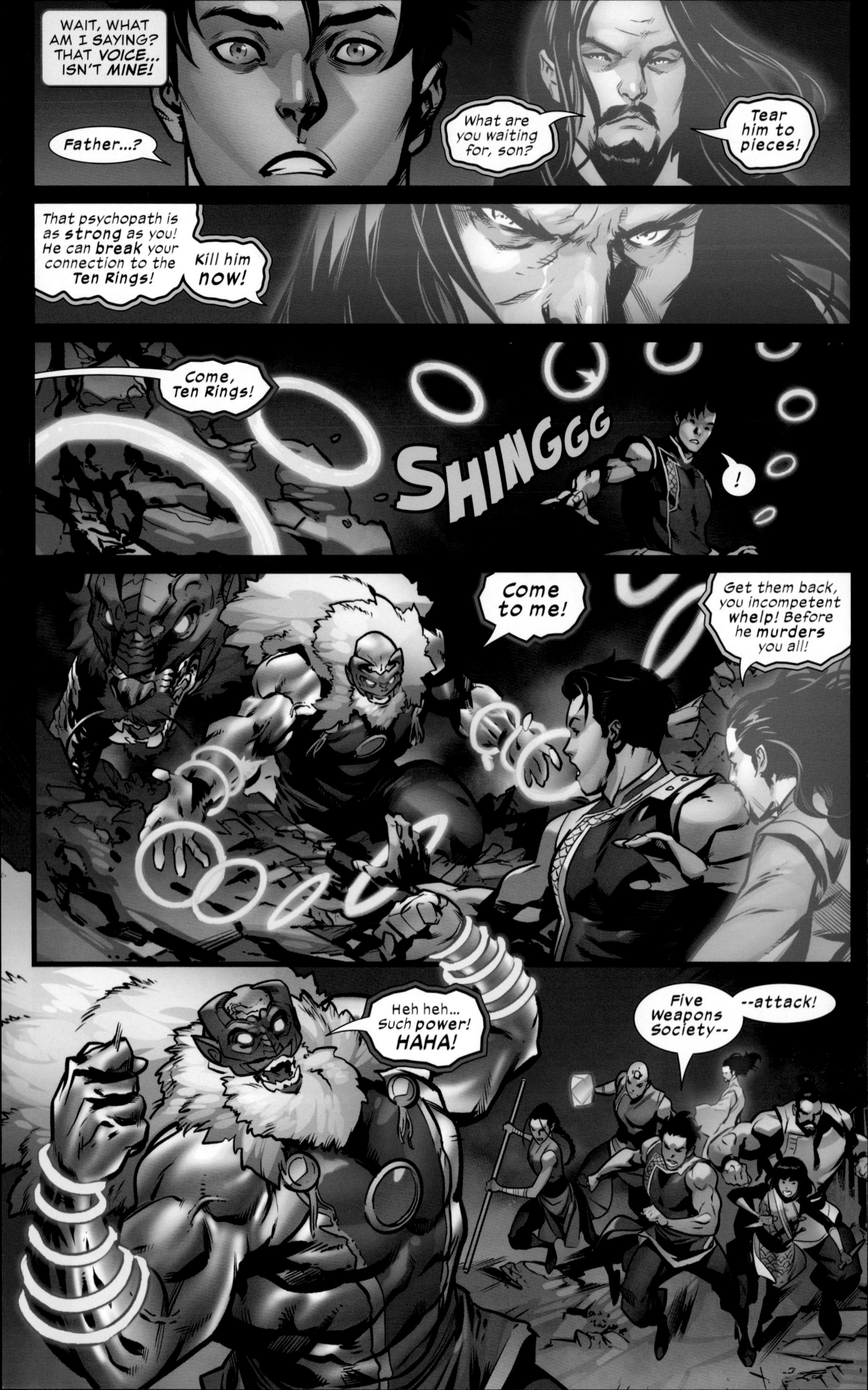
WAIT, WHAT AM I SAYING? THAT VOICE... ISN'T MINE!
Father...?
What are you waiting for, son?
Tear him to pieces!
That psychopath is as strong as you! He can break your connection to the Ten Rings!
Kill him now!
Come, Ten Rings!
SHINGGG
!
Come to me!
Get them back, you incompetent whelp! Before he murders you all!
Heh heh... Such power! HAHA!
Five Weapons Society--
--attack!

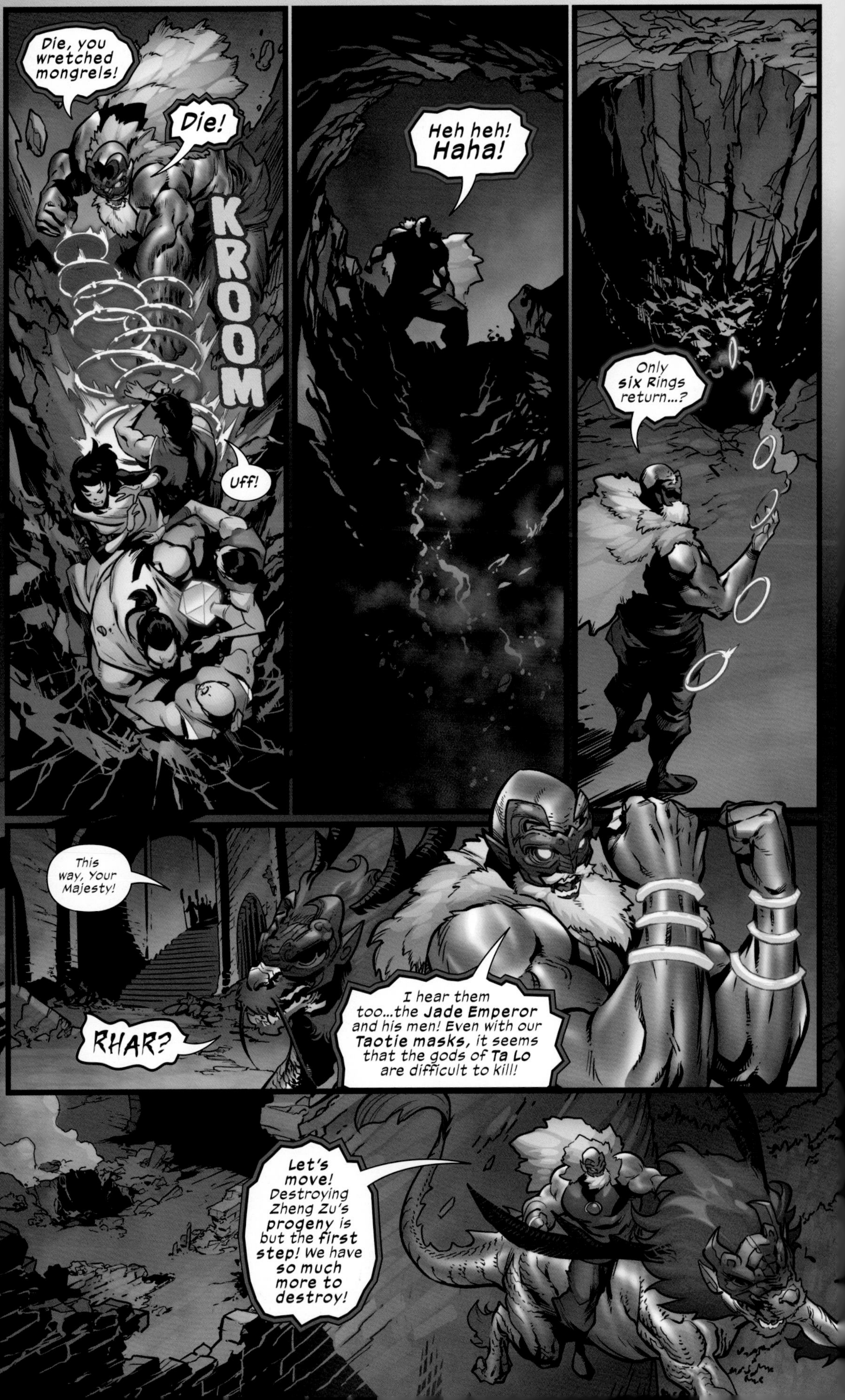
Die, you wretched mongrels!
Die!
KROOM
Uff!
Heh heh! Haha!
Only six Rings return...?
This way, Your Majesty!
RHAR?
I hear them too...the Jade Emperor and his men! Even with our Taotie masks, it seems that the gods of Ta Lo are difficult to kill!
Let's move! Destroying Zheng Zu's progeny is but the first step! We have so much more to destroy!

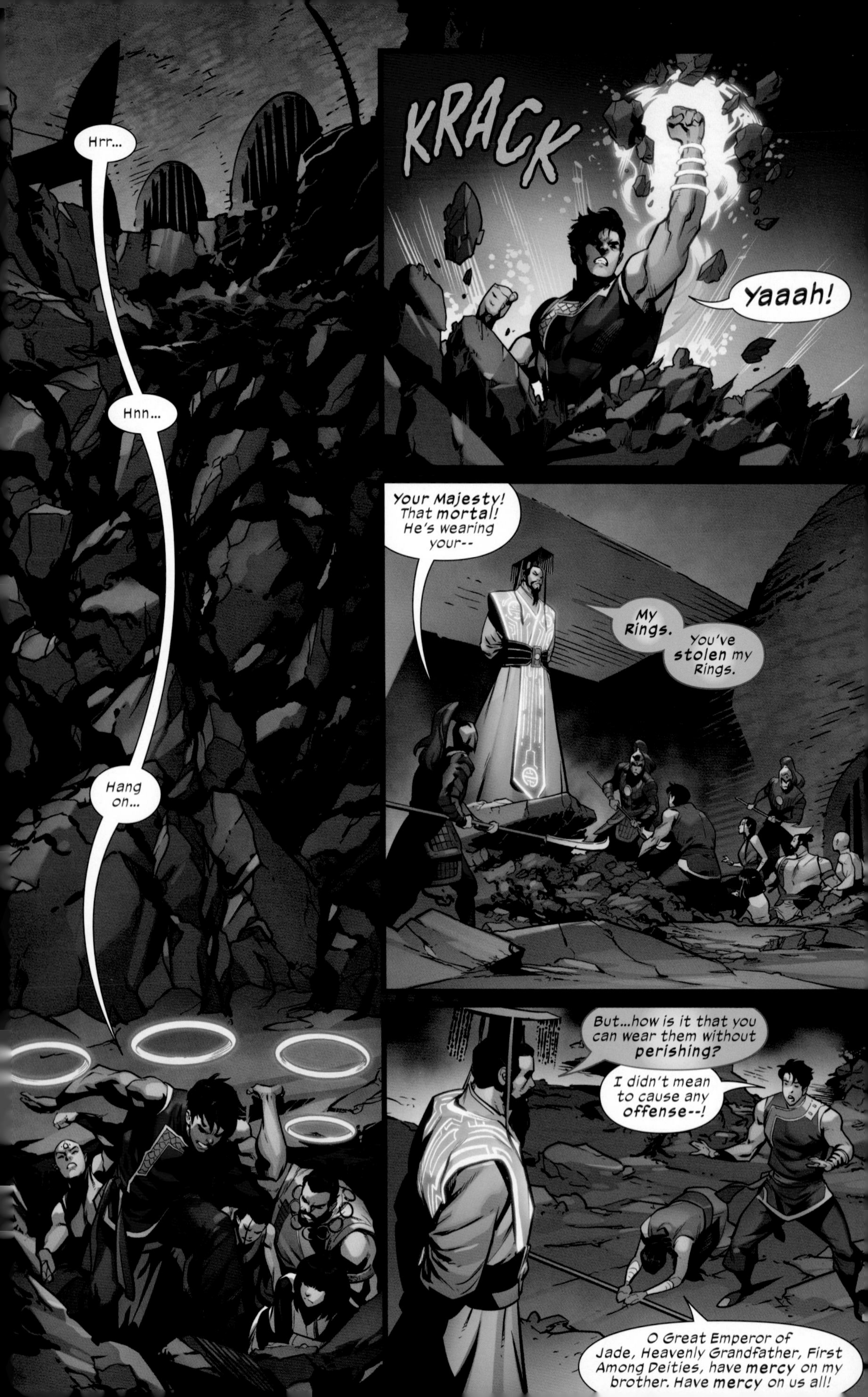
Hrr...
Hnn...
Hang on...
KRACK
Yaaah!
Your Majesty! That mortal! He's wearing your--
My Rings.
You've stolen my Rings.
But...how is it that you can wear them without perishing?
I didn't mean to cause any offense--!
O Great Emperor of Jade, Heavenly Grandfather, First Among Deities, have mercy on my brother. Have mercy on us all!

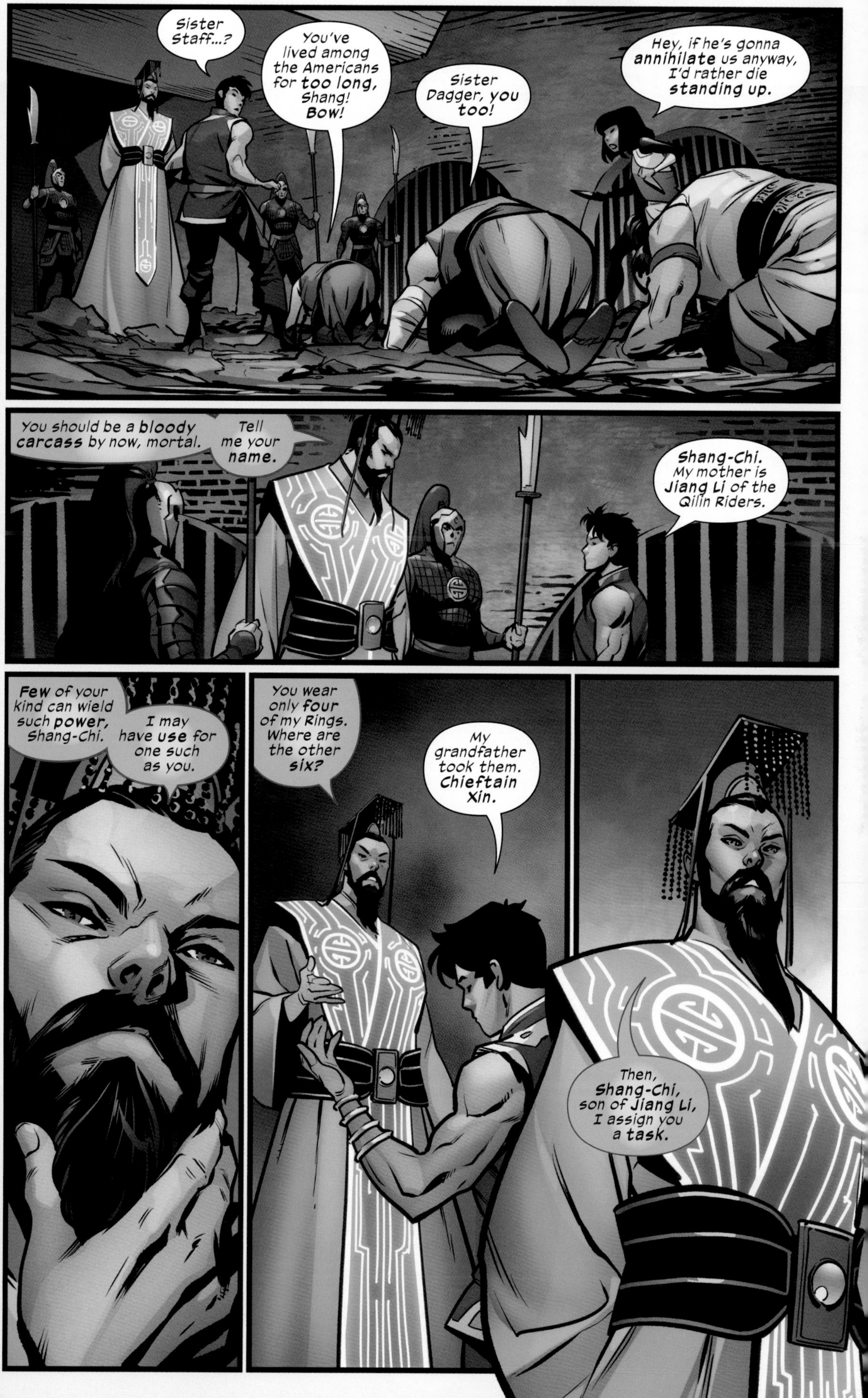
Sister Staff...?
You've lived among the Americans for too long, Shang! Bow!
Sister Dagger, you too!
Hey, if he's gonna annihilate us anyway, I'd rather die standing up.
You should be a bloody carcass by now, mortal.
Tell me your name.
Shang-Chi. My mother is Jiang Li of the Qilin Riders.
Few of your kind can wield such power, Shang-Chi.
I may have use for one such as you.
You wear only four of my Rings. Where are the other six?
My grandfather took them. Chieftain Xin.
Then, Shang-Chi, son of Jiang Li, I assign you a task.

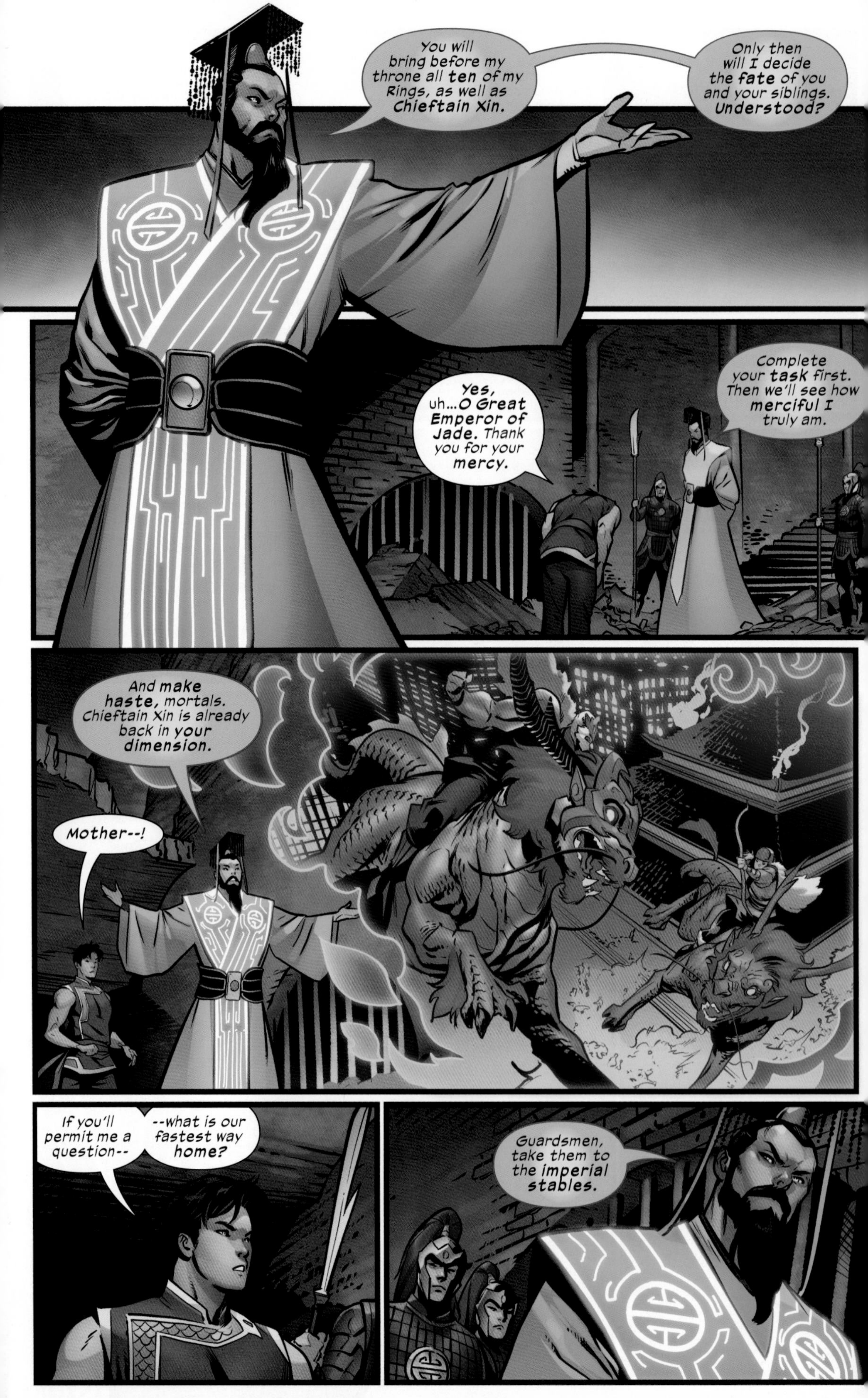

You will bring before my throne all ten of my Rings, as well as Chieftain Xin.
Only then will I decide the fate of you and your siblings. Understood?
Yes, uh...O Great Emperor of Jade. Thank you for your mercy.
Complete your task first. Then we'll see how merciful I truly am.
And make haste, mortals. Chieftain Xin is already back in your dimension.
Mother--!
If you'll permit me a question--
--what is our fastest way home?
Guardsmen, take them to the imperial stables.

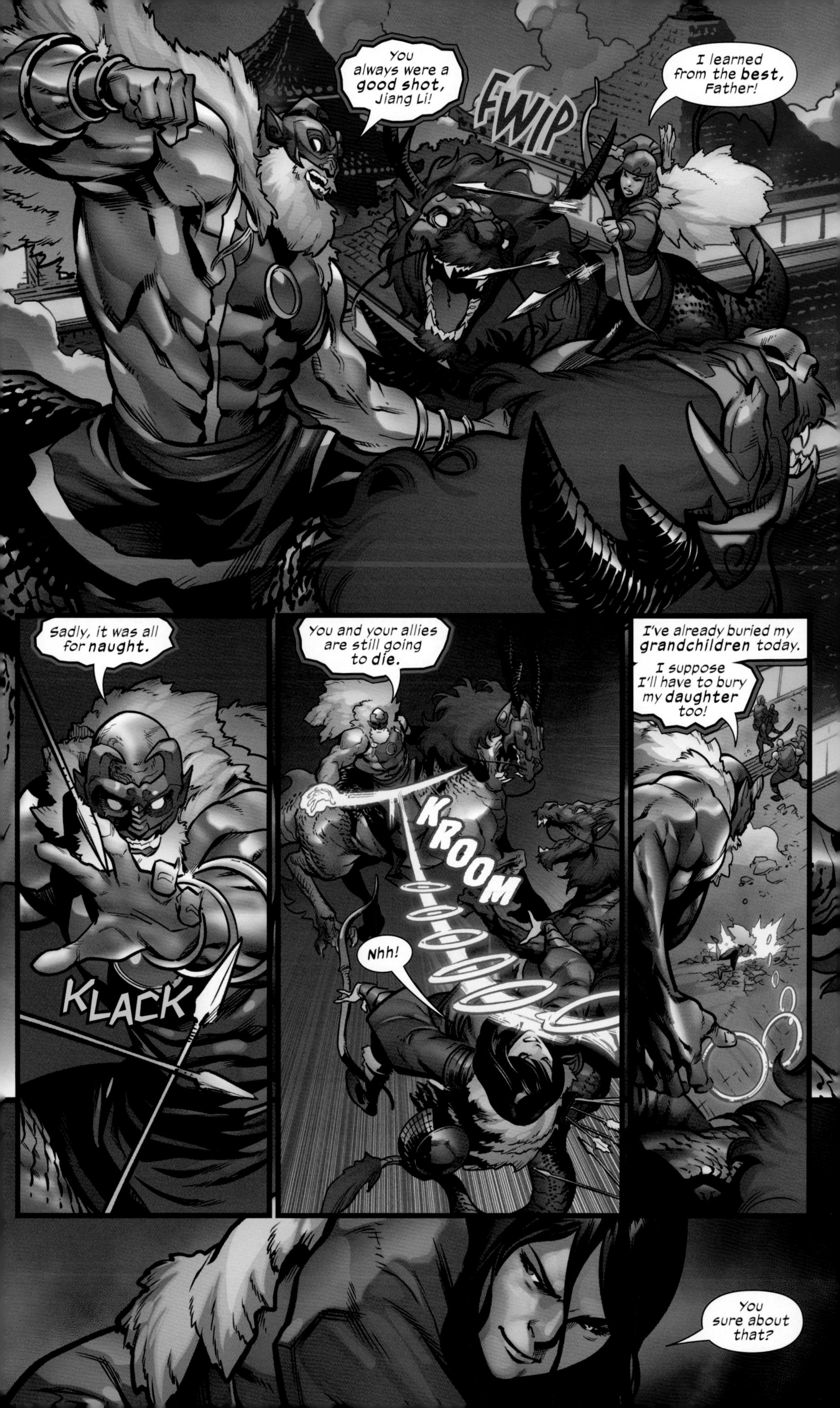

You always were a good shot, Jiang Li!
FWIP
I learned from the best, Father!
Sadly, it was all for naught.
KLACK
You and your allies are still going to die.
KROOM
Nhh!
I've already buried my grandchildren today.
I suppose I'll have to bury my daughter too!
You sure about that?

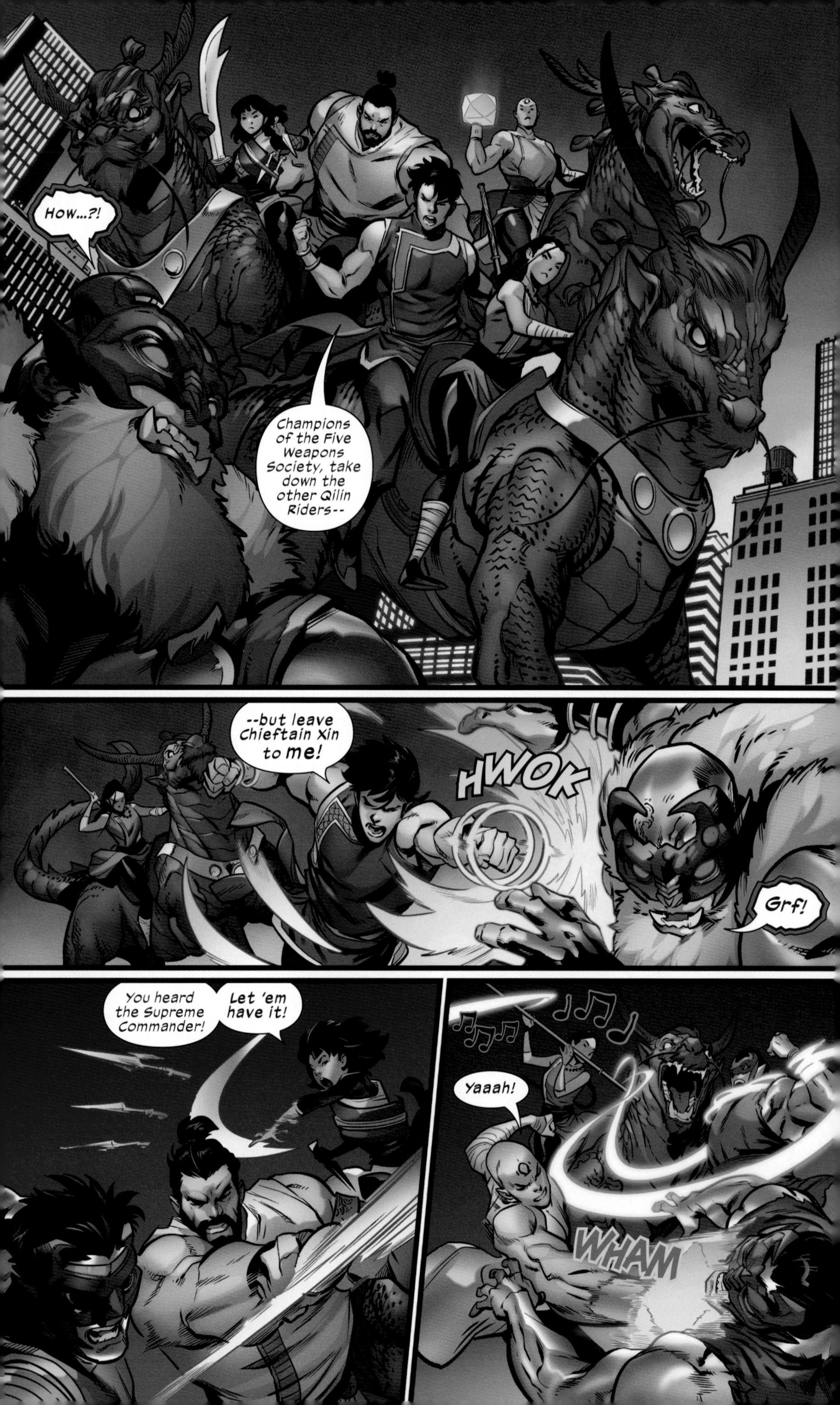
How...?!
Champions of the Five Weapons Society, take down the other Qilin Riders--
--but leave Chieftain Xin to me!
HWOK
Grf!
You heard the Supreme Commander!
Let 'em have it!
Yaaah!
WHAM

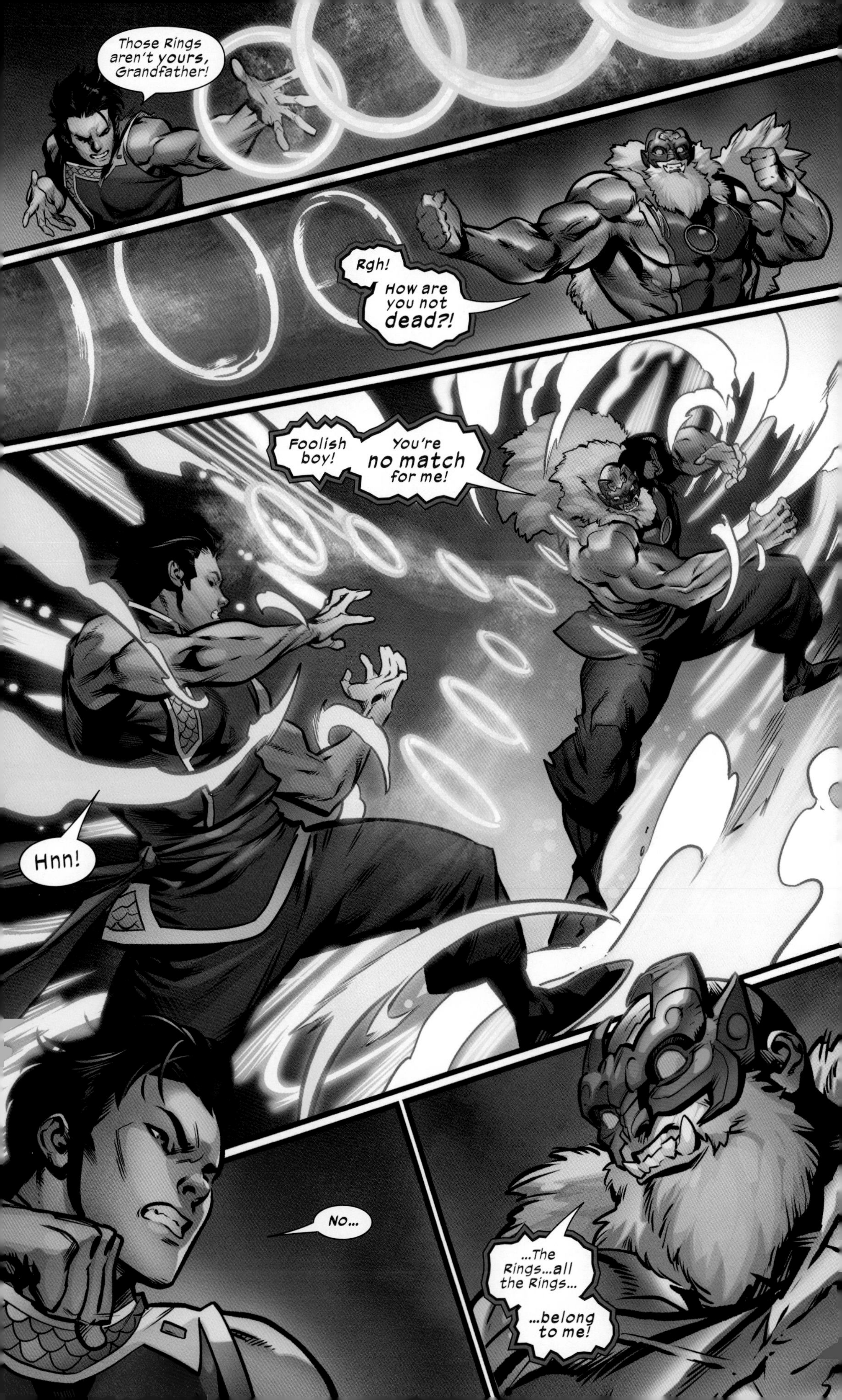
Those Rings aren't yours, Grandfather!
Rgh!
How are you not dead?!
Foolish boy!
You're no match for me!
Hnn!
No...
...The Rings...all the Rings...
...belong to me!

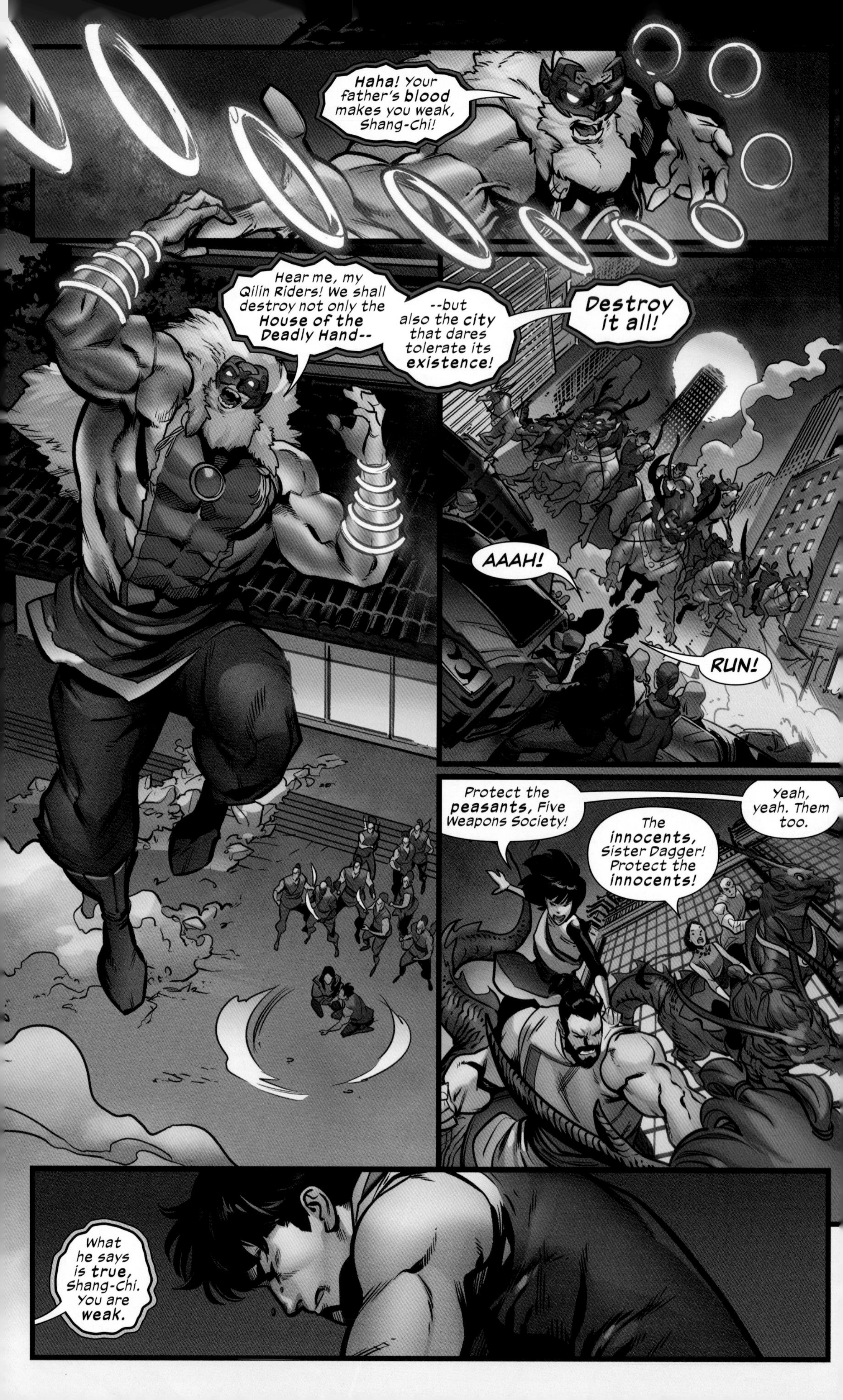
Haha! Your father's blood makes you weak, Shang-Chi!
Hear me, my Qilin Riders! We shall destroy not only the House of the Deadly Hand--
--but also the city that dares tolerate its existence!
Destroy it all!
AAAH!
RUN!
Protect the peasants, Five Weapons Society!
The innocents, Sister Dagger! Protect the innocents!
Yeah, yeah. Them too.
What he says is true, Shang-Chi. You are weak.

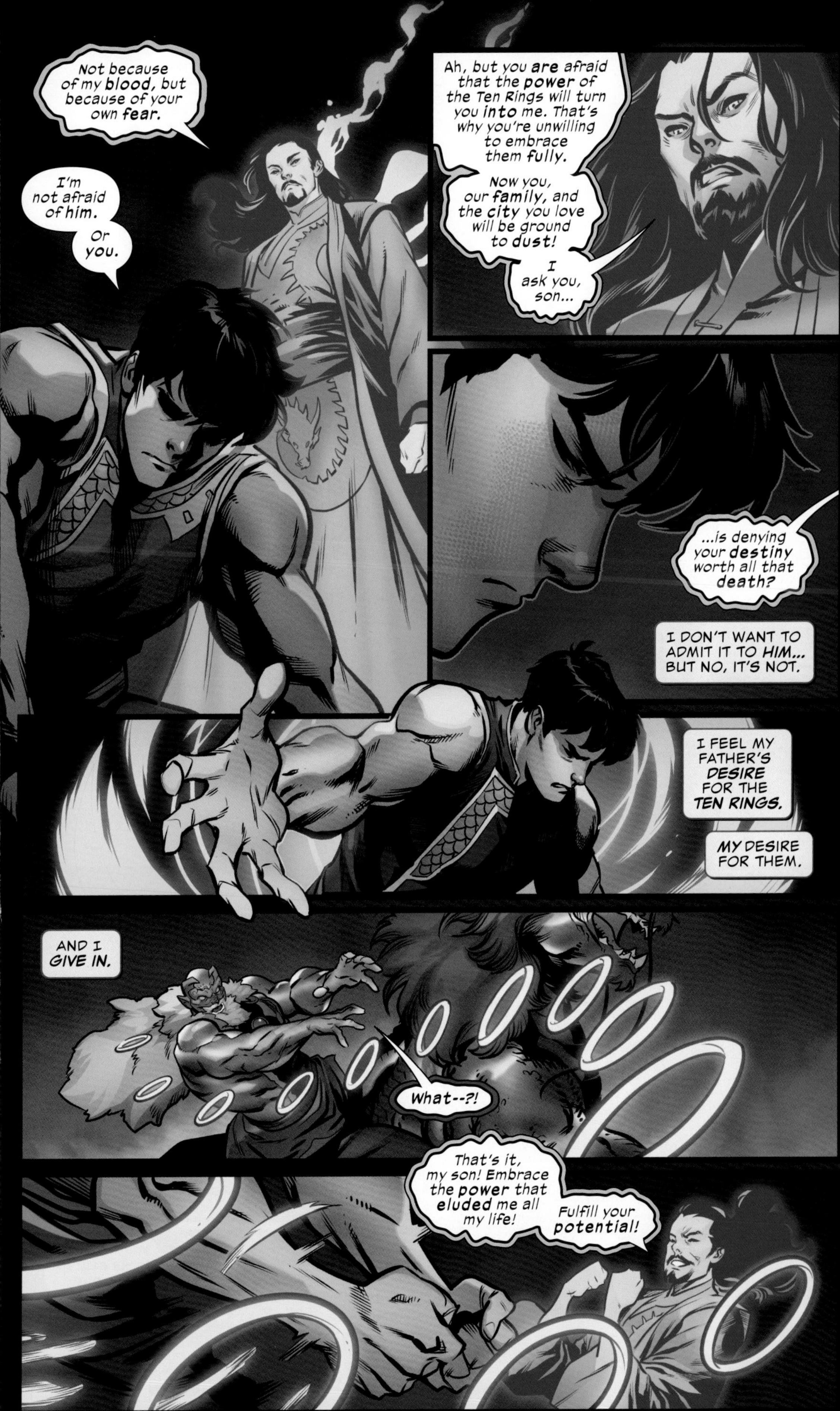
Not because of my blood, but because of your own fear.
I'm not afraid of him.
Or you.
Ah, but you are afraid that the power of the Ten Rings will turn you into me. That's why you're unwilling to embrace them fully.
Now you, our family, and the city you love will be ground to dust!
I ask you, son...
...is denying your destiny worth all that death?
I DON'T WANT TO ADMIT IT TO HIM... BUT NO, IT'S NOT.
I FEEL MY FATHER'S DESIRE FOR THE TEN RINGS.
MY DESIRE FOR THEM.
AND I GIVE IN.
What--?!
That's it, my son! Embrace the power that eluded me all my life!
Fulfill your potential!

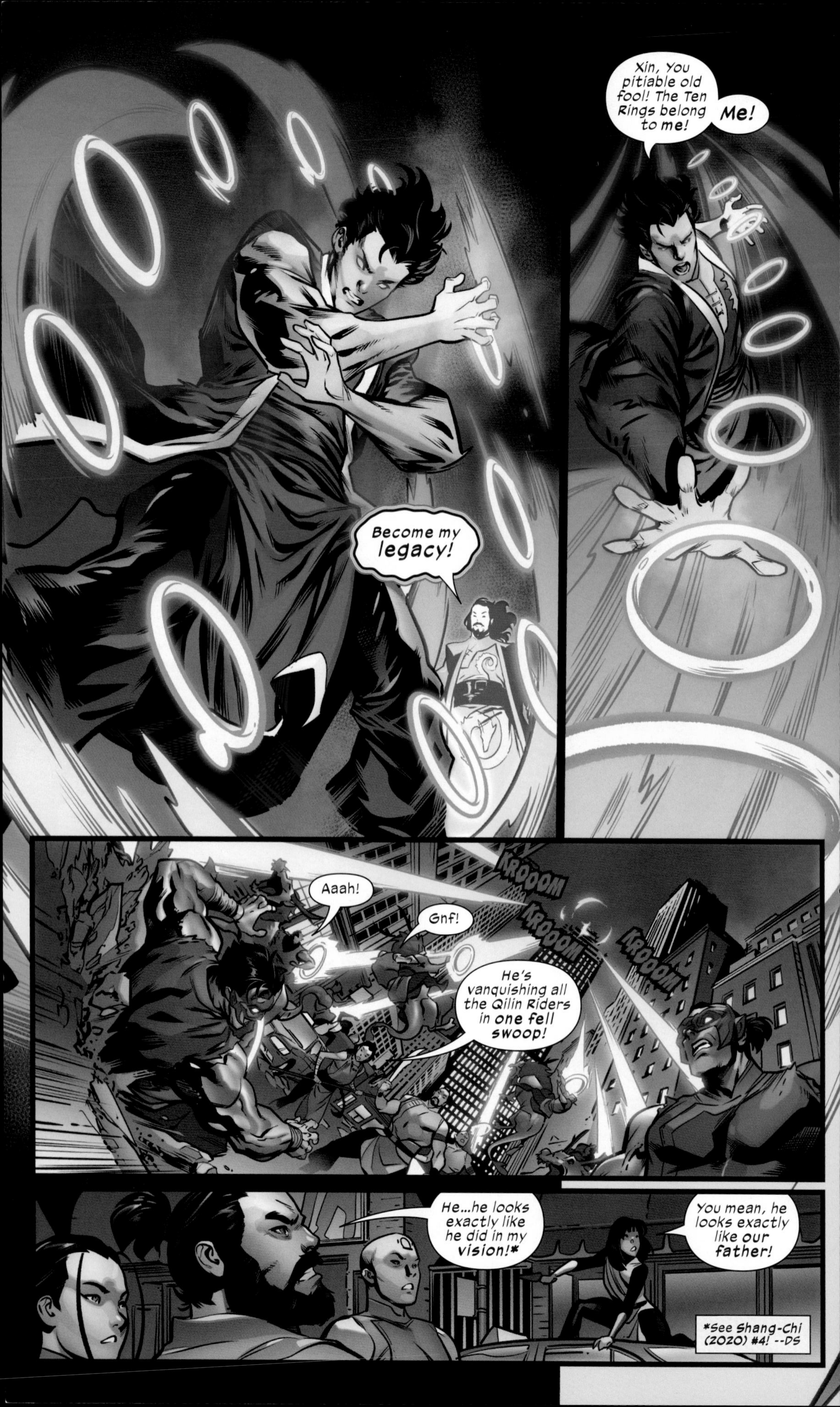
Become my legacy!
Xin, You pitiable old fool! The Ten Rings belong to me!
Me!
Aaah!
KROOOM
Gnf!
KROOOM
KROOOM
He's vanquishing all the Qilin Riders in one fell swoop!
He...he looks exactly like he did in my vision!*
You mean, he looks exactly like our father!
*See Shang-Chi (2020) #4! --DS

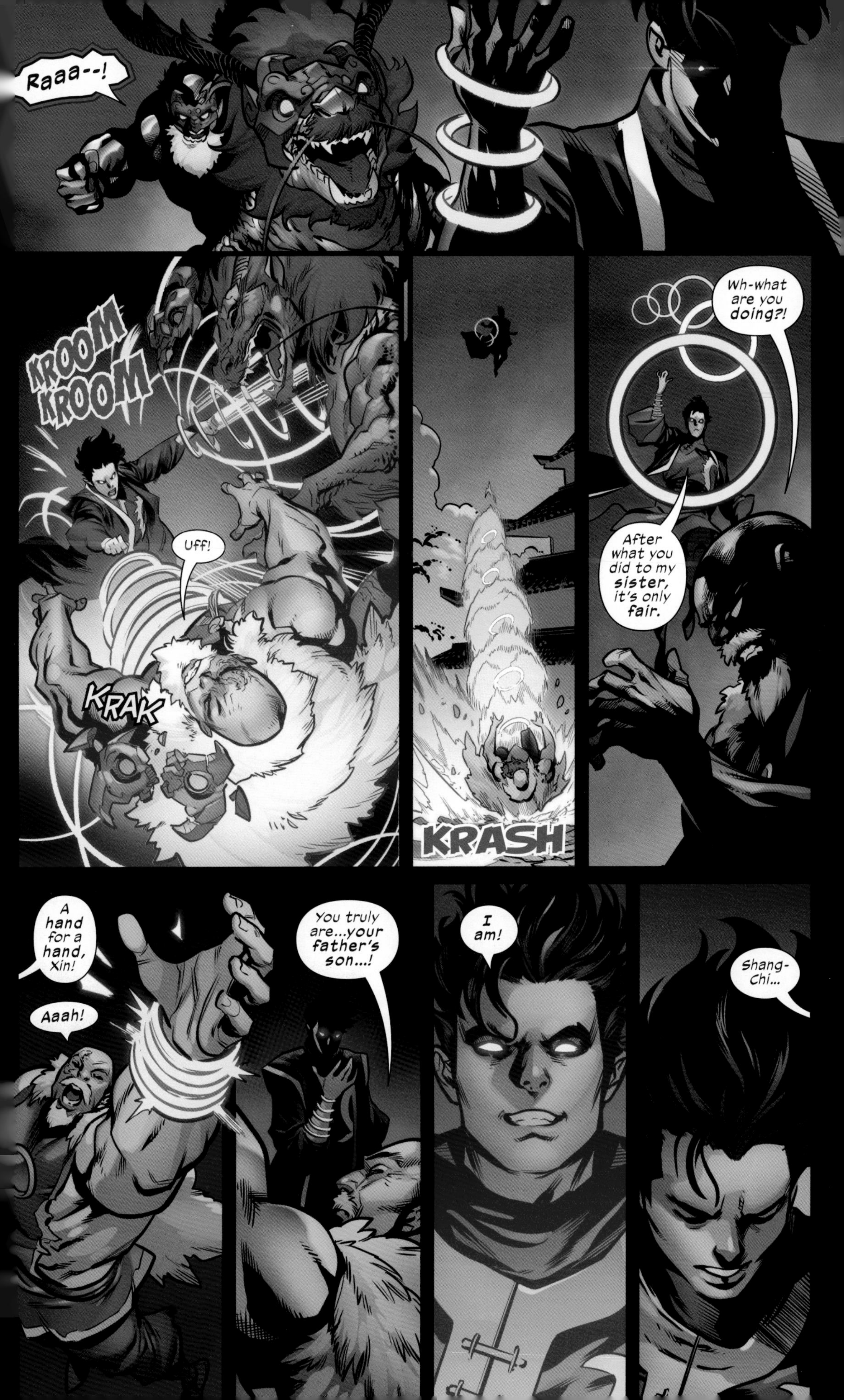
Raaa--!
KROOM KROOM
Uff!
KRAK
KRASH
Wh-what are you doing?!
After what you did to my sister, it's only fair.
A hand for a hand, Xin!
Aaah!
You truly are...your father's son...!
I am!
Shang-Chi...

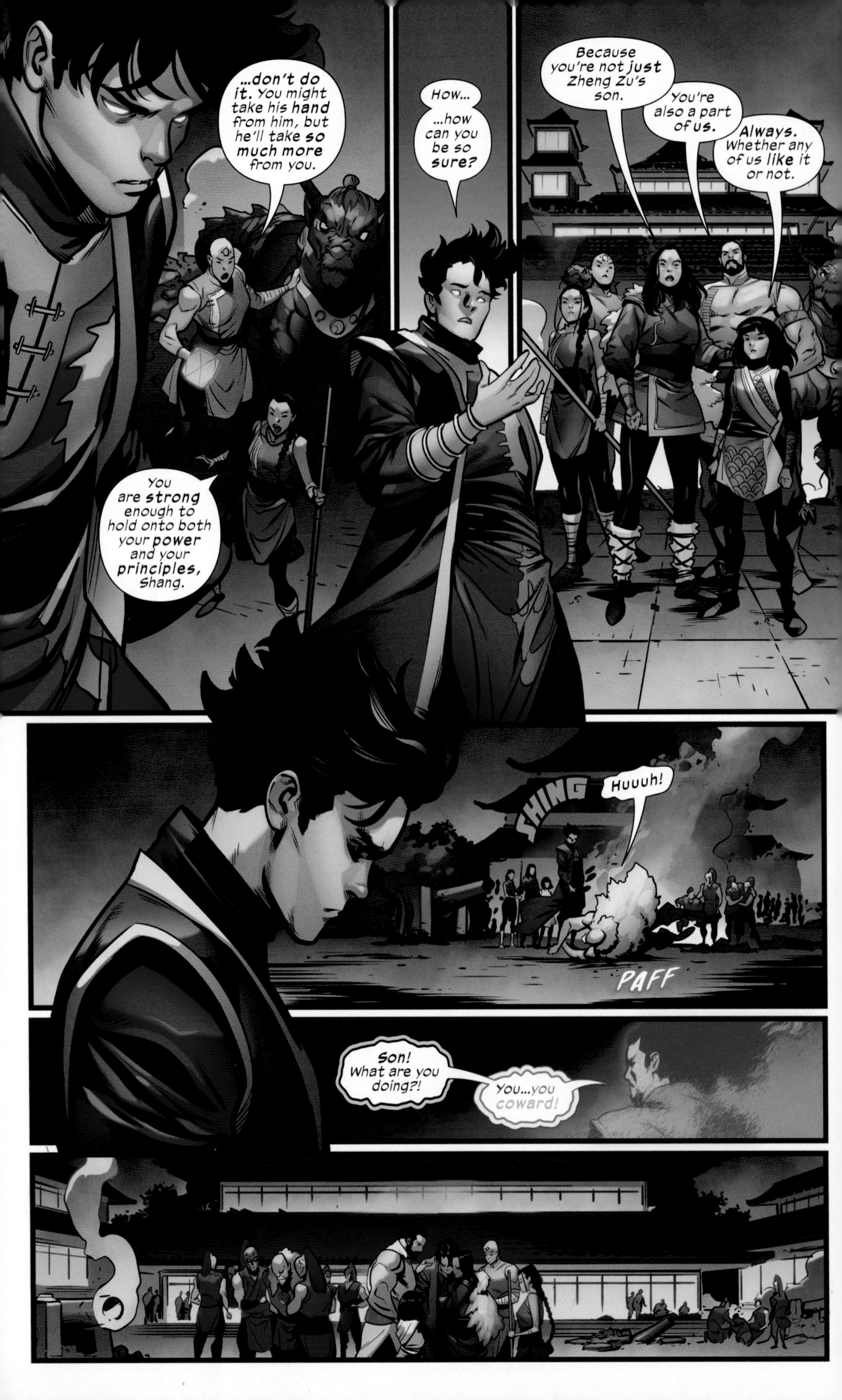

...don't do it. You might take his hand from him, but he'll take so much more from you.
You are strong enough to hold onto both your power and your principles, Shang.
How...
...how can you be so sure?
Because you're not just Zheng Zu's son.
You're also a part of us.
Always. Whether any of us like it or not.
SHING
Huuuh!
PAFF
Son! What are you doing?!
You...you coward!

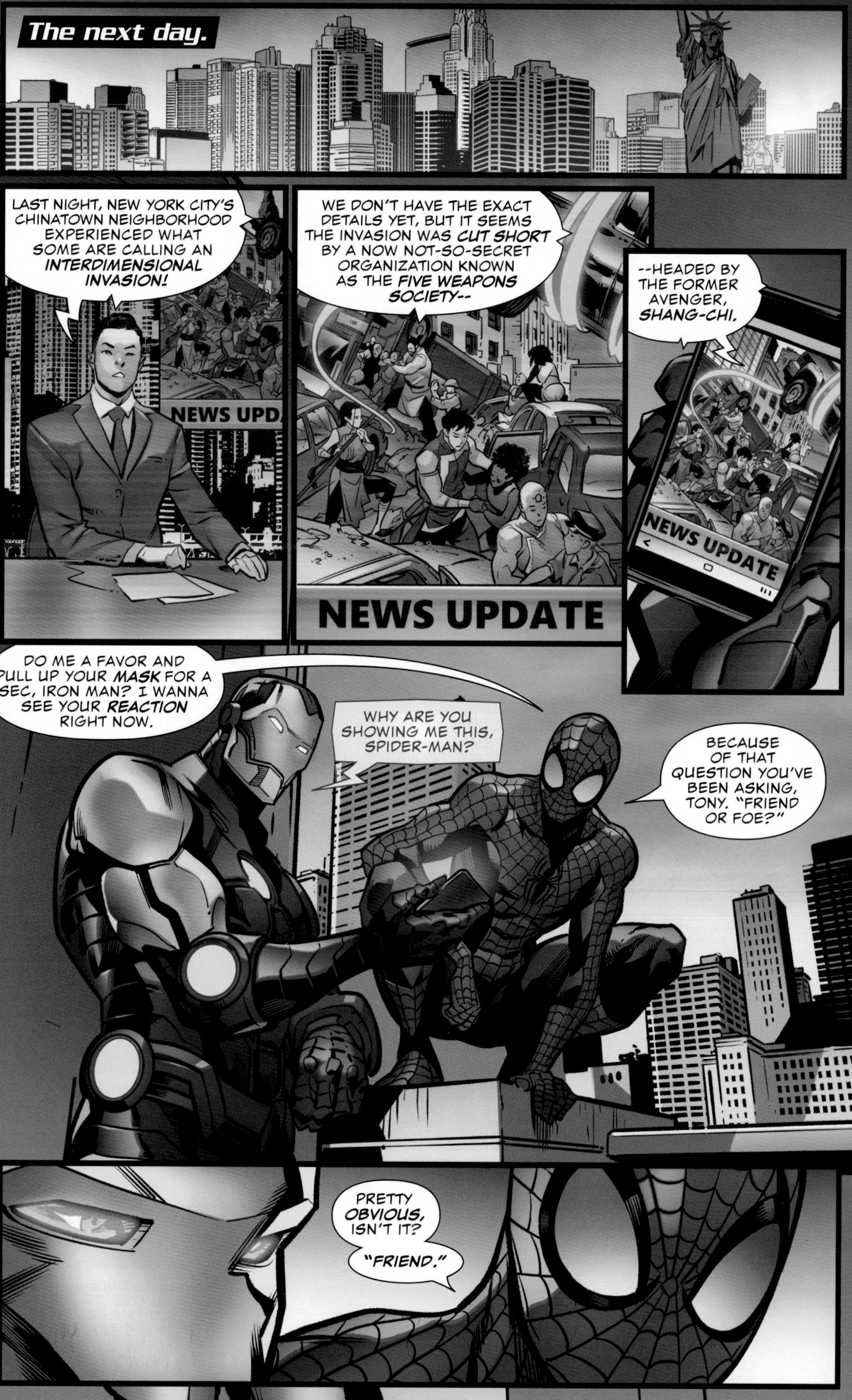
The next day.
LAST NIGHT, NEW YORK CITY'S CHINATOWN NEIGHBORHOOD EXPERIENCED WHAT SOME ARE CALLING AN INTERDIMENSIONAL INVASION!
NEWS UPDA
WE DON'T HAVE THE EXACT DETAILS YET, BUT IT SEEMS THE INVASION WAS CUT SHORT BY A NOW NOT-SO-SECRET ORGANIZATION KNOWN AS THE FIVE WEAPONS SOCIETY--
NEWS UPDATE
--HEADED BY THE FORMER AVENGER, SHANG-CHI.
NEWS UPDATE
DO ME A FAVOR AND PULL UP YOUR MASK FOR A SEC, IRON MAN? I WANNA SEE YOUR REACTION RIGHT NOW.
WHY ARE YOU SHOWING ME THIS, SPIDER-MAN?
BECAUSE OF THAT QUESTION YOU'VE BEEN ASKING, TONY. "FRIEND OR FOE?"
PRETTY OBVIOUS, ISN'T IT?
"FRIEND."

One month later.

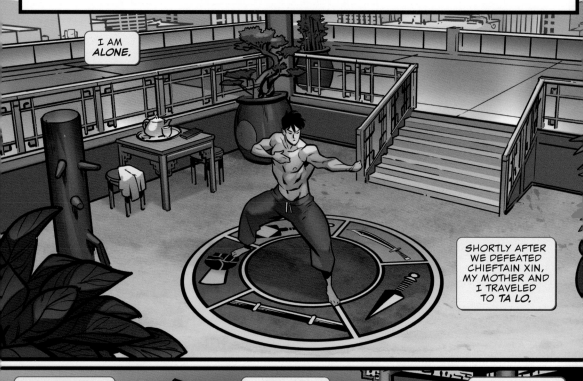

I AM ALONE.

SHORTLY AFTER WE DEFEATED CHIEFTAIN XIN, MY MOTHER AND I TRAVELED TO *TA LO.*

WE BROUGHT MY GRANDFATHER TO JUSTICE AND GAVE THE *TEN RINGS* BACK TO THEIR RIGHTFUL OWNER.

THE JADE EMPEROR, IN TURN, PROVED *MERCIFUL.*

HE ALSO APPOINTED MY MOTHER THE NEW *CHIEFTAIN* OF THE QILIN RIDERS, WHICH MEANT SHE HAD TO STAY.

IT WAS DIFFICULT TO SAY *GOODBYE*, OF COURSE, BUT SHE WAS AS *AT PEACE* AS I'D EVER SEEN HER.

TAKESHI CHOSE TO SERVE OUT THE REMAINDER OF HIS SENTENCE IN *THE VAULT.* "IT'S THE *PRINCIPLED* THING TO DO," HE SAID.

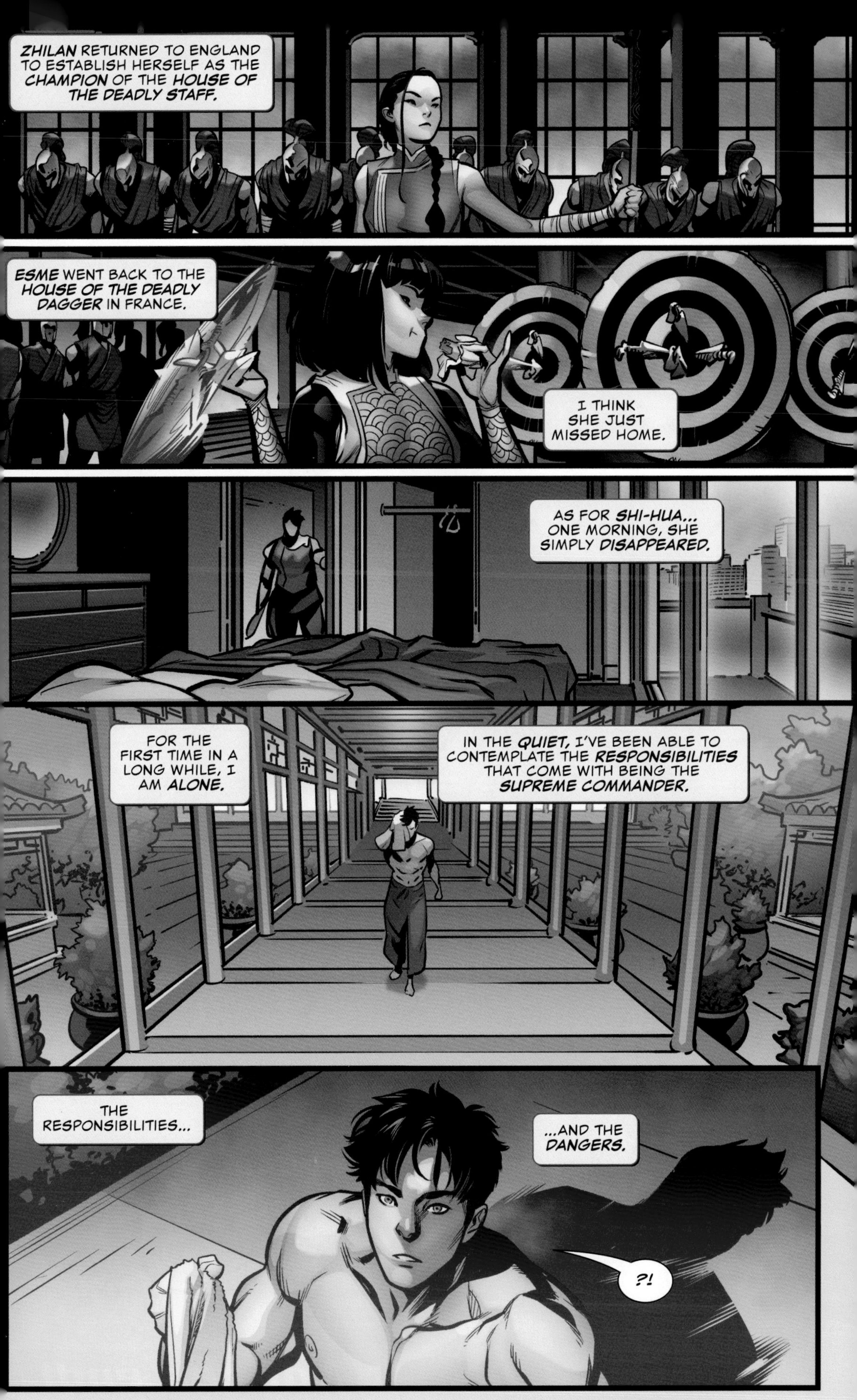
ZHILAN RETURNED TO ENGLAND TO ESTABLISH HERSELF AS THE CHAMPION OF THE HOUSE OF THE DEADLY STAFF.
ESME WENT BACK TO THE HOUSE OF THE DEADLY DAGGER IN FRANCE.
I THINK SHE JUST MISSED HOME.
AS FOR SHI-HUA... ONE MORNING, SHE SIMPLY DISAPPEARED.
FOR THE FIRST TIME IN A LONG WHILE, I AM ALONE.
IN THE QUIET, I'VE BEEN ABLE TO CONTEMPLATE THE RESPONSIBILITIES THAT COME WITH BEING THE SUPREME COMMANDER.
THE RESPONSIBILITIES...
...AND THE DANGERS.
?!

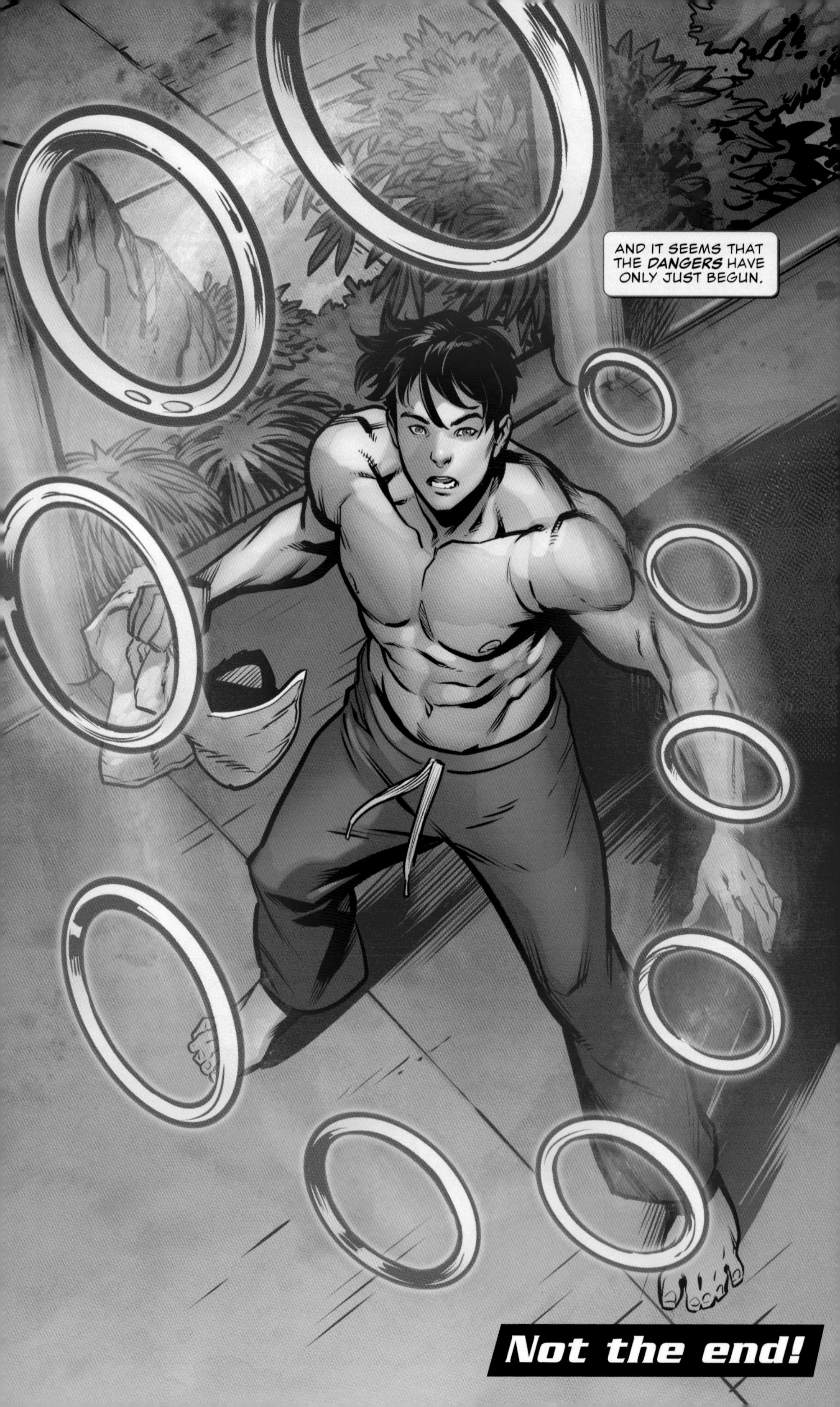
AND IT SEEMS THAT THE DANGERS HAVE ONLY JUST BEGUN.
Not the end!

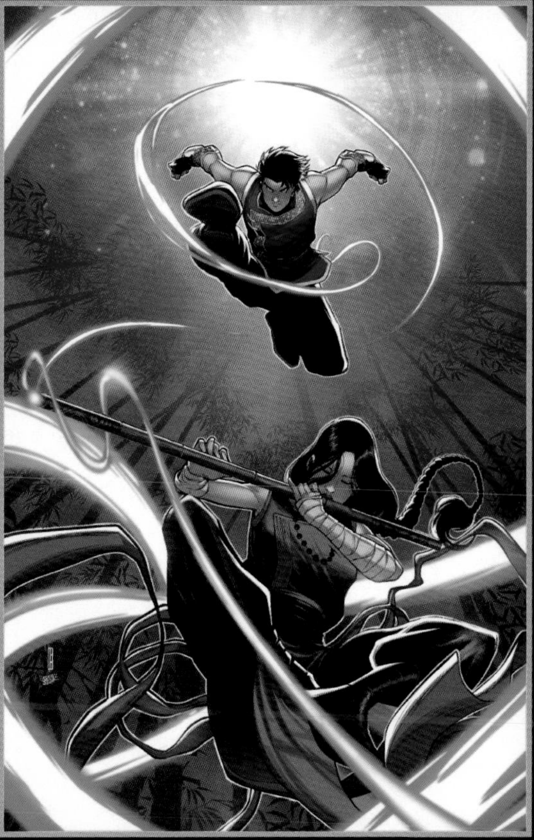

#9 VARIANT BY VARIANT BY
DAVID BALDEÓN & ISRAEL SILVA

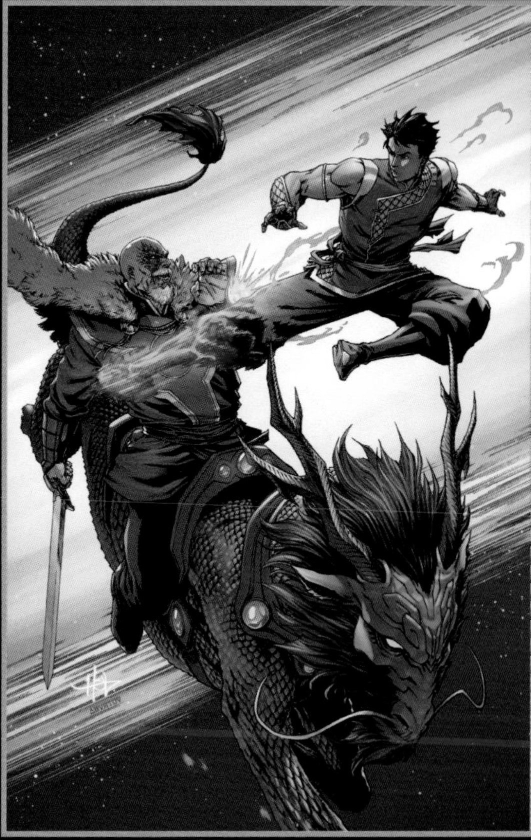

#10 VARIANT BY
CREEES LEE & JESUS ABURTOV

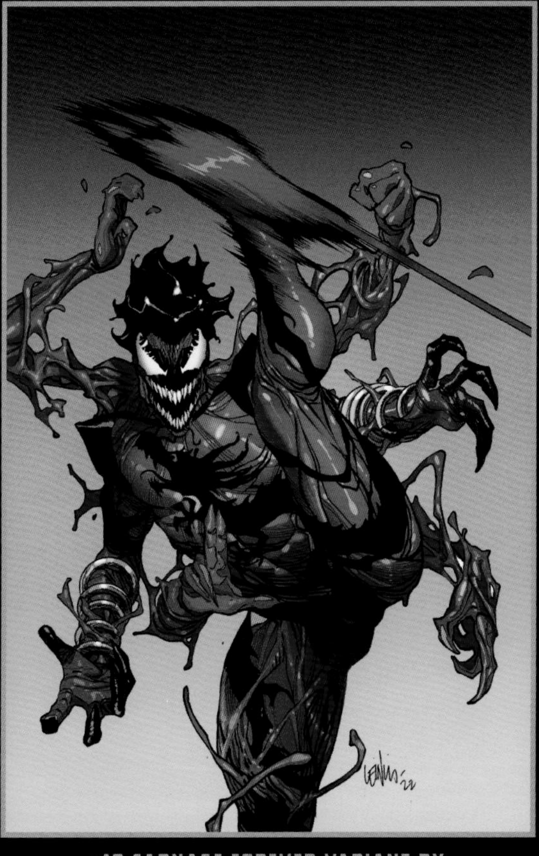

#10 CARNAGE FOREVER VARIANT BY
LEINIL FRANCIS YU & SUNNY GHO

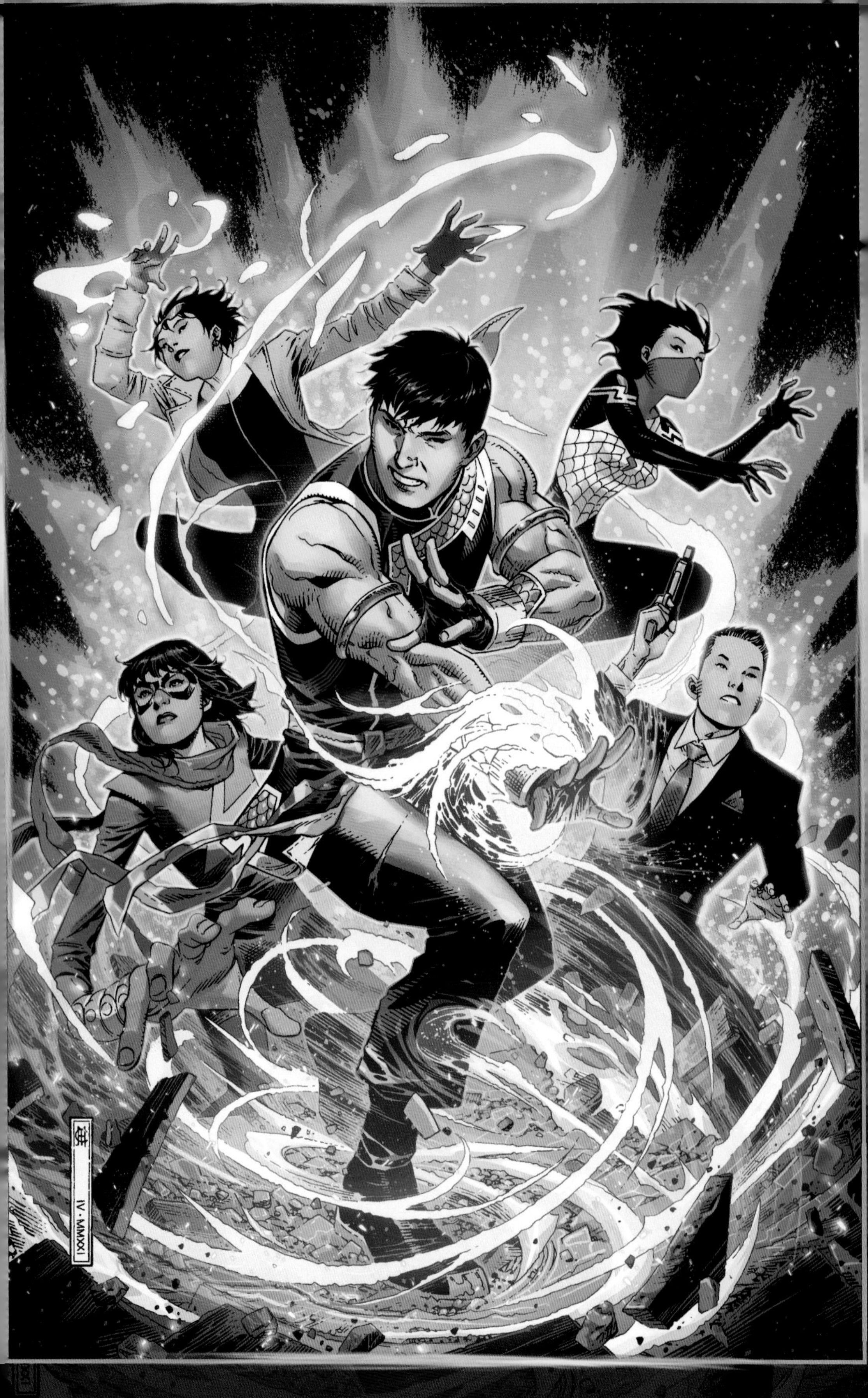
IV · MMXXI

MARVEL'S VOICES- IDENTITY

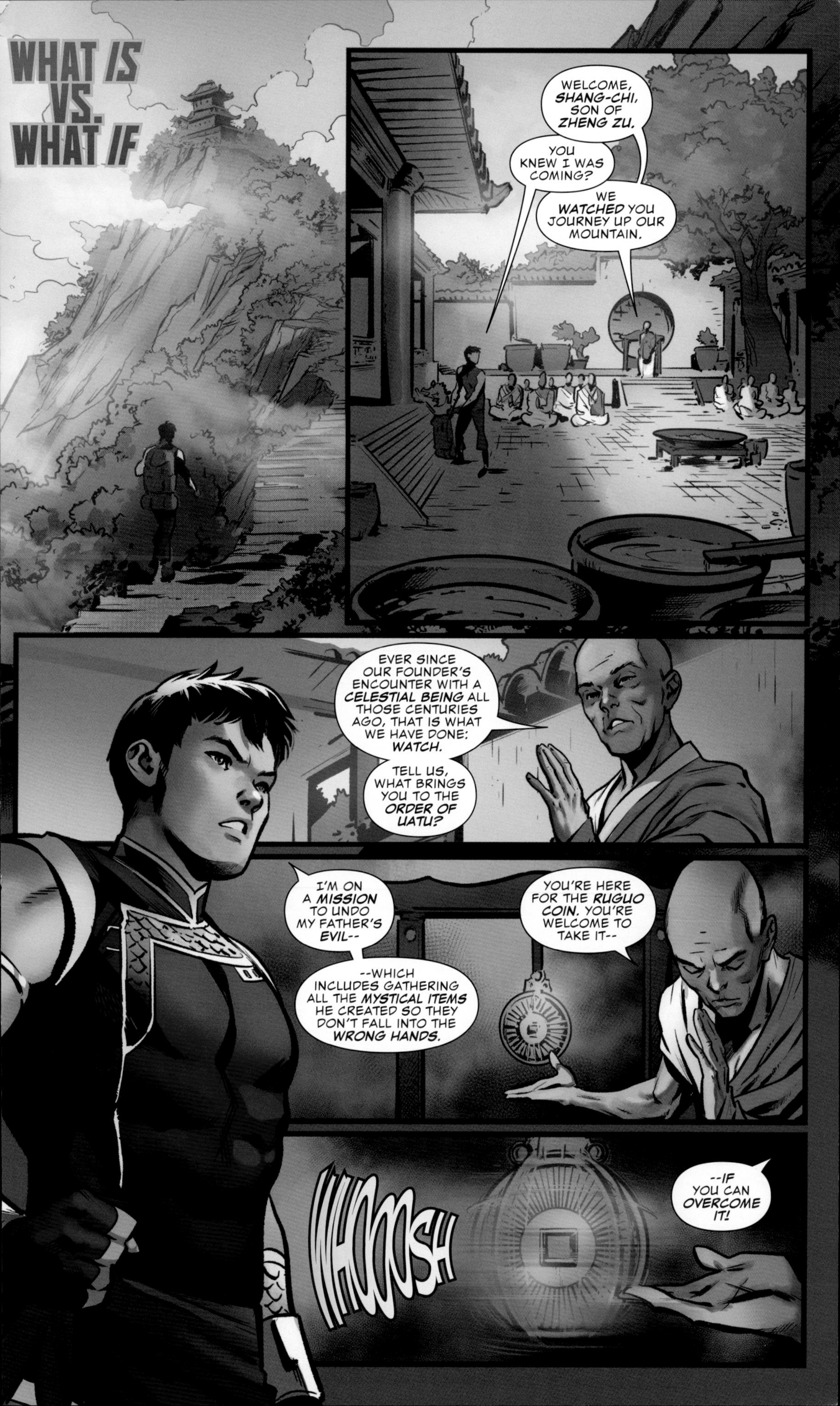
WHAT IS VS. WHAT IF
WELCOME, SHANG-CHI, SON OF ZHENG ZU.
YOU KNEW I WAS COMING?
WE WATCHED YOU JOURNEY UP OUR MOUNTAIN.
EVER SINCE OUR FOUNDER'S ENCOUNTER WITH A CELESTIAL BEING ALL THOSE CENTURIES AGO, THAT IS WHAT WE HAVE DONE: WATCH.
TELL US, WHAT BRINGS YOU TO THE ORDER OF UATU?
I'M ON A MISSION TO UNDO MY FATHER'S EVIL--
--WHICH INCLUDES GATHERING ALL THE MYSTICAL ITEMS HE CREATED SO THEY DON'T FALL INTO THE WRONG HANDS.
YOU'RE HERE FOR THE RUGUO COIN. YOU'RE WELCOME TO TAKE IT--
WHOOOSH
--IF YOU CAN OVERCOME IT!

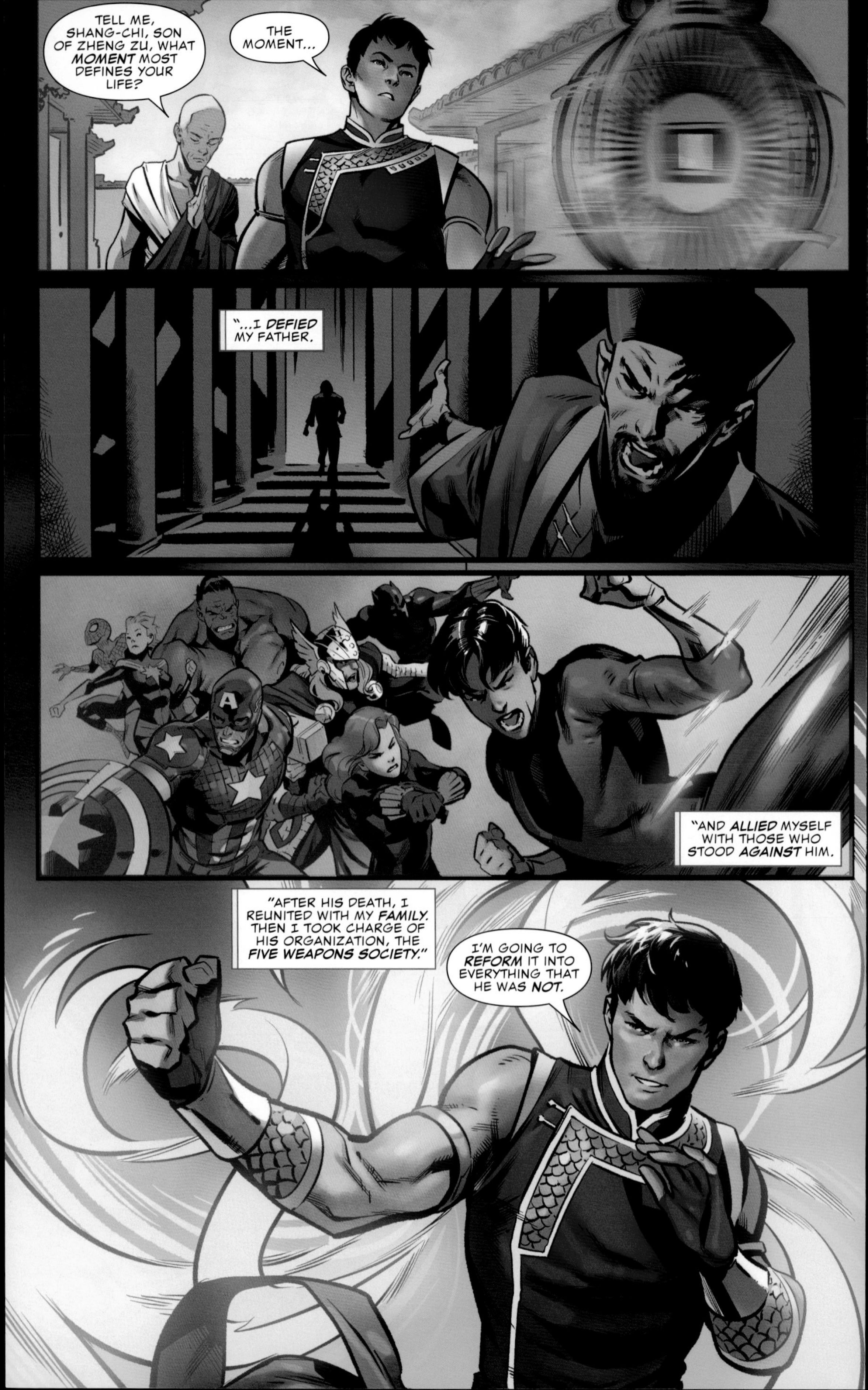
TELL ME, SHANG-CHI, SON OF ZHENG ZU, WHAT MOMENT MOST DEFINES YOUR LIFE?
THE MOMENT...
"...I DEFIED MY FATHER.
"AND ALLIED MYSELF WITH THOSE WHO STOOD AGAINST HIM.
"AFTER HIS DEATH, I REUNITED WITH MY FAMILY. THEN I TOOK CHARGE OF HIS ORGANIZATION, THE FIVE WEAPONS SOCIETY."
I'M GOING TO REFORM IT INTO EVERYTHING THAT HE WAS NOT.

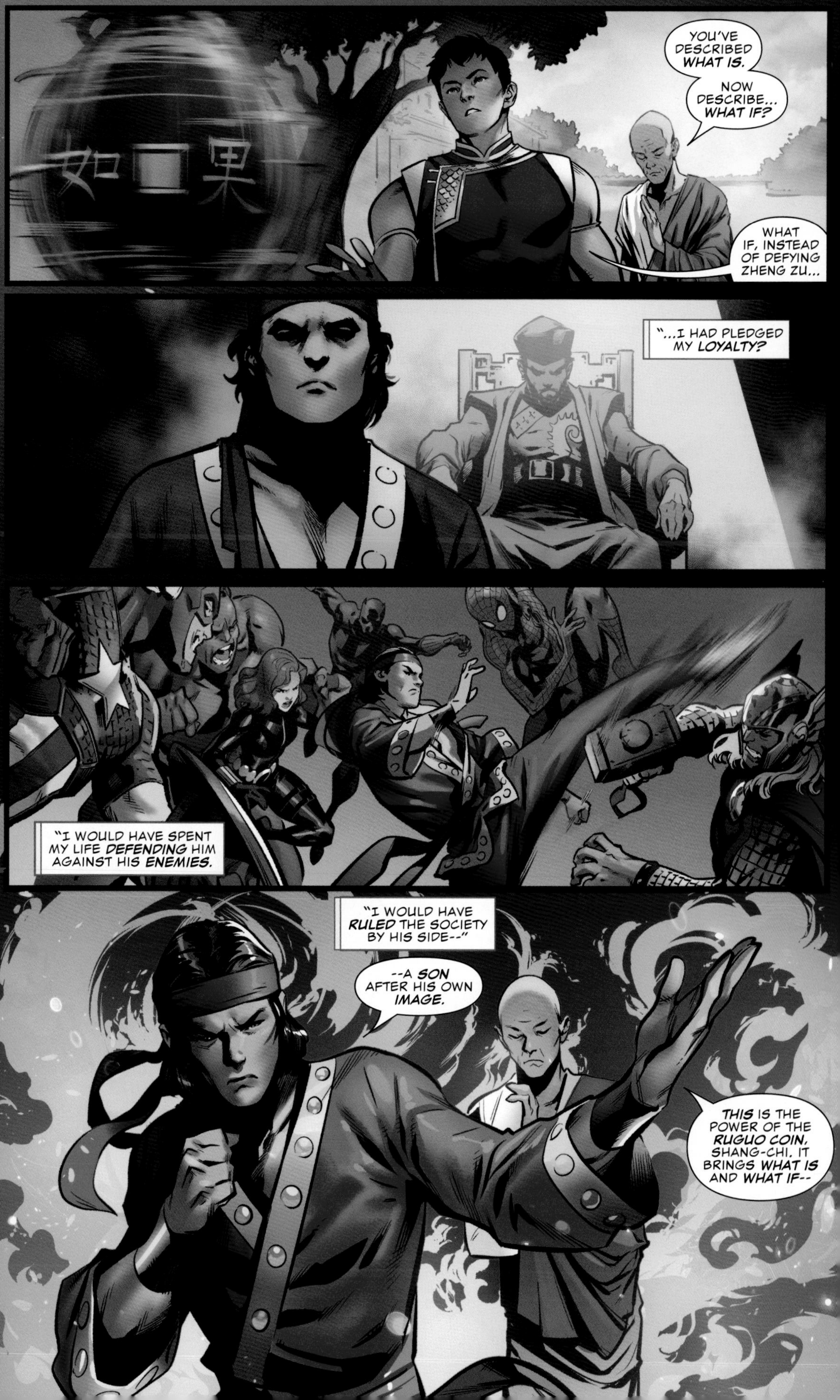

如果
YOU'VE DESCRIBED WHAT IS.
NOW DESCRIBE... WHAT IF?
WHAT IF, INSTEAD OF DEFYING ZHENG ZU...
"...I HAD PLEDGED MY LOYALTY?
"I WOULD HAVE SPENT MY LIFE DEFENDING HIM AGAINST HIS ENEMIES.
"I WOULD HAVE RULED THE SOCIETY BY HIS SIDE--"
--A SON AFTER HIS OWN IMAGE.
THIS IS THE POWER OF THE RUGUO COIN, SHANG-CHI. IT BRINGS WHAT IS AND WHAT IF--

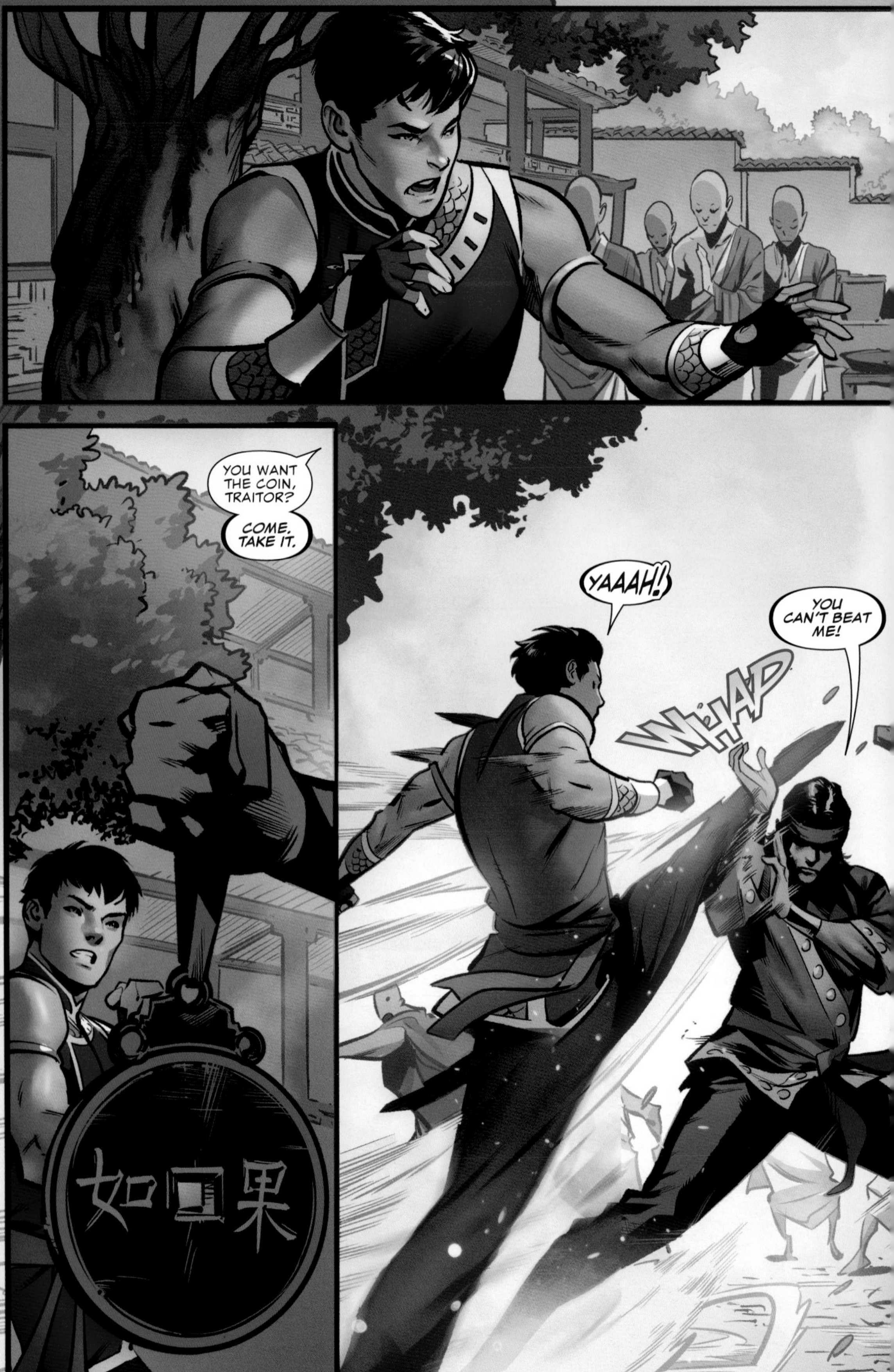

YOU WANT THE COIN, TRAITOR?
COME. TAKE IT.
如□果
YAAAH!
WHAP
YOU CAN'T BEAT ME!

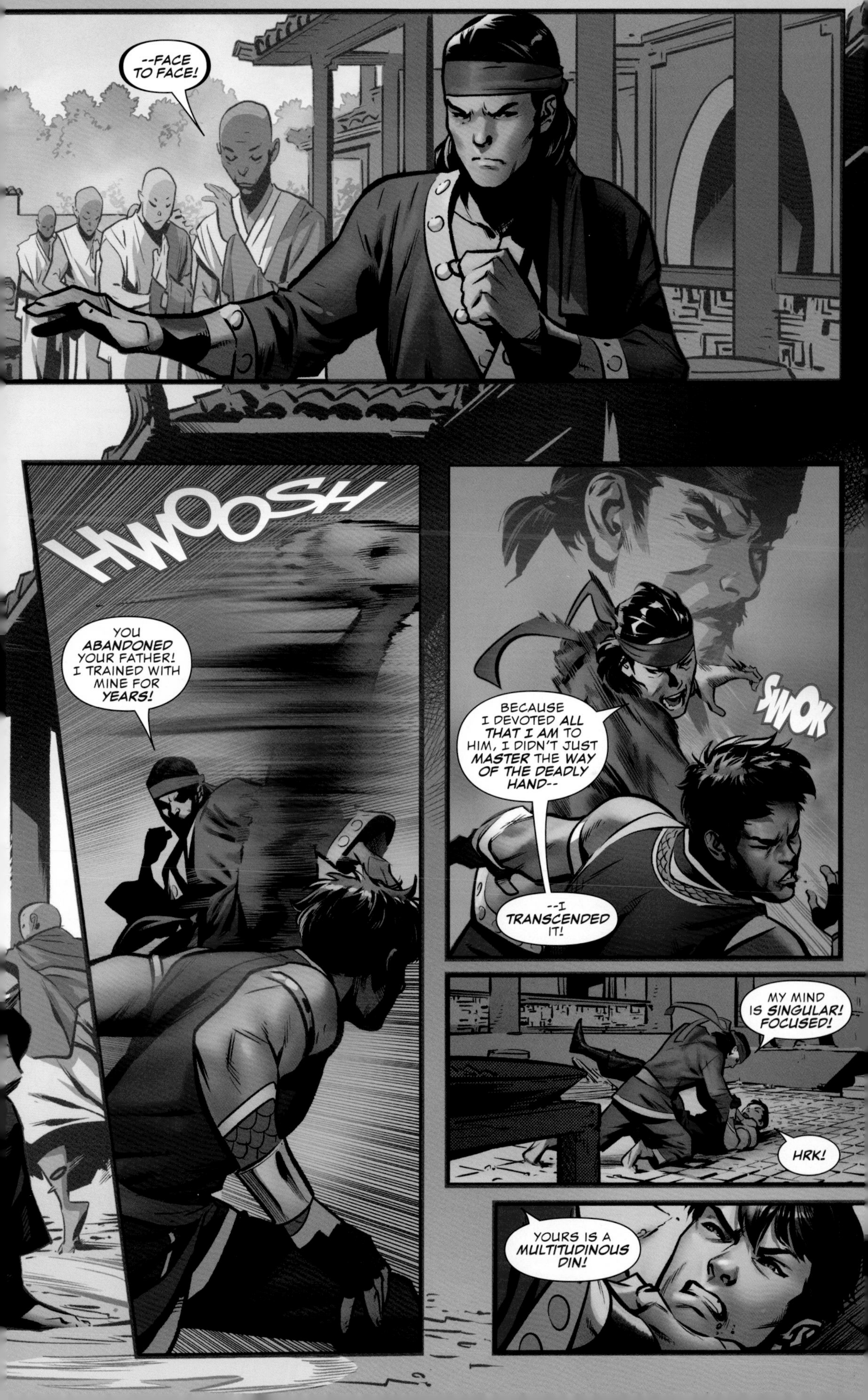
--FACE TO FACE!
HWOOSH
YOU ABANDONED YOUR FATHER! I TRAINED WITH MINE FOR YEARS!
BECAUSE I DEVOTED ALL THAT I AM TO HIM, I DIDN'T JUST MASTER THE WAY OF THE DEADLY HAND--
SWOK
--I TRANSCENDED IT!
MY MIND IS SINGULAR! FOCUSED!
HRK!
YOURS IS A MULTITUDINOUS DIN!

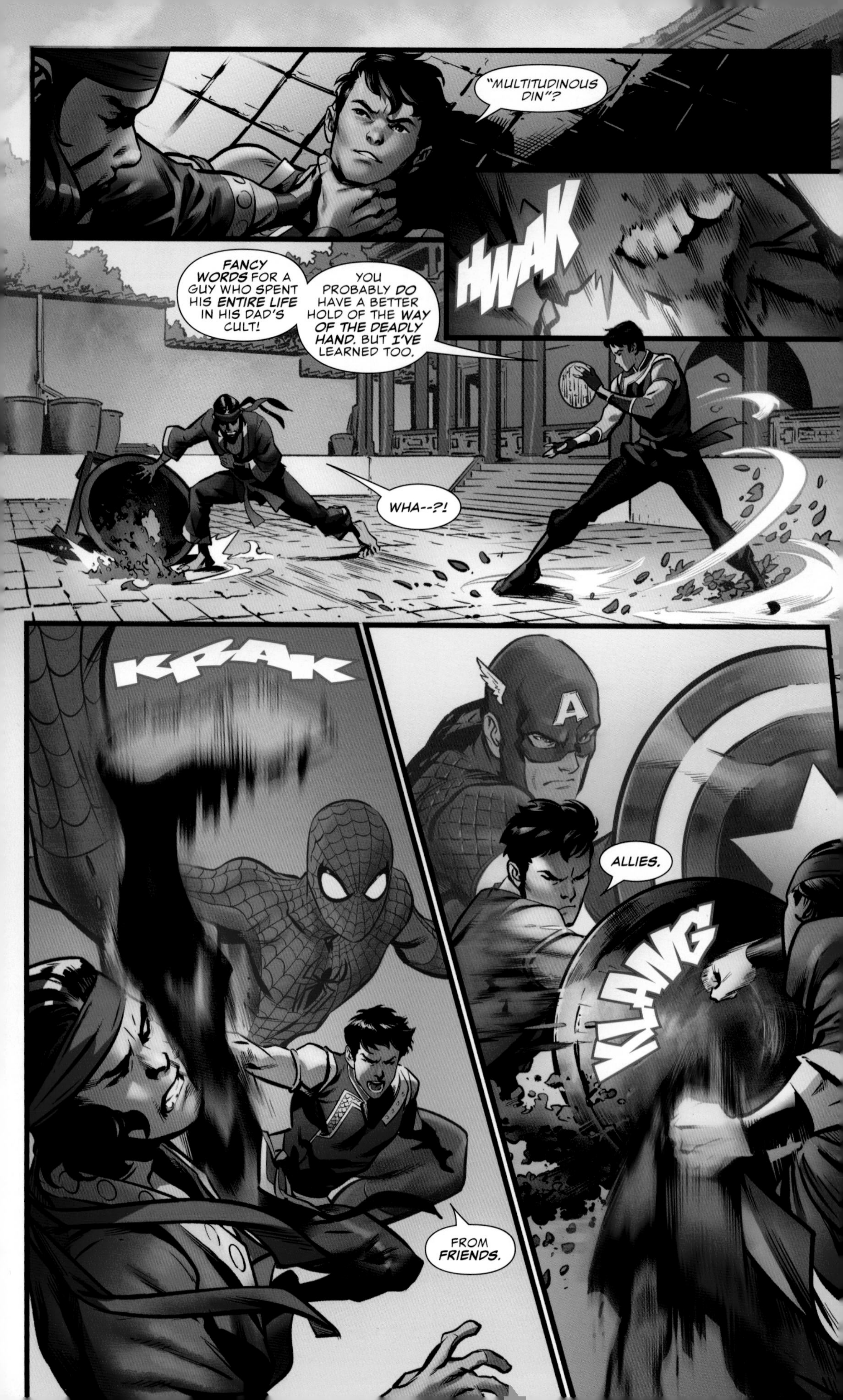
"MULTITUDINOUS DIN"?
HWAK
FANCY WORDS FOR A GUY WHO SPENT HIS ENTIRE LIFE IN HIS DAD'S CULT!
YOU PROBABLY DO HAVE A BETTER HOLD OF THE WAY OF THE DEADLY HAND. BUT I'VE LEARNED TOO.
WHA--?!
KRAK
FROM FRIENDS.
ALLIES.
KLANG

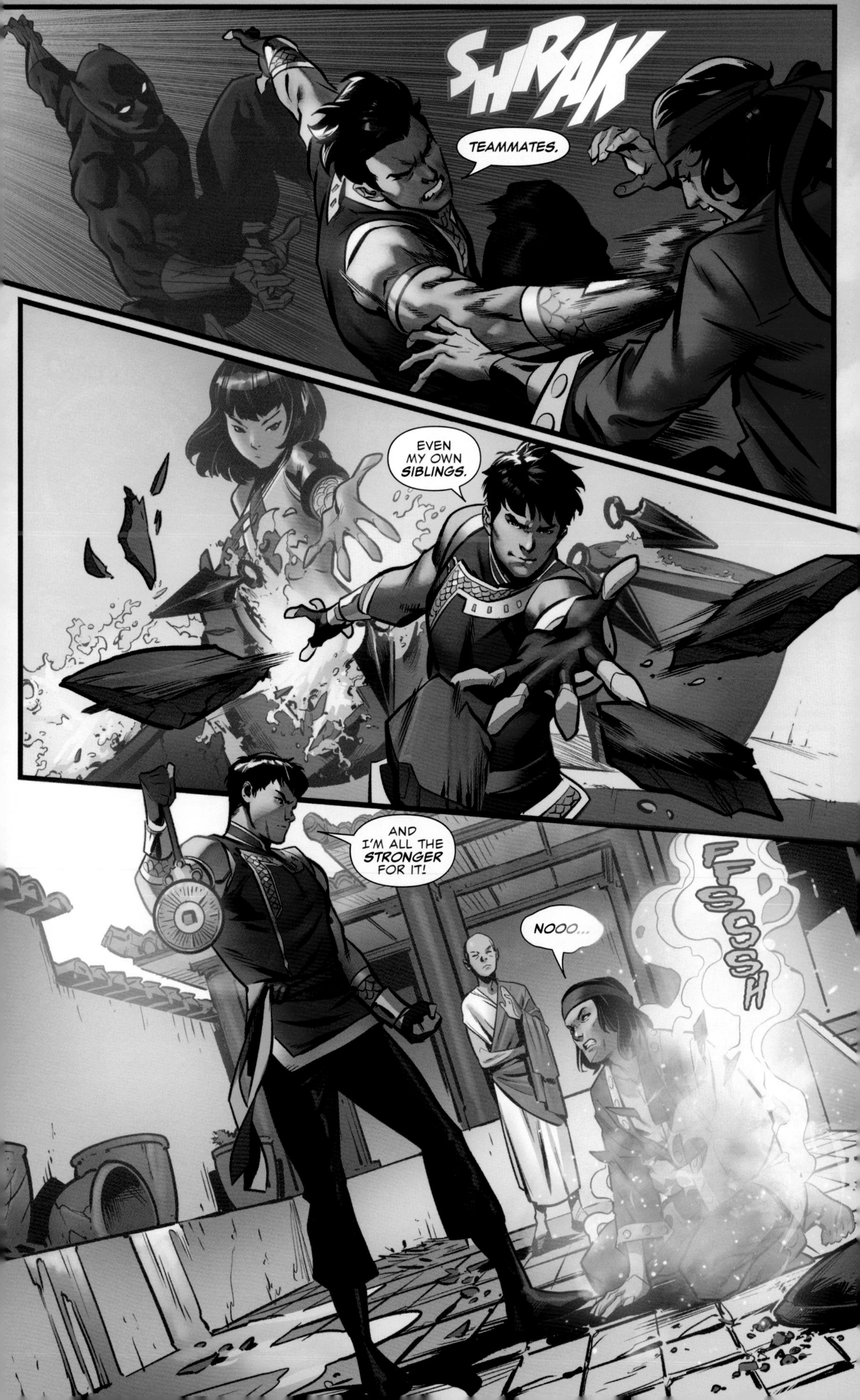
SHRAK
TEAMMATES.
EVEN MY OWN SIBLINGS.
AND I'M ALL THE STRONGER FOR IT!
FFSSSH
NOOO...

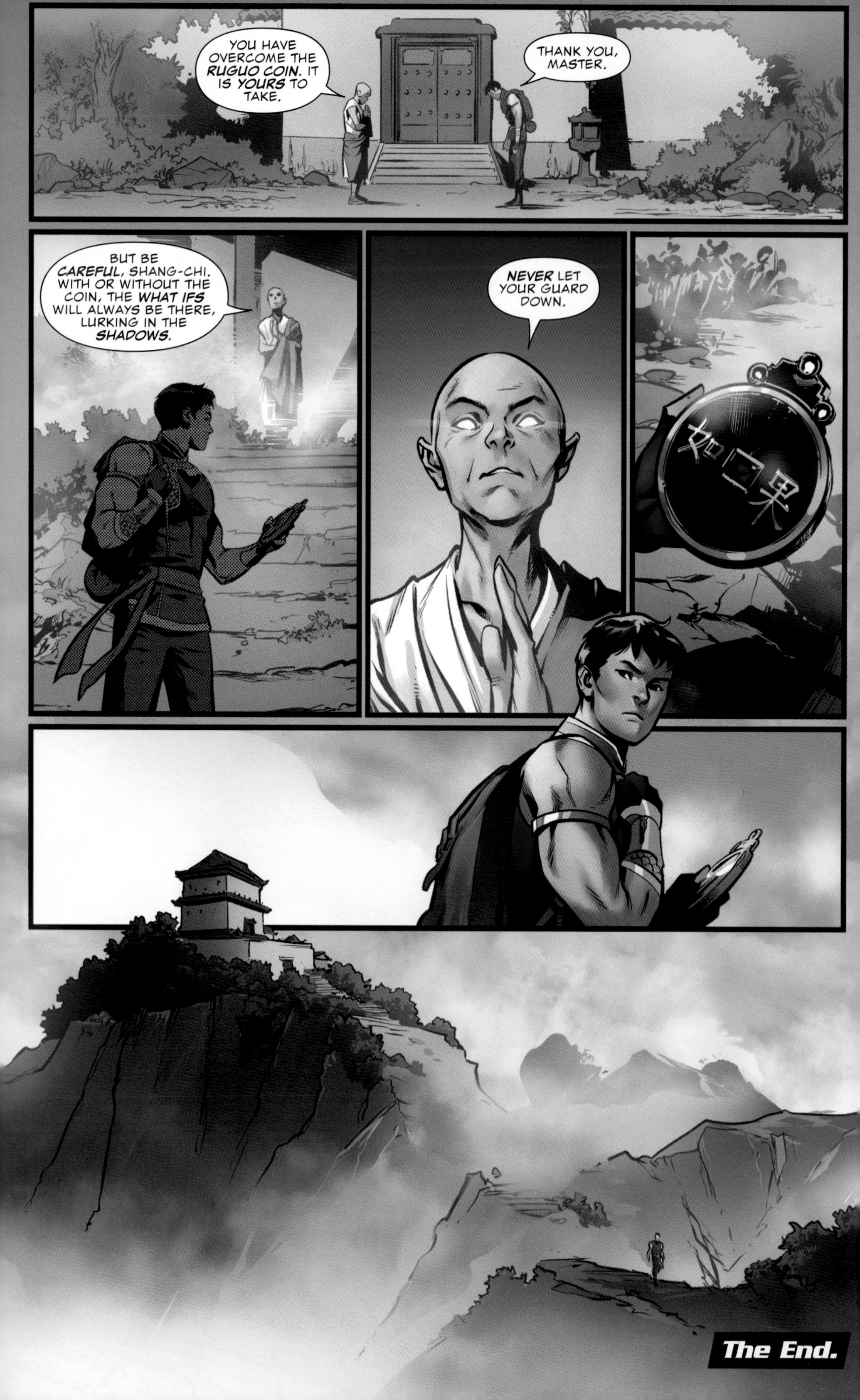

YOU HAVE OVERCOME THE RUGUO COIN. IT IS YOURS TO TAKE.
THANK YOU, MASTER.
BUT BE CAREFUL, SHANG-CHI. WITH OR WITHOUT THE COIN, THE WHAT IFS WILL ALWAYS BE THERE, LURKING IN THE SHADOWS.
NEVER LET YOUR GUARD DOWN.
如果
The End.

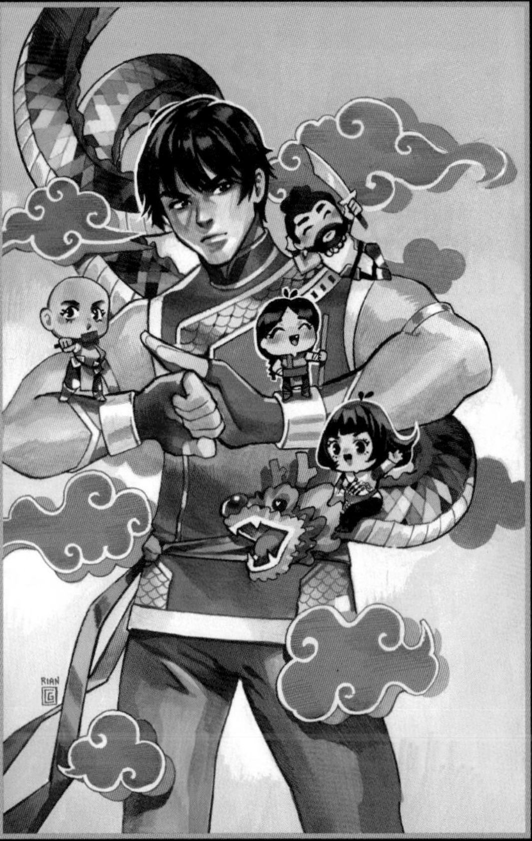

#11 VARIANT BY
RIAN GONZALES

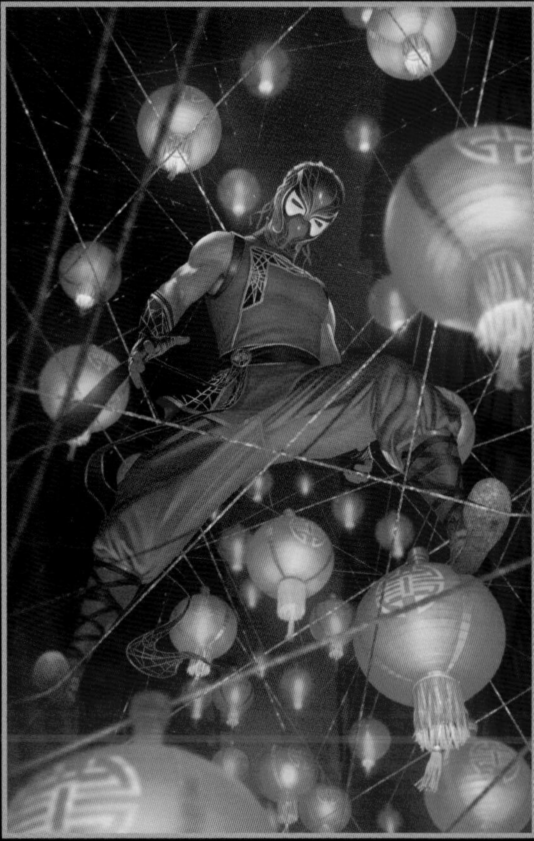

#11 SPIDER-MAN 60TH ANNIVERSARY VARIANT BY
RAHZZAH

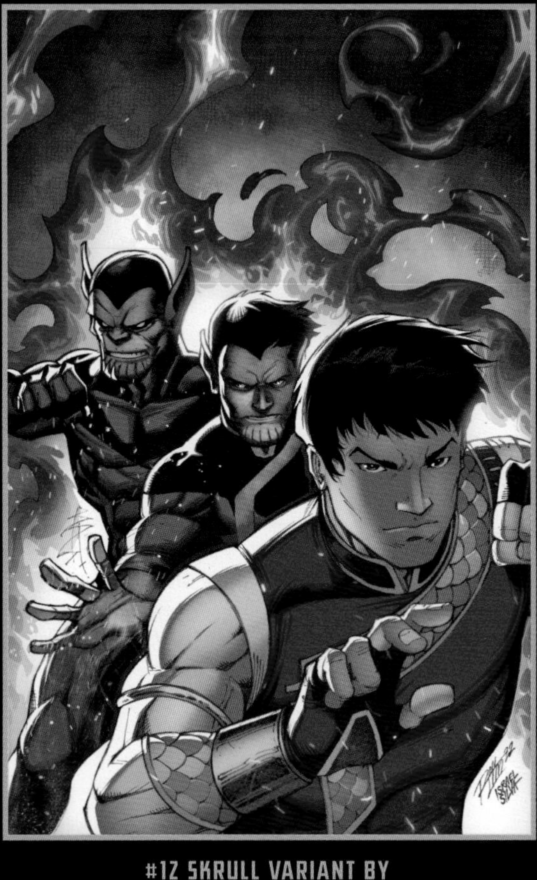

#12 SKRULL VARIANT BY
RON LIM & ISRAEL SILVA

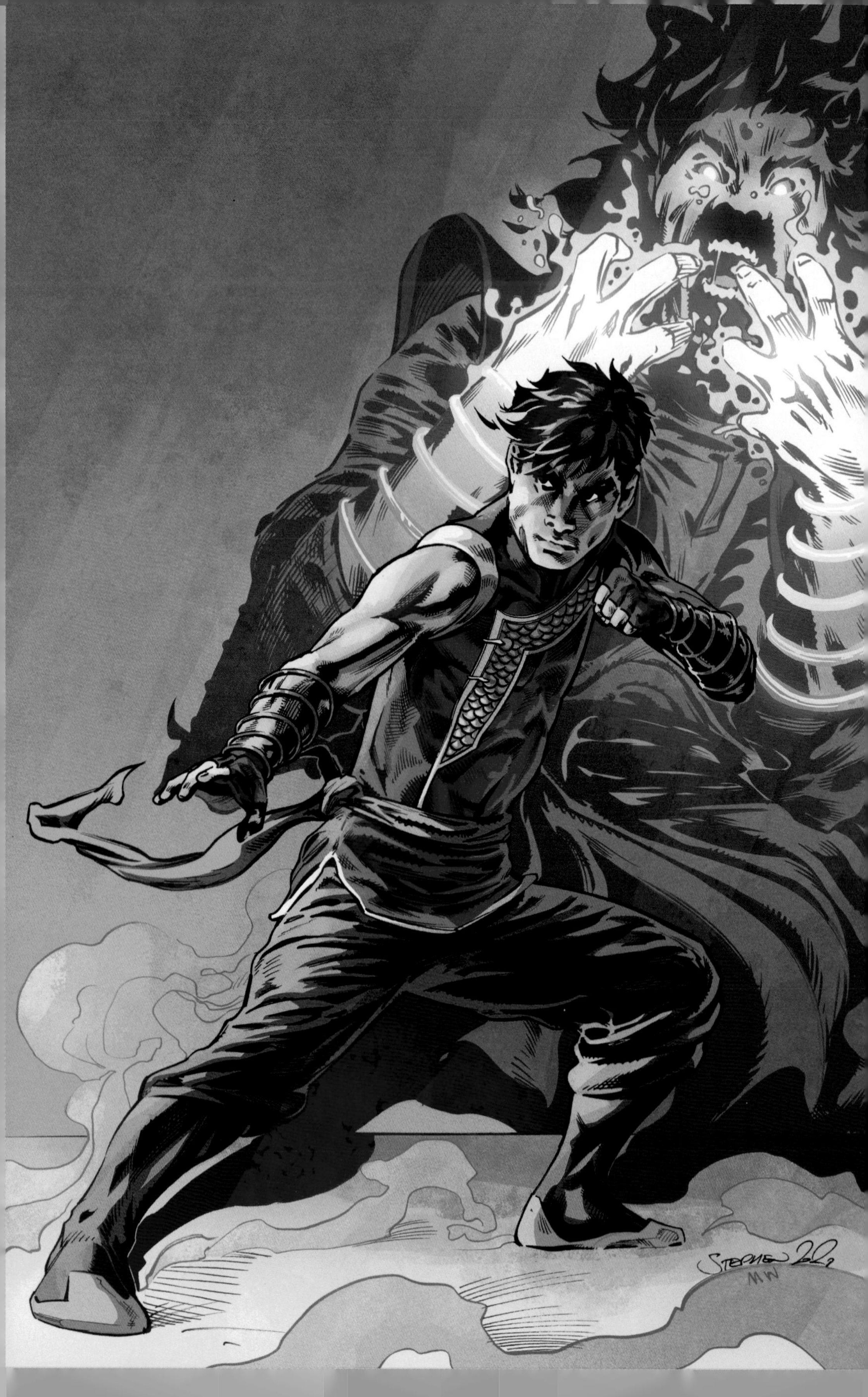

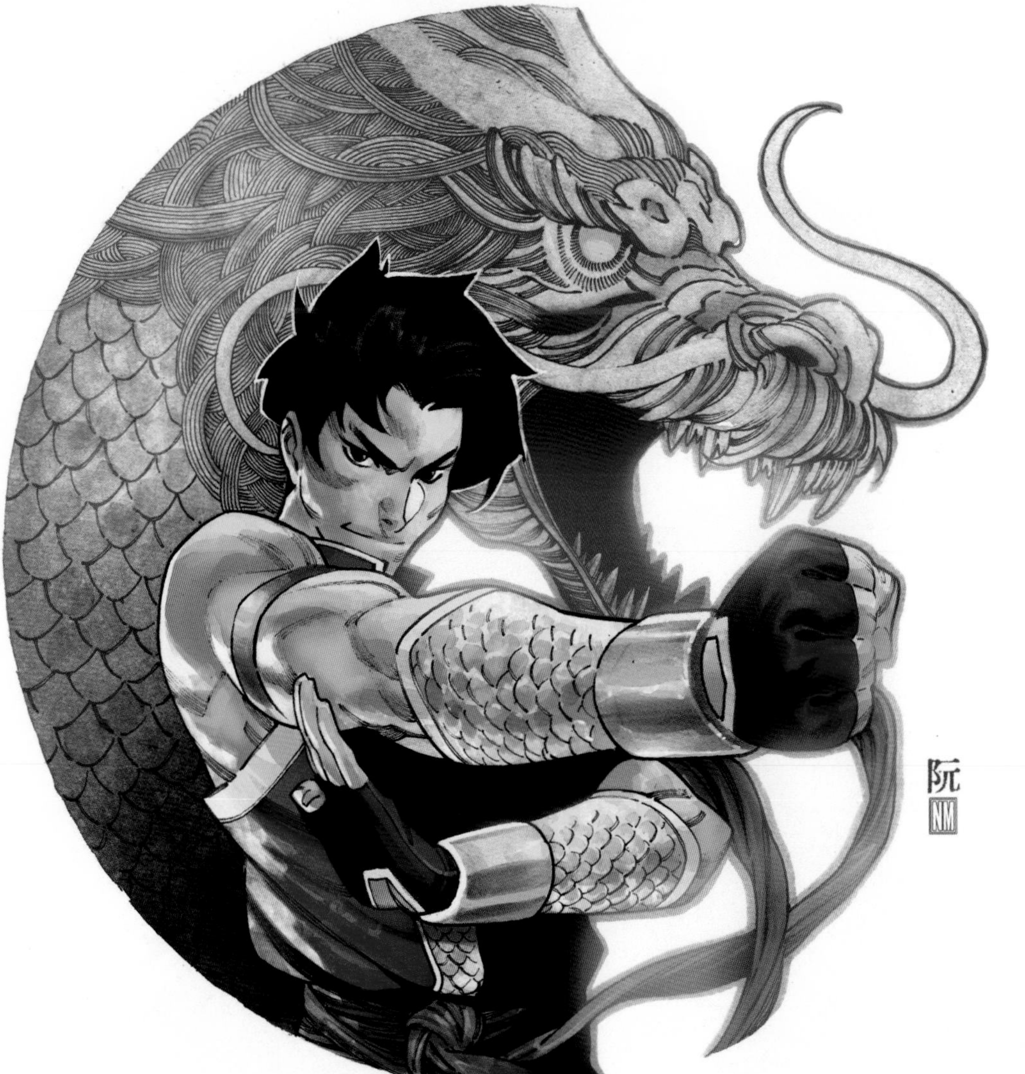
阮
NM

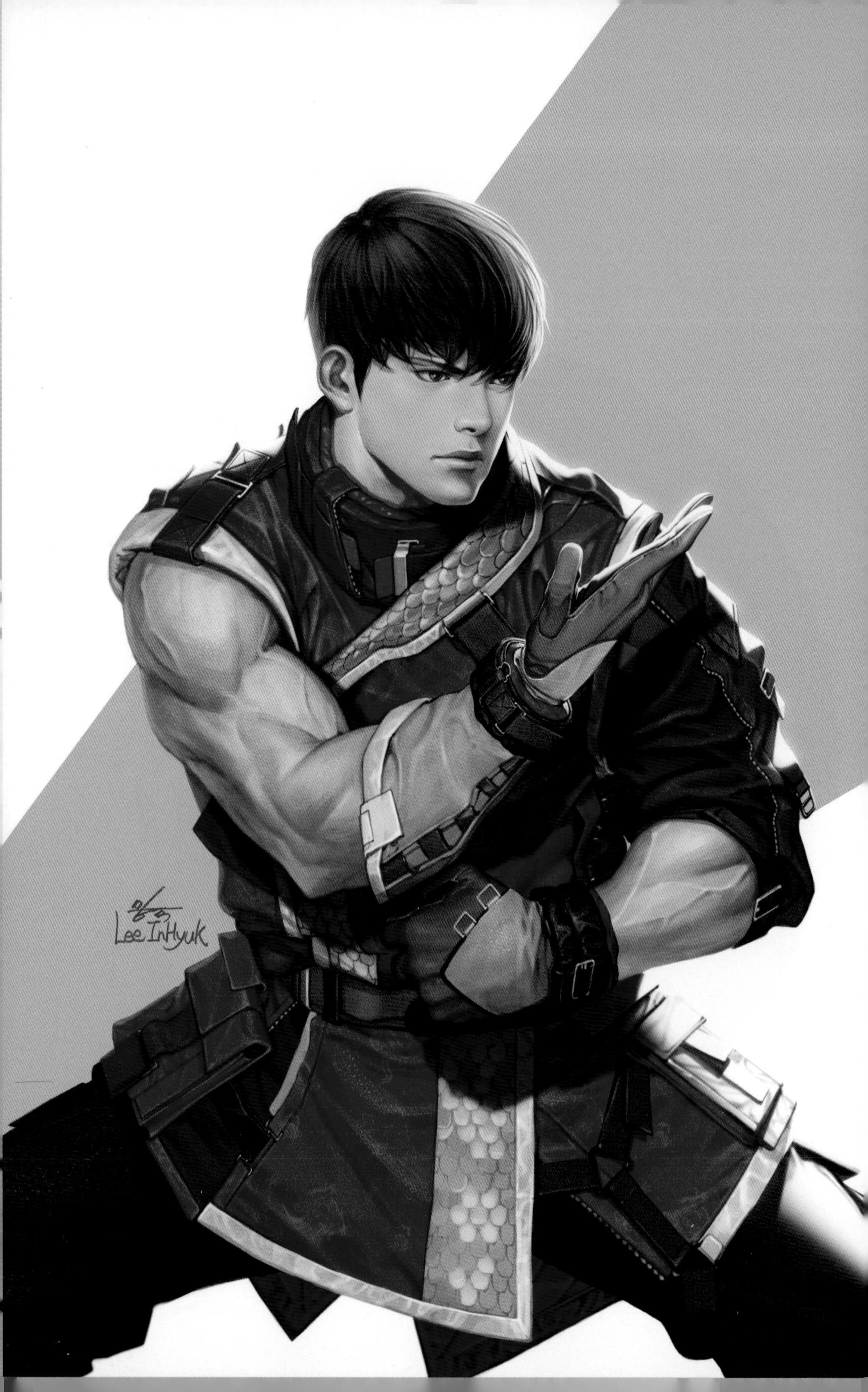
Lee InHyuk